Advance praise for NAKED LEADERSHIP

'Peter Stephenson's leadership methodologies have helped hundreds of executives cut through the confusion that exists for leaders in today's business world and achieve superior levels of success for themselves and their organisations. I am very fortunate to have been one of those executives and have been so completely impressed by the effect this approach can have, I have joined Peter's organisation and his quest to help develop truly great business leaders.

By stripping away the mystique and mythology surrounding great leadership and defining it in a way that is simple, practical and implementable, *Naked Leadership* offers a path to great leadership which any executive can traverse, even with the omnipresent weight of the modern business world on their shoulders. As such, *Naked Leadership* is the perfect book for executives leading their organisations into the 21st century.

Don't miss this chance to catapult yourself and your organisation towards great leadership and true business success.'

**Rob Balmer, Executive Partner, The Stephenson Partnership
and former Divisional Director of Compaq Computer Australia**

'Every phase of economic, social and business development demands different styles of institutions, different organisation structures and, importantly, different approaches to leadership. What Peter Stephenson has done in this book is to distil the essence of effective leadership regardless of the specific circumstances of the leader. In a practical, easily understood way, he explodes a series of leadership myths and simplifies a number of truths so that readers can see through trendy fads to become truly and consistently effective as executive business leaders.'

Meredith Hellicar, Company Director

NAKED LEADERSHIP
CONFRONTING THE
TRUTH ABOUT LEADERSHIP

PETER STEPHENSON

Pearson Education Australia
Unit 4, Level 2
14 Aquatic Drive
Frenchs Forest NSW 2086

www.pearsoned.com.au

Publisher: Nella Soeterboek
Managing Editor: Susan Lewis
Cover and text design: Liz Seymour
Typeset by Midland Typesetters, Maryborough

Printed in Australia by Griffin Press

1 2 3 4 5 06 05 04 03 02

National Library of Australia
Cataloguing-in-Publication Data

Stephenson, Peter, 1945- .
    Naked leadership: confronting the truth about leadership.

    Bibliography.
    Includes index.
    ISBN 1 74009 598 7.

    1. Leadership. 2. Executives - Training of. I. Title.

    658.4092

Prentice Hall is an imprint of Pearson Education Australia.

Contents

Chapter 1 Executive leadership effectiveness

Chapter 2 Influencing

Chapter 3 Synergising

Chapter 4 Enabling

Chapter 5 Energising

Chapter 6 Trusting

About the author

Peter Stephenson is managing director of The Stephenson Partnership Pty Ltd. He has specialised in executive coaching and monitoring since 1990, although he first designed and marketed assessment and development processes more than 25 years ago.

Peter has worked in a number of company director positions in Australia, Canada and the UK. He was NSW and ACT director of Davidson & Associates, Australia's leading outplacement company; the founding managing director of Deloitte Consulting Group; founding managing director of Hospital Extension Services; director and general manager of Lucas Marine; and divisional chief executive of a food group.

He has extensive management consulting experience in the ASEAN region, South Asia, Japan and the People's Republic of China and has lived and worked in Pakistan. He has taught, trained and coached people of a broad range of Asian and other ethnic origins, both overseas and in Australia.

Peter has an exceptional understanding of the issues involved in organisational change and its impact on executives and staff. He has worked with many of Australia's top 100 companies on planning and implementing change and on providing executive coaching and mentoring for more than 600 directors, executives and other key people. Earlier in his career, he also coached more than 300 proprietors of small and medium-sized enterprises.

Educated in the UK, Peter holds a postgraduate Diploma in Management Studies specialising in Behavioural Sciences. He is a Fellow of the Australian Institute of Management and of the Australian Institute of Company Directors. He is the author of *Executive Coaching* and *The Bulletproof Executive*, and of eight audio cassette workbook programs on personal development and career success.

Preface

You may wonder why *Naked Leadership*.

Just a gimmick to get you to take it off the shelf and have a look? Perhaps.

But now I have your attention, the title reflects a growing passion I have, if not anger, that it's about time some executives came out of their executive suites and got real about the subject of leadership!

Over the past eleven years, having worked with more than 600 executives and other key people in various forms of executive coaching and mentoring, having provided input in more than 70 organisational restructures, having hosted or facilitated 100 executive focus group discussions, forums and off-siters, involving about 1500 executives—I can honestly say that I am appalled by the feedback I continue to receive about the state of executive leadership or, rather, in many cases, its complete and utter absence.

I have therefore settled on the title of *Naked Leadership*. It's time to uncover the myths and reveal the truth about leadership. There should be nowhere to hide for executive leaders—they have to come out into the open, lead for real, full frontal!

That's what this book is all about, and I call it *executive leadership effectiveness*.

In seeking to enhance your own and your organisation's executive leadership effectiveness, you can use the book in three ways:

➢ first, by reading the chapters, which comprehensively address this topic, and then reviewing them in the context of your own organisation's progress (daily review guidelines are included at the end of each chapter);
➢ second, by personally completing the assignments in Appendix A, which are designed to help you implement new, more effective leadership practices and behaviours;
➢ third, by using Appendix B to help you coach and mentor your direct reports and others in executive leadership effectiveness, with a view to cascading this through your organisation.

Naked Leadership is the third book in a trilogy, the two earlier books being *The Bulletproof Executive* and *Executive Coaching*.

The Bulletproof Executive is a survival guide for individual executives transitioning their way through their careers and included a range of key success factor guidelines. These guidelines were subsequently developed further, in fact they continue to be developed, and are used by The Stephenson Partnership in our executive coaching and mentoring.

Executive Coaching moves to the next stage and demonstrates to executives and leaders how to use such guidelines, together with a broad range of other approaches and processes, in their own internal coaching and mentoring applications—putting leadership into action!

Naked Leadership goes to the next stage and distils the essence of executive leadership effectiveness from my first two books, from my continuing empirical research on the topic and from international best practice.

The statistics cited in *Naked Leadership* are all estimates based on my empirical research and compared with a broad range of other input from international sources.

One Caveat! Should you require external coaching or mentoring support in your own organisation in applying executive leadership effectiveness from *Naked Leadership*, please make sure you use a coach or mentor whom I have personally trained and accredited. Let me know and I'll confirm if this is the case.

If you have a query or observation on any of the principles and practices in *Naked Leadership*, you are invited to email me at: peter@thestephensonpartnership.com.au

Finally, my thanks to my commentators who have kept me on the straight and narrow, and for their contributions throughout this book:

David Hearn, Chief Executive, Goodman Fielder
Lyn Cobley, Chief Executive Officer, tradingroom.com.au (a joint
    venture between Fairfax and Macquarie Bank)
Meredith Hellicar, Company Director
Peter Macdonald, Chief Executive Officer, James Hardie Industries
Peter Scott, Chief Executive Officer, MLC
Peter Wilkinson, Chief Executive, David Jones
Rob Balmer, Executive Partner, The Stephenson Partnership and
    former Divisional Director at Compaq Computer Australia

Good reading, and good luck in applying *executive leadership effectiveness.*

PETER STEPHENSON
Sydney, Australia

Foreword

The subject of leadership in the corporate world is not a new one. For centuries, aspects of leadership in business and commerce have been described and discussed in many a management training text, self-help guide and corporate development program. For many executives, becoming an effective leader has been, and remains, a primary objective in their career development. Yet, for all the texts, guides and programs, truly effective leadership has remained an elusive butterfly for most.

In the business environment in which we find ourselves today, the requirement for executives to exhibit what are deemed 'desirable' leadership traits has never been greater. Among other things, executives are expected to fit in with the corporate culture, demonstrate vision, co-operate and communicate well with all around them, manage their staff effectively, build an environment that is invigorating and fun, 'walk the talk' and maintain a proper work/life balance. All this is taken for granted—'part of the job'—as is consistently meeting required business objectives, operating with fewer resources and less expense than ever before, 'dotting the Is and crossing the Ts' and facing the ever increasing likelihood of restructures, mergers, downsizings and other major changes within their immediate work environment.

And so it was with me. Early in 1999 I was promoted to become a divisional director in Australia's largest PC company (and next-to-largest IT company)—Compaq Computer Australia. I had been with the company for nearly seven years and was five years the junior of the next youngest director. The division I was responsible for—the Consumer Division—was the fastest-growing part of the entire business and had become very significant in size with revenues in the hundreds of millions of dollars.

My role? To keep the growth going at 50+% per annum, to reduce operating expenses by 25% and, consequently, to amplify dramatically the operating profit of this division. I was also to introduce two very major and controversial (internally as much as externally) distribution channels to the business, so that the future growth of the division was assured. I had to continue to manage the small core team that existed and introduce new specialist members. I had to become an active and useful member of the management board of the company. And I had to improve the relationships between my division and the others in the company (many of whom viewed my group as 'cowboys' and 'too radical').

Fortunately, at the same time as promoting me, Compaq had the fore-sight to realise that I might need a helping hand in all this, and appointed Peter Stephenson of The Stephenson Partnership as my executive coach and mentor. In the subsequent two years, I have pursued the leadership philoso-phies, principles and practices that are enunciated in this book. With Peter's guidance, I was able to implement them in a very practical way, and they made a hugely positive contribution to my own success and that of the business I ran.

I believe passionately that Peter Stephenson's approach, and that of The Stephenson Partnership, provides all executives with a net to catch the 'elusive butterfly' of effective leadership. So much so that, earlier this year, I accepted Peter's invitation to join The Stephenson Partnership as executive partner and now actively champion this approach to major Australian and international companies and government enterprises.

This book does away with rhetoric and gives every executive a way of looking at leadership which can be implemented in the real world and which can lead to real business bottom-line improvements. To help demonstrate this in a 'real-world' way, throughout the book I've added a commentary by way of case studies and highlights from my own experi-ences of implementing the strategies Peter espouses. I hope this proves helpful and that it demonstrates why my belief in his approach is so strong.

Don't hesitate to contact me at rob@thestephensonpartnership.com.au if you'd like to find out more about my experiences in implementing the techniques for enhancing executive leadership effectiveness, as described in this wonderful book.

ROB BALMER
Sydney, Australia

CHAPTER 1

Executive leadership effectiveness

Executive leadership effectiveness starts with balancing leadership and management, and knowing when to emphasise each—a real juggling match!

KEYNOTES FROM THE COMMENTATORS

A big challenge for any CEO is balancing some of the inevitable corporate restructuring and financial markets' requirements with ensuring the executive team remains focused on business objectives. Another challenge is the fluidity of funds management, when stocks can go out of favour overnight. This requires a focus on quarterly results, but in the context of also pursuing business strategy. *Just* focusing on quarterly results becomes 'death on wheels'.

Peter Macdonald, Chief Executive Officer James Hardie Industries

Executives have so many balls in the air—and they are all supercritical, all A1 priorities! Speed, rate and pace of change, and the need for quick decisions represent a critical challenge, fuelled by the media explosion which makes anyone instantly accessible—by email, fax, mobile. The corollary can be the quantity and quality of information also instantly accessible, leading to the obvious issues of focus and prioritisation. So business is getting more complex, while great efforts are being made to simplify it! The 'lower hanging fruit' has been picked—quick and easy wins are getting rarer and harder.
David Hearn, Chief Executive Goodman Fielder

The complexity, breadth and physical demands on executives and their constancy of intensity is like drinking from a fire hose! And executives feel guilty if they are not on top of it all. But successful executive leaders don't take themselves too seriously. Managers were supposed to know everything. Leaders may not, and are not afraid to declare this.
Peter Scott, Chief Executive Officer MLC

Having come through the year 2000 where business was highly unusual—Y2K, GST and the Olympics—many executives I work with have looked forward to 'business as usual'. What does this look like?

Business as usual sees Australia among the top five countries in spending on telecommunications and information technology, with a trend towards continuing growth in these sectors and also in communications and financial, business and other services. At the other end of the scale, the decline of conventional manufacturing and agricultural industries will continue, in terms of their contribution to the economy.

Much of the growth will come from smaller, faster-moving companies capitalising on cheaper resources—yesterday, for example, semiconductors, tomorrow bandwidth.

Many of the large, heavy-investment, slower-moving organisations will falter. 'Small, fast and timely' is today's and tomorrow's maxim for success. 'Big, bureaucratic and slow' can be a recipe for disaster (not discounting the benefits of economies of scale but, rather, 'big' needs to think and act *small*, i.e. focus on the individual customer and sales transaction, focus on the individual employee).

Beyond our shores, the mighty momentum in North America and Western Europe continues. Eastern Europe remains stagnant. Asia-Pacific will out-accelerate the rest.

CHANGES IN THE EXECUTIVE ENVIRONMENT

Set against my introductory backdrop, the following changes pose both opportunity and threat, and certainly a challenge for most executives:

> *Customer needs and wants.* They can change as fast as the channels on a digital TV; and, just as these channels are multiplying, so will the availability of information on, and channels of supply for, *any* product or service internationally.

> *The global village.* Deregulation (particularly of capital controls) and lower technology costs have enabled, and will foster exponential growth in, cross-border trade, investment, mergers, acquisitions and 'reveal-all' communication. So watch out for those who might come and compete in your own backyard, while you're trying to compete in theirs!

> *Information technology and telecommunications (IT&T).* A tripling of data traffic in five years; a capacity for anyone to be 'wired into the world'; Internet traffic doubling every three months; bandwidth availability/cost breakthroughs imminent; the mammoth storage and communication capacity of digitalisation; the convergence of IT&T with broadcasting, media, entertainment and publishing; IT&T effectively the new utility. The possibilities are boundless! Particularly when you consider it has been predicted that 50% of the jobs that will exist 15 years from now have not yet been invented.

> *Overseas competitors.* Focusing more, diversifying less; outsourcing non-core activities and disposing of fixed hard assets, replacing them with variable or soft assets (buildings leased not owned, stock reduced through just-in-time); greater emphasis on intellectual property than on physical assets; emphasis on leadership rather than management; developing various forms of alliances rather than going it alone/self-sufficiency.

> *Changing business fundamentals.* Continuing economic rationalisation; more downsizing; more flattening of organisation structures and broadened spans of control; and different types of work including distance working, or teleworking (i.e. home-based).

> *Demographic and social change.* The gender revolution; high consumption of tranquillisers and antidepressants; record divorce rate; the multicultural revolution; alarming and rising rate of attempted youth suicides; lowest marriage and birth rates; high levels of personal debt; increasing single-parent households; work/life balance out of control for many; faster, forced adaptation

to the increasing pace and rate of change; for some, increasing focus on self and shorter-term self-gratification; for others, the quest for a sense of belonging.

- *aging workforce, fewer young executives.* As the baby boomers age, there will be a shortage of younger people coming through; this will create employment opportunities for older executives and managers who wish to keep working, although not necessarily in senior positions.
- *regular job changes.* Executive mobility among jobs and organisations is increasing as people look not only for more money but also for opportunities to learn and grow in their careers.
- *greater utilisation of talent.* The executive, managerial and professional talent existing within an organisation is often greatly underutilised. As we move through the new century, every individual has to count in the leaner, keener organisations.
- *end of lifelong employment with loyalty to one employer.* Individuals will stay only as long as they are meeting their personal career goals. This doesn't mean they don't commit themselves fully to the job at hand while they are there.
- *high level of restructures, mergers, acquisitions and divestments.* The search for increased efficiencies and profits by these means will continue, with their resulting wholesale change in executive and management ranks.
- *dual-career marriages.* As more and more women enter the executive world it can no longer be assumed that either partner will give up a lucrative career to follow the other. Offers of promotion and transfer will increasingly be evaluated in terms of both careers, and decisions to accept or refuse made on this basis.
- *better-educated executives.* Higher education will be appreciated and rewarded even more, with master and doctorate degrees becoming more common in executive suites. Psychologists and others interested in the utilisation of human resources will be even more in evidence.
- *flexible work arrangements.* Work schedules will continue to be replaced by part-time, project and contract arrangements to take advantage of high-level skills and know-how, as and when needed.
- *leisure time.* The time demands of work may or may not decrease because of technological innovation and more efficient work methods, leaving more or less time for non-work pursuits. The jury is divided!

– *continuing emphasis on productivity.* In response to the need to keep costs down and profits up, executives, managers and their teams will have to be even more efficient and productive. This will enhance but not guarantee individual job security and advancement.

In a nutshell, faster-paced companies, more emphasis on intellectual capital, higher-tech, higher-touch leadership, a global marketplace—for talent too. Unlimited opportunity, unlimited threat, unlimited challenge!

IMPACTS ON EXECUTIVES

Although this is by no means a comprehensive list (and your list is more important than mine!) some of the impacts on executives include:

➤ be computer literate for survival;
➤ keep up to date, in your business sector, around your business sector, internationally, technically, functionally, managerially, and about leadership;
➤ focus and do it best; be diffused or distracted and you'll fail;
➤ focus on your people—get results through them and with them, not simply imposed on them;
➤ invest in talent and then harvest it (it's getting harder to attract and retain);
➤ communicate, communicate, communicate—and that means listen twice as much as tell, to those all around you;
➤ balance leadership with management, creativity with control, people with output;
➤ focus on customers: today's and tomorrow's products and services are there only to satisfy their fast-developing needs;
➤ predict, pre-empt and create change; wait to adapt to it and you'll have missed the boat;
➤ build on such strengths at hand as:
  – our Asia-Pacific proximity
  – our increasing world competitiveness
  – our IT&T literacy and uptake
  – our heritage based on quick adaptation: a capacity to change fast, once the need is acknowledged and the means of change owned by those involved in it;
➤ attend to such challenges as:
  – still too product-centred, rather than customer-centred

- declining business spending on R&D
- productivity gains still too slow
- the generation gap: baby-boomer managers failing to maximise the potential of a younger, vastly different thinking and acting workforce; the young, in fact, are often better equipped than their forebears to create the change shaping the developing executive environment
- underestimating the wisdom and corporate knowledge vested in the more mature, who are being cast out of their organisations in droves
- expired prematurely? Please note, the average age of leading CEOs in the USA is around 60; the average age in Australia around 50.

If all this hasn't put you off, read on!

THE CHANGING NATURE OF EXECUTIVE LEADERSHIP

It doesn't seem so long ago that we were all schooled in managing the factors of production—namely, land, labour, buildings, plant, equipment and raw materials. Indeed, many organisations are still in the industrial age where executives have tight control over these physical assets, the capital of the company.

However, with the emergence of the personal computer and its linkage with advanced telecommunications, the door is open to assets over which executives have far less direct control. These intellectual assets comprise customer and supplier information, processes, skills, experience, global alliances, patents and technology, along with an increasingly mobile and younger workforce with different mindsets from their forebears (see Chart 1.1).

As we move from the industrial age into the information and knowledge age, the capital of the company changes from purely physical assets (over which the executive has tight control) towards intellectual assets (over which the executive has far less direct control), along with a vastly different workforce. *And this is where the trouble can start!*

The industrial age executive 'controlled the what' by managing the factors of production through conventional top-down management, a relatively simple command and control model that was accepted, however grudgingly, by the workforce.

The information and knowledge age executive needs to 'create the

CHART 1.1   The information and knowledge revolution

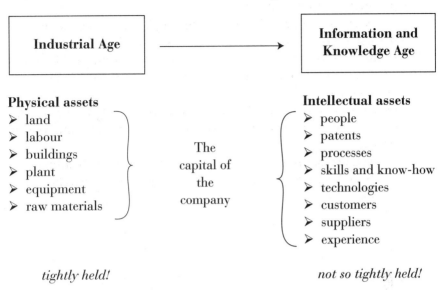

how' by facilitating people and processes via enlightened 360° leadership (360° means leading up, outside, sideways and down) and with a strong customer orientation. This far more complex leadership and facilitation model is expected by today's customers, other stakeholders and employees, who from early schooldays have been taught, it seems, to question almost everything. Thank the Lord they have! See Chart 1.2.

The complexity is compounded because most organisations are in transition between these two 'ages' and are likely to retain one foot in each half of the playing field for many years to come.

This means that executives need to hasten their development within the leadership and facilitation paradigm, yet retain elements of the command and control paradigm while reducing their dependence on them. In other words, increasingly 'create the how' and yet continue to 'control some of the what', according to situations and priorities.

The final ever moving target is the organisation's expectations in terms of desirable management practices and leadership traits within this transition, compared with the executive or manager's perception of how they should act and behave. Clearly, opportunities abound for these expectations and perceptions to be poles apart, with some executives still stuck in command and control mode, and others keen to win the popularity stakes in the feel-good, be-nice-to-everyone, happy-happy school of mismanagement.

CHART 1.2 Impact on executives

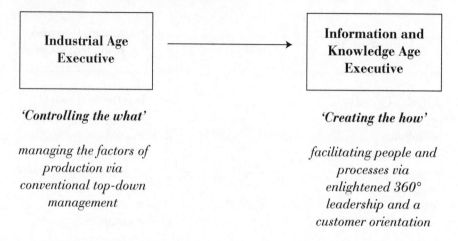

Industrial Age Executive	→	Information and Knowledge Age Executive

'Controlling the what'

managing the factors of
production via
conventional top-down
management

'Creating the how'

facilitating people and
processes via
enlightened 360°
leadership and a
customer orientation

Many executives believe that leadership is all about leading 'down', leading their direct reports. But this is a given these days. Leading down and getting good results with your direct reports is the baseline for performance.

Leading up (your line manager, the executive committee, the board of directors—who need to be led via influence if they are to make optimal decisions about the company); leading outside (key customers, suppliers, the community); leading sideways (your peers, rather than operating solely in your own functional silo); and leading down—*all* these underpin true five-star executive leadership performance and career development potential.

But 360° leadership is complex, particularly if you consider the large number of potential contact points to be led, as demonstrated in the larger company shown in Chart 1.3.

Because all the contact point groups are interconnected in some way, the possible number of communication lines can be demonstrated by multiplying them (up and outside times sideways times down), which in this case computes to 4416!

Executive 360° leaders certainly have their hands full leading those around them, but fortunately they are not alone. Leaders can enlist the support of their team, their direct reports, to 'mark' (in the sports sense) other significant contact points, allowing the leader to focus on key contact points (I call this *internal key account management*).

In the business setting, 'marking' means keeping a careful eye on, communicating with and *engaging* with the person you have been designated

CHART 1.3   360° leadership

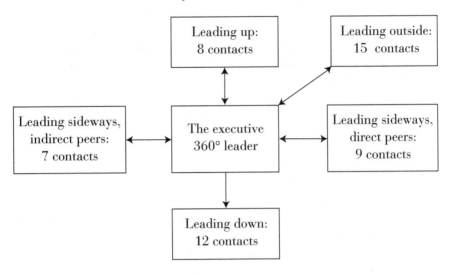

to mark, with appropriate feedback to the team captain—the leader. This is a powerful approach in today's complex 360° environment. See Chart 1.4.

Compounding all this is the fact that, because of flatter organisation structures, the increasing rate and pace of change, and faster job tenure and turnover, many people are promoted into substantial executive leadership roles quite quickly, often from technical and functional

CHART 1.4   Changing leadership emphasis

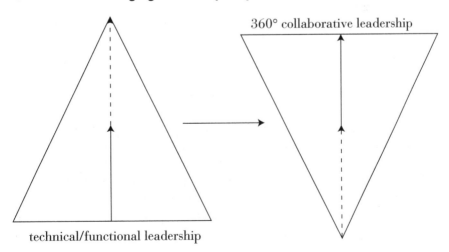

backgrounds. Even those promoted from straight management roles can fail to realise that their leadership roles need to have a true 360° emphasis. This new leadership paradigm is shown in Chart 1.5.

All this is happening and changing at such a pace that it is indeed a 'revolution' we are experiencing, rather than evolution, and for many it is an uncomfortable revolution. The keys to succeeding in the transition from 'controlling the what' to 'creating the how' are the five essential drivers that form the basis of *executive leadership effectiveness* (discussed later in this chapter).

LEADERSHIP MYTHS

In the course of my work I meet many outstanding individuals in leadership and executive positions. But what if they could really attain their full potential, for themselves and for the organisation? What might be the effect—if they could achieve maximum leverage through people and processes—on attaining financial and other results?

I have found that most organisations, particularly during *major change*, fail to unlock the full potential of their most valuable and variable assets,

CHART 1.5   Changing leadership focus

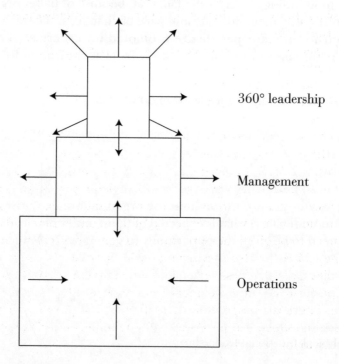

their people. Many try a range of management and leadership approaches, which often turn out to be nothing more than trend-driven, quick-fix solutions. And these quick-fix solutions often attend to leadership myths!

The *first myth* is that executive life is all about results. But results are a given these days and what actually separates successful executives from also-rans is how they behave, the degree to which they exhibit 'desirable' leadership traits, and how they manage and lead not only their direct reports but their peers, senior colleagues, stakeholders and external contacts.

The *second myth* is that executive success is all about leadership. While leadership is a vital ingredient, success also depends on basic management and administrative competence in order to maximise the bottom line and shareholder returns. Success is also about motivation: no matter how skilled an executive may be as a leader or manager, without high levels of self-motivation at work these skills will be underdeployed.

The *third myth* is that an organisation's success requires a team of stars at the executive level. While a team of stars clearly helps, what has an even more powerful effect is a *star team*. Developing teamwork through interpersonal relationships lies at the heart of this, so that each team member harmonises rather than competes with the others. This generates a powerfully synergistic effect, whereas the internally competitive team may eventually self-destruct.

The *fourth myth* is that a new CEO or a new senior executive automatically needs fresh blood, a new team, their own team—out with the old and in with the new! Coupled with this is the theme that people won't change and that the organisation is better off replacing apparently less than satisfactory performers.

Such loss of intellectual capital, the huge costs associated with 'fire and hire', the time and cost it takes for new people to get up to speed, and the erosion of employee trust and morale that this can cause all suggest there must be a better way. And there is a better way. Starting at the top and cascading down throughout the organisation, executives and staff need to understand what is expected of them under new leadership and they need to be given the opportunity to generate great outcomes.

The *fifth myth* is that downsizing works. Invariably, it doesn't! A range of studies shows that two-thirds of organisations that downsize fail to attain their performance improvement objectives in terms of quantum and time frame. There is a range of more graduated options than 'big bang' in downsizing, which if applied invariably generate better outcomes in the medium to longer term.

Such options include more attention to staffing planning, succession planning, natural attrition, early retirement, part-time work, job sharing, study leave, 'encouraged' holiday leave, leave of absence, secondment and discretionary voluntary redundancy. But, for now, 'big bang' seems to remain very much in vogue.

The *sixth myth* is that executives and staff should now manage their own careers. This may be a natural reaction at times of organisational turbulence, so that individuals develop a sense of personal security in place of job security. However, if an organisation abdicates this responsibility to its staff, one outcome may be that the talent manages its way out of the organisation!

While I am not disputing the need for individuals to become more career resilient, I am not in favour of the career theme being abdicated to them. It would seem to make economic sense for line managers to put some energy and time into seeking greater career alignment for their staff—individual and organisational goals coinciding as far as possible—in order to generate a 'You win, I win, we all win together' outcome. The bottom line is a degree of shared responsibility in career management to ensure, at least, that the talent is nurtured and retained.

The *seventh myth* is that an executive (or indeed anyone in a company) needs to conform and play it safe these days. But an organisation of clones is not going to go very far, and nor is the clone. Differences in personal operating styles and views on strategy and operations need to be encouraged, rather than scorned.

For this to happen, the onus is on the organisation to create an environment that engenders motivation and thinking outside the square. And the onus is on individuals to communicate their ideas in a way whereby they are taken seriously and listened to, rather than too easily rejected. Personal selling and presentation skills clearly play important roles. So, too, does a sense of personal confidence which can be developed through a greater understanding of self-image and career direction and destiny, no matter who the future employer might be.

LEADERSHIP TRUTHS

Most organisations fail to address the key fact: that sustained success in any business boils down to leadership and teamwork in action, which need to cascade powerfully throughout the organisation. This is the main opportunity facing most organisations today, and the challenge is *how to make it really happen!*

Training is not enough. Most conventional training and development programs can provide new knowledge or self-awareness. The trouble is, they do not make it happen, or they do not make it happen fast enough. Or they do not make it happen intensively or sustainably enough. This is because they often miss the point. They try to do it for leaders and executives by encumbering them with often largely unnecessary and ineffective processes, rather than emphasising leadership content—in other words, focusing on *how actually* to lead and manage for high performance.

Leaders, executives and teams can only do this for themselves. This is my approach, using proven implementation processes based on extensive empirical and international research and experience—the basis of *executive leadership effectiveness.*

With such input, executives can attain new levels of effectiveness through high-performance leadership, management and teamwork, and cascade this throughout the organisation, making this the culture—'The way we do things around here!'.

Executive leadership effectiveness can make this happen, consolidating and building on conventional leadership and management development, rather than being 'just another leadership approach'.

The theme of *leadership myths and truths* is continued throughout this book, at the end of each chapter.

THE EMOTIONAL INTELLIGENCE BACKDROP

In attaining new levels of effectiveness, leaders and executives will be exhibiting and developing their emotional intelligence (EI), which is now being validated as the heart of executive leadership effectiveness.

Why? Because emotional intelligence is about recognising and dealing effectively with the way we think and feel, understanding 'self' better and underpinning high levels of personal motivation, performance and self-control. Similarly, it's about understanding others better.

Next, it is about understanding how we are perceived by others and our impact on others. Emotional intelligence is also about how to understand and handle other people and their feelings: improving interpersonal relationships is the first step in inspiring and leading others towards positive goals.

In my model, emotional intelligence is also about understanding our 'atmospheric' or motivational needs and values, and how to exercise more self-control when they are not met.

Emotional intelligence requires empathy and active listening skills, and a full understanding of how to deal with and harness individual differences. See Chart 1.6.

CHART 1.6   Emotional intelligence

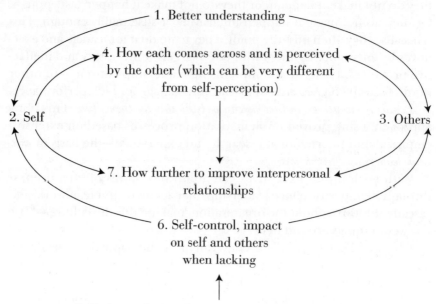

1. Better understanding

4. How each comes across and is perceived
by the other (which can be very different
from self-perception)

2. Self

3. Others

7. How further to improve interpersonal
relationships

6. Self-control, impact
on self and others
when lacking

5. Better understanding our atmospheric needs and
values and degree to which they are met/not met

Over the years I have found that emotional intelligence, as defined, is at the heart of executive leadership effectiveness, whereas many organisations and leaders believe it's more about intellect (IQ). In fact, it's about both, and the model in Chart 1.7 enables you to contemplate them both in the context of executive leadership effectiveness potential.

Yes, it is proven that all the attributes of the information-age, collaborative and facilitative executive leader who exhibits superior emotional intelligence actually *do* generate superior results. Not that leaders should be soft—rather, leaders must be able to leverage people and teams to the full by treating them appropriately as human beings, rather than as physical assets.

Which, in a nutshell, is what *executive leadership effectiveness* is all about!

THE DRIVERS OF EXECUTIVE LEADERSHIP EFFECTIVENESS

After eleven years of Australian empirical research entailing the coaching of more than 600 executives and other key people, together with over

CHART 1.7 Executive leadership effectiveness potential

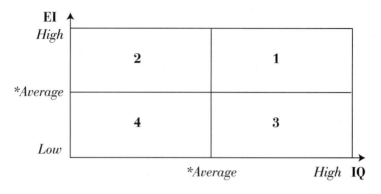

Code
* compared with your leading competitors' executives
1 the potentially highly effective executive leader
2 may be very good with people, but would you entrust them with potentially complex
  issues, such as leading business strategy development or process re-engineering?
3 may be very good with complex issues, but how good are they at leading, attracting,
  developing and retaining talent, and getting results with and through them?
4 any room for them in your leadership ranks?

70 organisational restructures, and overlaid with my assessment of international best practice—I have found five essential drivers (see Chart 1.8):

1. *Influencing*—attaining superior results with individuals over whom
   we have no direct control, yet whose decisions affect strongly the
   ongoing performance and development of the organisation (CEO,
   line manager, board of directors, and external contacts such as key
   customers, suppliers and the community).
2. *Synergising*—attaining superior results with our peers, with whom
   close interface leads to better decisions for the total organisation,
   rather than just operating in our own particular functional silo.
3. *Enabling*—attaining superior results with individuals for whom we
   are responsible, by managing, leading and coaching our direct
   reports forward and attaining superior results with and through
   them.
4. *Energising*—attaining superior results ourselves by optimising our
   motivational alignment with the organisation, and by applying the
   necessary principles and practices for this in dealings with other

CHART 1.8   Executive leadership effectiveness

How to leverage human potential: the five essential elements with universal and time-enduring application for the information and knowledge age executive

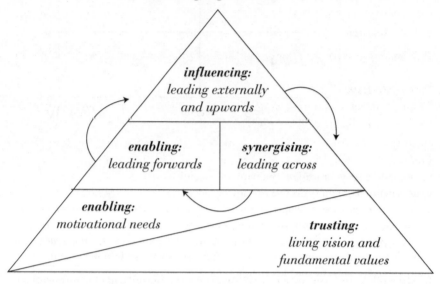

individuals, to create a strongly motivational environment for one and all.

5. *Trusting*—attaining superior results through the belief of direct reports and other individuals in the reliability of the organisation through the consistency of its leaders—'walking the talk' through living the vision and continuously upholding the fundamental values of the organisation—and thereby giving direct reports and other individuals the confidence to act to the full in their roles.

To provide further insight into these five essential drivers and how I address them through executive coaching, each is covered in more detail below and forms the focus of a subsequent chapter.

Influencing

I often start with an examination of power and where it resides in organisations, and describe how to deal with it and succeed in influencing it. This is done by selling yourself assertively and by building a strong network of allies—internally and externally—rather than by indulging in the darker side of political struggles and power plays.

Setting personal selling goals, time management and prioritisation are also important and are addressed in terms of their impact on building loyalty and expanding influence.

Performance at meetings and in group presentations is examined in some detail, as most executives have to work with groups and present to senior internal and external audiences—a great opportunity and challenge for influencing! Written communications are also addressed.

Influencing—attaining superior results with individuals outside our direct control.

Synergising

The initial focus of synergising is leading across the organisation. My operating style is discussed to show how it can be applied to the team and peer setting, all in the context of harnessing diverse operating styles and maximising interpersonal relationships—the key to developing synergy.

Team composition is discussed, together with strategies for dealing with imbalances. The group dynamics of teams also requires an understanding of in-team behaviour characteristics, as well as selection and use of optimal approaches, and conflict resolution.

Finally, team processes are addressed and reviewed with a particular emphasis on when the team should operate like a bona fide cross-functional leadership team with mutual accountability, and when it should orient itself towards individual functions and single leadership from the top—the team leader.

Synergising—attaining superior results with peers.

Enabling

The initial focus of enabling is managing, leading and coaching our direct reports forward. Clearly, techniques for *influencing* and *synergising* are equally applicable to leading individuals forward.

Management practices, including the power of combining motivation and delegation, are addressed together with definitive delegation principles—when to 'abdicate', when to delegate (in its true sense) and when to direct. 'Fast and simple!' is also explained, and represents my new core management competency.

Our own perceptions of leadership traits, and those of others, are examined, with guidelines to which of the leadership trait options to adopt situationally.

Finally, coaching for results is examined, one of the most underutilised yet powerful approaches for putting leadership into action.

Enabling—attaining superior results with individuals for whom we are responsible.

Energising

Job fit is at the heart of *energising*, when our occupational interests and capabilities are represented in our work. I help executives assess this for themselves and for their direct reports.

We all have a range of different motivational needs at work, some of them relating to compensation, others to preferred type of organisation structure or management style, others relating to interpersonal relationships and preferred management style, and others to such emotional needs as self-esteem or sense of achievement.

Understanding and pursuing our motivational needs and the needs of others makes for a more energised, conducive and effective work environment. Adopting and advising on appropriate coping mechanisms when these needs are not fulfilled staves off negative and even destructive individual reactions. This approach is about self-control and avoiding, in its absence, the adverse or even punitive reactions by both ourselves and others around us.

Finally, *energising* correlates to an organisation's capacity to attract, retain, develop and motivate its people: talent management. Potential strategies are addressed in full.

Energising—attaining superior results individually.

Trusting

Many leaders articulate organisational vision and values but fail to follow through and 'walk the talk'. Often this is because vision and values statements are something of a shopping list. Also—because of business imperatives, or for purposes of satisfying financial analysts, the board of directors or shareholders—vision and values are periodically placed 'on hold', at least as far as employee perceptions go.

Through the theme of 'living vision' and 'fundamental values', I help senior executives bring the vision alive and shorten the values shopping list and focus on core, high-level values. The notion here is 'Get these right and walk them, not just talk them'—and the rest, more or less, will take care of themselves.

The key? Leaders in vision- and values-based organisations behave consistently and thereby instil trust. Trust from customers and employees creates a greater sense of freedom, allowing them to act as 'business leaders' in their own roles.

Leadership of change and the best and worst ways of restructuring are also addressed, building or destroying trust according to the approaches selected or avoided. I believe that trust is such an integral element of leadership that I refer to it as 'The Quintessence of Leadership' (see Chart 1.9).

Trusting—attaining superior results through people believing in the reliability of the organisation through the consistency of its leaders in walking the talk of vision and values.

CHART 1.9   Trust

TRUST
The Quintessence of Leadership

'Quintessence. 1. Fifth substance, apart from four elements . . . entirely and latent in all things. 2. Most essential part of any substance, refined extract; purest and most perfect form, manifestation, or embodiment, of some quality or class.'

The Concise Oxford English Dictionary

LINKAGE TO LEADERSHIP COMPETENCIES

These five essential leadership drivers link well to the more conventional lists of leadership competencies. Typical leadership competencies include the following, showing their linkage to my five essential drivers:

➢ *Helicopter perspective*—rises above day-to-day operational routine and sees and understands the bigger picture; sees and exploits the linkages between areas or issues of significance; while capable of detailed analysis, makes decisions and solves problems in their wider context; intuitive and instinctive (links to *enabling*).
➢ *Strategic perspective*—focuses on external trends and projections relating to relevant aspects of international affairs, the economy, government, society, markets, customers, consumers, suppliers, technology and competitors; thinks outside the square and pursues opportunities for innovation and new paradigms (links to *enabling*).
➢ *Visionary leadership*—develops vision; articulates the vision; inspires others to participate; supports, values and empowers them in their progress towards attaining the vision (links to *enabling* and *trusting*).

➤ *Developing others*—helps others to identify and acquire development needs in the context of attaining the vision; inspires continuous learning; prioritises coaching; acts as role model through continuous self-development (links to *enabling* and *energising*).

➤ *Teamwork*—works cooperatively with direct reports, peers and other teams; a dual focus, i.e. on team priorities as well as on functional priorities; displays cross-functional rather than silo perspective; synchronises diverse capabilities and operating styles of team members to optimise synergy; operates efficient team processes (links to *synergising*).

➤ *Advanced team leadership*—in leading/facilitating their team of direct reports, ensures members operate flexibly between both a functional group and a mutually accountable and committed leadership team, selecting times and events judiciously for operating as a *leadership team*, i.e. where *real* opportunities exist for collective input and cross-functional results, and as a *functional group*, where a functional orientation and strong overall 'single' leadership should prevail (links to *synergising*).

➤ *Influencing*—sees situations from others' points of view; flexible approach in dealing with people; 'pulls' them persuasively and convincingly, rather than 'pushes'; listens as much as talks in communication; assertive and a strong negotiator when needed, but seeks win–win; continuously maintains, develops and leverages off strong internal and external networks; uses politics, power and influence positively (links to *influencing*).

➤ *Commanding*—when the going gets tough or the magnitude or urgency of tasks at hand require, can take a firm stand and call others to required action, even if this creates resistance or unpopularity; in this, displays courage and gets the required results (links to *enabling*).

➤ *Managing ambiguity*—copes well with ambiguity, risk, and diverse and complex tasks; sustains the morale and productivity of others in times of change and uncertainty; controls what can be controlled rather than waste time on matters outside their control; displays a sixth sense of what might be around the corner and pre-empts/adapts accordingly (links to *enabling* and *trusting*).

➤ *Leveraging diverse knowledge*—in response to the information age, the era of knowledge, 'creates the how' by facilitating people and processes via enlightened leadership with a strong customer orientation; rather than simply 'controls the what' by managing via conventional top-down management; in this, understands, adapts to, and leverages diversity in gender, ethnic background and age, e.g. Generation X-ers (in their twenties and early thirties) and Y-ers (just entering the workforce) are independent, self-directed and resourceful, often sceptical of authority and institutions, their first loyalty being to themselves and their own careers (links to *enabling* and *energising*).

➢ *Efficiency and effectiveness*—maximises efficient deployment and use of all resources through appropriate practices, processes and procedures; benchmarks internally and externally; helps others establish, monitor and develop their performance against agreed expectations; recognises individual and team contributions, and provides candid developmental or corrective feedback (links to *enabling*).

➢ *Decision making*—engages in systematic analysis yet retains broad perspective; reviews alternatives; thinks creatively; involves others in decision making; learns from lessons of the past; makes sound, timely decisions; exhibits sound commercial judgment (links to *enabling*).

➢ *Achieving results*—understands and pursues their primary business objective, supporting objectives and main drivers of the primary objective; in this, displays energy, a sense of urgency, tenacity, initiative and adaptability; enlists appropriate organisational support; aligns others, gaining their commitment to achieve sought outcomes (links to *enabling*).

YOUR ORGANISATION
In assessing the potential for the further development of *executive leadership effectiveness* in your own organisation, I now table the following thought-prompters.

Newly appointed executives
Organisations often find that it takes newly appointed executives nine months to become 'profitable'. Over 40% of newly appointed executives are seen as not performing at their best within their first year, and a significant proportion of them leave within 20 months of starting in their new roles.

➢ What if your organisation could halve the time needed for newly appointed executives to get up to speed?
➢ What if they could progress more quickly and securely in their new roles, delivering results faster?

➢ What if the risks associated with executive turnover after the honeymoon period could be reduced?

Established executives

Many executives still live in the industrial age and manage via top-down 'controlling the what'. In today's information and knowledge age, superior results come from 'creating the how' through enlightened 360° leadership with a strong customer orientation. Effectiveness as a leader is only part of the success equation; motivation through a sense of full alignment with the organisation is also a prerequisite for success.

➢ In the pursuit of continuous improvement in results, what if all your executives further developed their effectiveness quickly and sustainably . . .
  – in such areas as leadership, teamwork, interpersonal relationships and communication?
  – and through their motivational alignment with the organisation?

Executives potentially in transition

The costs and missed opportunities caused by the resignation of a talented executive, together with the costs of replacement hiring, can run to hundreds of thousands of dollars. As can the problems associated with underperforming executives, or those mismatched with their roles. Similar costs are associated with dismissal and replacement hiring.

➢ What if your organisation improved its ability to retain motivated executive talent for longer?
➢ And turned around any executive square pegs in round holes?
➢ Or, when necessary, and through a positive approach, enabled executives to see for themselves the benefits of reconsidering their career directions or options, including redeployment or moving beyond the organisation?

Change leadership

Two-thirds of restructures (including mergers) do not yield sought-after bottom-line improvements on time, less than 20% produce satisfactory outcomes, and one-third yield unsatisfactory levels of performance improvement or take an unacceptable time to achieve it. About 70% of organisations that downsize find no immediate increase in productivity and more than 50% fail to improve profitability in the following year.

➢ After restructuring, what if your organisation could halve the time it takes executives in new roles or reporting relationships to get up to speed?

➢ What if newly constituted executive teams galvanised far more quickly, yielding the much needed synergy and leverage they can produce?

➢ What if each of your executives demonstrated further capability in the change leadership competence areas of adaptability, entrepreneurism (innovation balanced by risk management), resilience and open, two-way communication?

➢ What if restructuring did not leave any executives in new roles or reporting relationships demotivated, performing poorly or with a sense that they had lost out, or that their future promotional prospects were limited?

➢ At times of major change, what if you were able to reduce the risks of your key people being poached?

Executive teams

In thinking about a particular team or teams, what stage have they reached in their development?

➢ A *new or young team*—a collection of executives operating more or less independently, their main dependence being on the appointed leader for direction and support.

➢ A *divergent team*—affected adversely by a number of issues that it needs to resolve before team members can work together effectively.

➢ A *convergent team*—strong interpersonal relationships and alliances. However, independent thinking is not particularly valued; the danger of cloning is high.

➢ A *synchronised team*—a highly developed team of independent team members, combining star players with a star team; often team decisions exceed what individual team members working by themselves would be able to achieve.

Thinking further about this team, or teams, are they avoiding unsuccessful team makeup, which can include:

➢ just all very clever people: disaster-prone;

➢ too many idea generators: good ideas produced but never taken up;

➢ just idea generators and all-rounders: team looks brilliant but is always beaten by better balanced, broader-based teams that can accomplish things;

➤ fewer than six people: secondary roles/doubling up as needed;
➤ more than eight to ten people: difficult group dynamics where you must be careful about the balance?

THE BOTTOM LINE

If any of these thought-prompters suggest there may be some potential for further improving *executive leadership effectiveness* in your own organisation, then this book is clearly for you!

Executive leadership effectiveness is based on your reading, learning, applying (with the help of the assignments in Appendix A) and even coaching your direct reports and others (using the guidelines in Appendix B) in the five essential drivers described earlier. Your direct reports themselves can then coach their direct reports in the same principles and practices, and so on in a full cascading sense. It's your choice as to how far you use the contents of this book.

If you choose to use the contents of this book to the fullest extent, then the fourfold advantage here is that, first, you and your direct reports can benefit from a powerful and sometimes transformational experience, adding immense value to your and their executive effectiveness as leaders, in teamwork and as internal coaches.

Second, coaching someone else in the development and implementation of new leadership and teamwork skills is one of the best ways of becoming proficient in them yourself.

Third, having each executive coach their direct report is an excellent way of engaging in, and demonstrating, *leadership in action.*

Fourth, with each of your direct reports undertaking this with their direct reports, the rollout and cascading effect throughout the organisation of new, effective approaches to leadership and teamwork is swift and powerful, generating great momentum in leveraging human talent.

MORE LEADERSHIP MYTHS	MORE LEADERSHIP TRUTHS
➤ Executive life is all about leadership.	➤ It's about balancing leadership with management and when to emphasise each.
➤ Leadership is all about leading your direct reports.	➤ Leadership is about leading people all around you!
➤ It's about the latest management and leadership techniques.	➤ It's about you as a manager and leader — in action!
➤ It's all about a high IQ.	➤ It's about a high IQ and a high EI!
➤ Leadership is all about a long shopping list of competencies.	➤ It's about just five activities: influencing, synergising, enabling, energising and trusting!

DON'T HIDE!

➤ Change isn't going to go away; it will just go faster and faster and faster.
➤ You have to develop yourself continuously, and that's *your* responsibility.
➤ Always walk the talk of your organisation's living vision and fundamental values.
➤ Leadership needs to be a proactive rather than purely reactive process.
➤ If you are not spending as much time on the process of executive leadership as you are on business processes, you are missing the main point.

YOUR WEEKEND REVIEW

1. Have we been thinking and acting 'small, fast and timely', focusing on the individual customer and sales transaction, focusing on the individual employee?
2. Are we tuned in to the fast changing customer's needs and wants, the global village, information technology and telecommunications, overseas competitors, changing business fundamentals, and demographic and social change?

3. Are we fully understanding, estimating and attending to the impacts of the need for leaders to be high-tech, high-touch, leading as well as managing, building on our Australian strengths, attending to our Australian challenges?

4. Are we focusing on the changing nature of executive leadership: leading up, outside and sideways, as well as leading down?

5. Are we overplaying up-to-date management and leadership processes and underplaying the fact that it's about ourselves as managers and leaders in action?

6. Are we working with and developing our emotional intelligence, together with the leadership drivers of influencing, synergising, enabling, energising and trusting?

7. As leaders, are we focusing in different ways on different needs: newly appointed executives, established executives, executives potentially in transition, change leadership and executive teams?

CHAPTER 2

Influencing

Influencing is about leading those outside your control—CEO, line manager, board of directors and key external contacts—so that they make better decisions affecting your area of the business!

KEYNOTES FROM THE COMMENTATORS

Less reliance on more formal authority and greater attention to getting results through influence—particularly influencing one's peers—represents a critical leadership development priority. Communication is at the heart of this, and communication means each party leaves the meeting with a clearer understanding of the other party. You need to tell people stuff, but they've got to hear it and listen to it. Effective communication means getting into the hearts and minds of people around you, at every level, in every way, and on every day. In this, greater competitive and organisational complexity underpins the need for 'clarity'—what's expected, what's the end game, what's the essence of our roles, and how do we express it simply?

David Hearn, Chief Executive Goodman Fielder

Executive leaders have to be in touch and in sync with all their stakeholders; they must always have successors in place; they need to emphasise continuous improvement and development, and not rely on just their base learning and education.
Peter Wilkinson, Chief Executive David Jones

Create a management team of influencers, rather than instructors! Executives need to be able to work well across a large range of stakeholders, including senior level staff in parent companies. When working with joint venture partners, establish strong working relationships within them, in a way that maximises the value of your joint venture offering. A minimum expectation should be positive participation in all relevant communication forums and ensuring outstanding issues are quickly brought to a close.
Lyn Cobley, Chief Executive Officer—tradingroom.com.au
(a joint venture between Fairfax and Macquarie Bank)

This chapter provides guidance to executives and managers on how to deal with and succeed at power, politics and influence. This is achieved by selling yourself assertively, individually and with groups, by building a strong network of supporters (allies) and by successful personal selling, rather than by indulging proactively in the darker side of political struggles and power plays.

POWER

Every organisation has its networks, and we are not talking here about the formal structure of lines of power and authority but the informal ones that operate behind the scenes (see Chart 2.1). The sooner you become aware of these networks, the sooner you can begin to use them for the further development of your image and your own career success.

This doesn't mean fighting or clawing at other people's expense— such an attitude will backfire on you eventually. What it does mean is that you do *not* stick your head in the sand about how the organisation really operates and who the real decision makers are. Take the time to look around and ask yourself the following questions:

➢ Whose advice is sought and followed?
➢ Whose criticism counts?

CHART 2.1
Formal structure

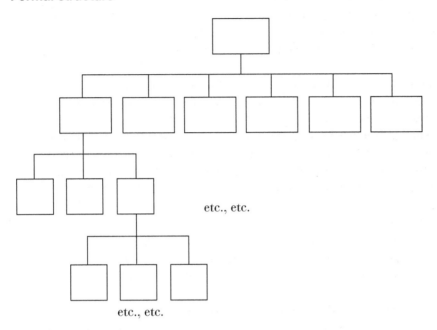

etc., etc.

etc., etc.

Informal structure

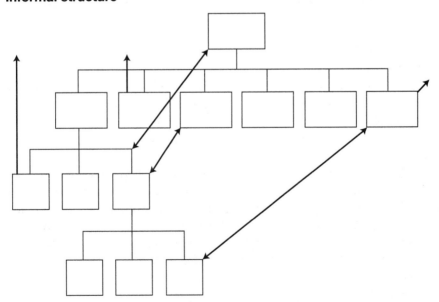

- ➤ Whose ideas carry weight?
- ➤ Whose opinion causes others to change theirs?
- ➤ At whom do people look when they make a recommendation?
- ➤ Who confides in whom?
- ➤ Who backs whose suggestions?

Endeavouring to answer these questions is not just an exercise in people watching but a necessary requirement for your own ongoing success, career protection and advancement. Once you have identified the power plays and networks, you will be in a better position to use them to your advantage and to enhance your influence. To do this effectively you will also need feedback on how you are seen, in terms of your work performance and your relationships with others. This feedback can come from the senior executive to whom you report, your peers and even your subordinates.

Be aware of how people respond to you in terms of tone of voice, their desire to know your opinion, and unspoken signals. Don't neglect to ask for feedback directly on how you are doing and where you may need improvement. In this way you can set up a channel for communication and feedback that will prevent potential problems and keep you informed, rather than isolated.

However, the biggest problem in the context of 'power'—and also the most significant opportunity—is to work out where the power *really* resides in your organisation.

Case Study

Take the case of the newly appointed CEO of a major division of a large company. He was appointed to follow through on some recommendations he had made earlier while acting as a management consultant and advising on divisional strategy and operations improvement. This newly appointed divisional CEO was told by his boss—the CEO of the overall group—to watch out for one of his direct reports, an older-style general manager who managed, in a highly autocratic fashion, one of the companies in the division. It went further than this. The division needed rationalising and part of that rationalisation might include the early retirement of the 'difficult' general manager, who had been a thorn in the side of the group CEO for years. However, the group CEO had lacked sufficient intestinal fortitude to do anything about it.

The new divisional CEO went about his task and found, indeed, that rationalisation and the phasing out of the general manager in question made sense. Pressure was applied in the context of the need for change and improved bottom-line performance. Just a few short months into the job, the divisional CEO was called into a meeting with the group chairman, who had flown in from the group head office. The meeting was a fight from start to finish. The chairman challenged the divisional CEO from the outset and it became obvious that he was in real trouble, although the reason for this was unclear at the time. The group CEO watched the confrontation like a salamander, watery-eyed and licking his lips, but making no comment and certainly not leaping to the defence of his new divisional CEO, who up to that point had made an excellent start in his new role. Shortly after this disastrous meeting, the divisional CEO received the bullet—several, actually, over a period of a couple of weeks—until the *coup de grâce* finally came. He never knew at the time what hit him, alas.

The group CEO did not, after all, hold the power. The power—and in this case the 'forces of darkness'—actually resided with the general manager. It turned out that he had a strong personal relationship with the group chairman because they had worked together closely, earlier in their careers.

The exiting divisional CEO learned a lot about power, politics and influence from this episode, although it took him quite a long time to recover from the experience. I should know—he was me!

INFLUENCE

I have been involved in executive and management development for more than 25 years, and during that time I have advised countless executives and others on how to become successful in organisational and business life, through winning at power, politics and influence.

One of the key success ingredients in this area is best described thus: 'It's not *what* you know, but *who* you know!'. Indeed, it is clear that personal selling—selling your views, ideas and yourself to others, networking to expand your contact base of allies, and effectively negotiating with others within and outside your immediate work environment—is a critical success factor in this.

Executives and managers can accomplish this by developing an understanding of professional consultative selling techniques, adapting them to their own unique circumstances and honing such skills to an advanced level. What the executive or manager is trying to achieve here is greater 'influence' and this can be accomplished only through effective personal selling and the development of alliances.

Let me define exactly what I mean by the terms 'contact', 'lead', 'prospect' and 'alliance'. A *contact* is just about anyone you know or seek to know, or who may seek to know you. A *lead* is a contact who *may* have an interest or need to develop an alliance with you. A *prospect* is a contact who looks like having such an interest or need. The term *alliance* means ongoing informal liaison and mutual support with allies. See Chart 2.2.

Leads can come from many sources, such as existing allies, newspaper announcements, social contacts, family and friends, and so forth. As most leads will not have a definite interest in you or a desire to develop an alliance with you, you may have to generate many leads to get the few who actually do have a need or interest.

CHART 2.2   Alliances

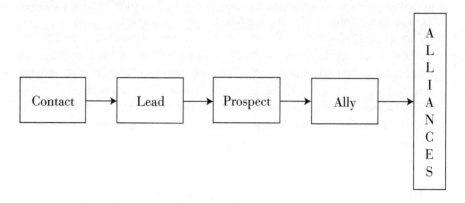

THE IMPORTANCE OF SELLING YOURSELF EXTERNALLY

Generating new allies within the organisation is a prerequisite for developing your internal influence and network of support. However, in today's turbulent economic and organisational environment, it is just as important to develop external influence and allies. Whatever the position you occupy, you are a representative of your organisation. If you have a strong network of external allies who think well of you, this will enhance your organisation's reputation. It will also enhance your reputation, and this will be fed back to those who matter in your organisation.

This strengthens your position and future. A strong external network of allies also balances your perspective and prevents you from becoming too introspective. Such a network of allies can tap you into a cadre of external experts and advisers who will not charge you a cent in fees!

Generating new external contacts is the first step in extending your external network of allies and influence, and your success in this is directly proportional to the number of people you contact (all else being equal). The importance of generating new external contacts cannot be overemphasised.

Case Study

I know of one major company which makes it a policy to use management consultants on a professional fee-paying basis only in extreme cases. Its senior executive team has developed the finest and largest informal 'Board of Management Advice' in the land—and it doesn't cost them a cent, other than the occasional lunch. They have even been able to implement Total Quality Management without using external consultants; instead, they used advice, tools and techniques sourced from other companies through their network of external allies. Neither do they use executive search consultants. They have such an expansive external network that any senior vacancy that arises can always be filled by the best and most relevant executive talent available, through word-of-mouth referral.

Another vital aspect is that all executives and managers need to become increasingly involved in customer contact and revenue generation. According to Richard Koch and Ian Godden, authors of *Managing Without Management*, the 'post-management' corporation will be aiming for a doubling of profitable sales in ten years, and in this context executives and managers will need to spend half their time dealing with customers, compared with only 5% currently. Get ready for the post-management era—step up your external personal selling efforts!

The first step in making a success of personal selling is to acquire the attitude of an entrepreneur: executives or managers seeking greater influence have a responsibility to run their business of personal selling efficiently and profitably.

Goal setting is the starting point of achievement. We have to know where we are heading and what we hope to achieve before we can take the necessary steps to get us there and effectively monitor our progress so that we stay on course. Goal setting in personal selling involves two principles:

➤ the setting of realistic, specific achievement goals; and
➤ monitoring those goals regularly.

SETTING GOALS

To be effective, goals must be realistic. They should be attainable, but set a little higher than would be required for easy achievement—you should have to work hard to achieve them. Setting them way out of reach, however, will only result in discouragement and eventually work against you.

Your goals should be specific, so that you can easily tell whether or not you are achieving them. To set a goal of 'improving personal selling influencing performance' or 'making more contacts' is so general as to be meaningless. Some examples of specific personal selling and influencing goals might be:

➢ Liaise with each member of the board of directors, monthly.
➢ Touch base with each senior executive in the organisation or division at least once a week.
➢ Make four presentations a year to external groups.
➢ Develop four new external contacts and two supporters or allies each quarter.
➢ Phone two former external contacts and one ally per week for an update.

Monitor your goals regularly

Make sure your goals remain realistic in the light of current developments and changing circumstances. Don't be tempted, however, to revise your goals downward at the slightest excuse. Your goals should stand, regardless of your current performance, unless there have been major positive or negative factors beyond your control. Continuous monitoring will keep you on track and help keep your personal goals and objectives in sight and attainable.

ORGANISATIONAL CONTACTS

In selling yourself and influencing at the executive and managerial levels you are not always dealing with independent contacts. You are often dealing instead with organisational contacts, who may be in some way involved, directly or indirectly, in helping you gain greater influence. These contacts may include executives in your own or other businesses, manufacturers, wholesalers, retailers, agricultural and resource companies, government agencies, associations and so forth.

In attempting to focus on organisational characteristics, you should realise that there are some major differences between independent and organisational contacts. For example, organisational contacts:

➢ normally associate with others, particularly those outside their employer organisations, for fewer *personal* reasons than do independent contacts;
➢ are sometimes restricted by well-defined company policies and practices, as well as the inevitable time pressures;

> typically distribute liaison with external contacts among several other people.

Thus, in trying to understand behaviour and motivation, you must consider not only the individual with whom you wish to develop an alliance but also the organisational characteristics that will influence this alliance. For example:

> What are the policies of the organisation?
> Apart from the contact I am targeting, how many other people are likely to be involved in developing this alliance?
> Who is the main influencer? Is it one individual or a group?
> If it is a group, who are the key people that tend to sway group opinion?
> What kind of individual operating style(s) am I likely to encounter, to which I must adapt and respond, in order to get desired results?

Being able to answer such questions, as they relate to each of your organisational contacts, obviously takes some preparation.

TIME MANAGEMENT AND PRIORITISATION

One of the toughest challenges facing executives and managers today is to make every hour of the day count for more. Challenging economic conditions and a highly competitive commercial environment have made efficient and profitable use of time essential for survival.

Working harder and longer is not necessarily the answer. What is needed is a good hard look at where you are spending your time and whether you are getting maximum payback for your efforts. Too much of your time may be spent on associating with marginal or non-productive allies, time that could be spent developing and maintaining the more profitable allies. This is just good business sense. Remember that, in selling yourself and further developing your influence, you are managing your own business and must keep one eye on the results, without rushing, pressuring or alienating any of your allies, whether external to the organisation or internal.

The best way of ensuring that your time is spent efficiently and profitably when interacting with your allies is to plan. Time management and planning is essential to your personal success, but is often ignored in favour of the 'hit and miss' approach. Planning takes time but, if undertaken in the evening or at weekends, it need not eat into your personal selling and business time. How and where do you get started?

A common pitfall in selling yourself and developing your influence is to devote too much time to low-potential allies and insufficient time to high-potential allies. If all this low-potential time can be recouped, it often improves personal selling efficiency by one-third or more. A close analysis of how you spend your time should point out where your plan may need some restructuring. To do this, you will need to complete a classification of your existing and prospective allies, and one way to do this is by a I, II, III analysis (Chart 2.3).

In this analysis I represents the high-yield/high-potential allies (existing and potential). You may find they make up 20% of your allies but 80% of your alliance and influence potential. Devote maximum time and attention to each 'I' ally. II represents the mid-yield/mid-potential allies. They may make up 30% of your contacts and 15% of your alliance and influence potential. Devote some time and attention to each 'II' ally. III represents the low-yield/low-potential allies. They may make up as many as 50% of your allies, yet offer alliance and influence potential of only 5%. Devote minimal time and attention to each 'III' ally and consider referring them to someone else in your organisation or dropping them altogether.

The first step is gradually to discontinue your low-yield/low-potential allies. The time saved can be used to increase the results from your existing, high-yield allies, as well as to cultivate those prospective allies with a high-yield potential. In submitting your existing and prospective

CHART 2.3 Ally prioritisation

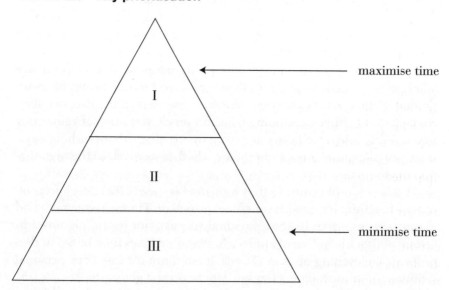

contacts to the I, II, III analysis, don't be too hasty in rejecting current low-yield allies, particularly if you have reason to believe that the yield will improve dramatically in the future. But as the manager of your own personal selling and influence development business, you should dedicate the major portion of your time and effort to those allies who yield the greatest return on your time, efforts and expense.

BUILDING LOYALTY
Building loyalty requires taking care of the interests of your allies. Stay in touch with them by planning and scheduling calls and visits.

Some executives and managers keep a daily 'reminder' file, so that they call their allies or visit them at predetermined times. There is no 'right' number of times to keep in touch, or 'right' amount of time to wait between making contact again. This will depend on each ally, the types of topics addressed with them and their importance to you as individuals. The main point to remember is to schedule call-backs and visits into your planning—this will ensure that each ally receives adequate attention.

EXPANDING YOUR INFLUENCE
Simply maintaining your current network of allies is not enough if you want to be really successful. It is consistent growth in the size of the support network that distinguishes the mediocre executive or manager from the outstanding one. There are basically three ways to increase the potency of your network: *increase dealings with current allies, develop new allies and win back lost allies.*

Increase dealings with current allies
Your best chance of developing your influence is to deal more with your existing allies, as they have already been won over to you. It is much easier to build on existing goodwill than to search out and win over new allies.

Dealing more with existing allies can mean developing your relationship more along its current lines, or meeting more of your ally's needs by addressing a wider range of topics. Also, as your know-how is being upgraded and improved constantly, there is a great opportunity to make your allies aware of this increased knowledge and how it can be applied to their interests and needs.

Let's take a professional selling example of increasing sales to existing customers. The prospect has been closed on a car insurance quote. The astute insurance agent then asks a raft of questions that supposedly relate to information needed to complete the application process, so that the car insurance policy can be issued. In fact, the insurance agent is certainly doing that, but more besides. They are finding out about potential additional insurance needs. When their new client drops by to collect the policy, the agent will be ready with alternatives for him for home insurance and other forms of cover.

This example, while not conventional personal selling, illustrates clearly a technique for developing your existing allies. Adapt it and, in the process, 'buy ownership' of your own adaptation.

Develop new allies

Existing, satisfied allies are an excellent source of leads for new allies. They can usually provide you with several names of good prospects, as well as offer suggestions on how to meet the prospect's interests or needs. Clues picked up in this way are one of your best sources of new allies. Remember, elitist executive and managerial networkers acquire up to half a dozen referrals for every alliance developed. Elitist networkers also dedicate more than 90% of their networking time to referrals.

Win back lost allies

Because personal selling to established allies forms the basis of successful networking, losing allies can greatly erode your current and future networking scope and potential influence. If you lose an ally other than through them moving away or going out of business, then something has happened to upset the status quo. If you value the ally, it is important to find out what happened. Perhaps their views about you have deteriorated, their interests and needs have changed, the effort entailed in your alliance has become too great, or others have done a better personal selling job. For whatever reason, if the loss of your ally comes as a complete surprise, you haven't been doing your job in staying in touch with your ally, or keeping up to date with developments in their field.

You may be able to win back lost allies if you find out the real reason and do your best to rectify the situation. Spend as much time and effort on trying to win back the ally as you feel is justified, considering the value of your alliance and your chances of being successful. Otherwise, you'll have to let the ally go—but learn from the experience in order to prevent such a loss happening again.

INFLUENCING AT MEETINGS

Meetings represent great opportunities for developing your alliances and thereby your influence, whether with allies outside the organisation or within. Meetings are where all your careful preparation, experience and training should come together to convince the other party to form an alliance with you. 'Alliance' may sound a strange and even somewhat strong term, as may the word 'allies', but this concept is one of the major outcomes of influence, if you think about it.

The main advantage of the face-to-face meeting is that it can be tailored to the prospect. It provides you with instant feedback on the other party's response, so that immediate adjustments can be made if necessary.

As the communication process is two-way, you are not only giving information but receiving it. In fact, most of those who are effective at personal selling act more as receivers than transmitters during a meeting by 'tuning in' to the prospect and practising active listening skills. Without a certain amount of empathy (where you sense reactions and respond to them), it is difficult to establish a relationship of trust, so essential to building a close alliance.

There are six steps to conducting an effective meeting: gaining attention, arousing interest, building desire, winning conviction, getting action, and writing notes of appreciation (Chart 2.4).

CHART 2.4   Effective meetings

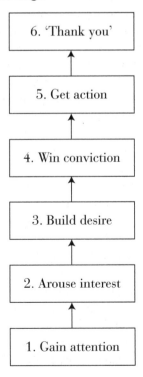

6. 'Thank you'

5. Get action

4. Win conviction

3. Build desire

2. Arouse interest

1. Gain attention

Gaining attention

Your opening statements should be such that you gain the prospect's attention immediately. This doesn't mean that you should turn somersaults or make wild, impossible claims! What it *does* mean is that you should have prepared an opening statement which introduces you (and your organisation) and then launches into the benefits of the topic you wish to discuss. This should grab the prospect's attention right away, as you know it to be a high priority for that particular individual.

Arousing interest

Once you have gained the prospect's attention, you must maintain it by arousing interest in what you are saying. This can be done by introducing a little touch of drama into your discussion. Don't let everything out of the bag at once—try to encourage the prospect to become involved by holding back on some aspects of the topic that you know will be of interest, and thus encourage questions.

Unless you can get the prospect to talk, you won't get very far. Encourage a dialogue, where both you and the prospect ask and answer questions. This will maintain their interest throughout the presentation and discourage mind wandering or 'tuning out'. If at any time you sense the prospect's attention is wandering, you can bring it back by asking an open question that needs some thought to answer, rather than just a yes/no response.

Building desire

Psychologically, before your prospect can make a positive decision to accommodate what you seek, they must actually want to do this. Once they reach this stage, they have a definite desire to follow through.

You can build them up to this desire by making frequent reference to how accommodating what you seek will benefit them, how their interests or needs will be satisfied or their problems solved. This should be explained in language they can understand: jargon and overly technical terms will turn them off, rather than build desire.

Winning conviction

This is where someone, or something other than you and the content of the discussion, convinces the prospect to accommodate what you seek. This can be a personal endorsement from another satisfied ally, a visit to your facilities, or a practical demonstration that gets the prospect more involved in what you seek. In other words, at this stage you must provide the prospect with proof that what you have been saying is true.

Getting action

The final step of the meeting should focus on getting the prospect to act, by signalling agreement to accommodate what you seek. There are several effective ways of doing what is often referred to as 'closing', and these are addressed later.

Writing notes of appreciation

'Thank you' is one of the most important phrases in personal selling; by sending notes that say 'Thank you', you will be leaving your mark or impression on the prospect. Thank-you notes should be sent:

➤ after first and all subsequent meetings with prospects and allies;
➤ after the prospect or ally has helped you in some way;
➤ to referrers;
➤ whenever you have had a positive telephone conversation with a contact, prospect or ally, or after an encounter with anybody who can potentially refer other prospects to you.

STRUCTURED vs PERSONALISED APPROACH

There has been a lot of controversy over the best type of approach to use in personal selling and meetings—structured, personalised or balanced.

In the *structured*, or 'canned', approach, you have total control as the whole meeting has been worked out ahead of time, right down to the exact wording to use. All possible objections that may be raised are anticipated and responses prepared. With this approach, you know that all key points will be covered and nothing will be missed. The advantage of this type of approach is that it can provide the new, inexperienced personal salesperson with confidence. It also simplifies personal selling self-development efforts, as one basic approach is developed, potentially to be used in all meetings.

The obvious disadvantage is that it doesn't allow for the differing needs, interests or behaviour of the other party. Also, it can sound stilted and unnatural and the other party may resent being treated 'just like the others'. We all like to think we are special and this goes for prospects, too. The totally structured meeting can also be a problem if the same person is visited several times. On the other hand, the problem with the completely *personalised* approach is that a different one must be prepared for each situation, and this can become unwieldy and time-consuming. And it can be confusing if you handle more than one or two personal sales meetings a day.

It has generally been found that a *balanced* approach is best, where some kind of framework or meeting outline is prepared which ensures that nothing important is overlooked—sample statements and questions can be written down. In this way, you can retain some control over the meeting. However, there is some flexibility in that decisions on the exact wording to use, what information to add, what to omit are left to your discretion at the time of the meeting. This leaves room for questions from the other party, as well as interaction in the process—essential ingredients in most successful meetings.

This brings us to an effective way to elicit participation by the other party—the use of visuals.

USE OF VISUALS

Visuals can help you develop a better discussion. They include brochures, presentation manuals, slides, overheads, videos and testimonials. By using visuals, you can often present more in a crisp and timely fashion (bearing in mind you have only 15–20 minutes to retain the other party's attention and interest).

Visuals can be used in structured, personalised or balanced meetings: you can stick rigidly to them or orient the main benefits in the visual to the specific needs of the other person. When using visuals, make sure your prospect or associate is seated in such a way that they can see the visuals clearly and you can see their reactions.

Whether you use presentation manuals, slides or overheads, it is recommended that you have one set relating to each topic you wish to address. In external meetings, visuals can reinforce an introduction to yourself and your organisation, information relating to what you or the organisation has accomplished or undertaken in the past and which is relevant to the meeting, and information relating to what you or your organisation can do for the other party—all related in the form of benefits.

When using visuals you need to be fully conversant with their contents. Point with a pen for emphasis, and look at the visuals yourself and then at the other party for reactions. This will ensure the prospect looks at your visuals and then at you, alternately.

With regard to brochures, underline or circle key points and leave the material with the other person.

CLOSING

Closing is the ultimate goal of your meeting. It helps your prospect or ally to make the right decision—in other words, to accommodate what you are seeking. If you cannot close, then you cannot accomplish this, no matter how good you are at planning, prospecting, approaching, questioning and overcoming concerns or objections. A football team might have all the moves, speed and techniques needed to get the ball near the goal, but it won't win if it doesn't score! Over the long term, success in closing determines the extent of your network of allies and influence, the achievement of your goals and even your level of income.

In spite of the importance of closing, many executives and managers engaged in personal selling fail to learn and practise closing techniques, and thus limit themselves to a network of allies, influence and income level much smaller than they could attain with a little extra knowledge and skill in closing.

There are certain times during a meeting when attempting to close may be appropriate. The trick is to learn how to recognise these opportunities. Closing doesn't have to wait until the end of the meeting; if the other party is ready, it can come very early in the personal selling process, sometimes right after the approach. Take the case of the football team, where goals can be scored in the last and *first* few minutes of play.

How do you recognise when the other party is ready to accommodate what you seek? There are certain closing signals that you must watch for. Those who learn to identify these signals will be more successful in closing than those who try to close indiscriminately throughout the personal selling process. Closing signals can be classified as *verbal* or *physical.* Some examples:

➤ *Verbal*
 – 'Yes, I guess that would solve our problem.'
 – 'Did you say you would consider providing some ongoing input?'
 – 'How soon can you get involved?'
 – The other party asks more questions about the topic being addressed, or starts to slow down—both may indicate a high level of interest.
➤ *Physical*
 – The other person nods in agreement.
 – They re-examine the visuals more closely.
 – They check something in the files or on their computer.

Verbal and physical clues are numerous—you can probably come up with many more from your own experience. Practice will improve your ability to recognise these signals of interest and readiness to form an alliance with you or accommodate your other needs.

Once you have determined an opportune moment for closing, there are several methods that can be used, and they can be built into the following sequence:

➢ Display a full understanding of the other party's requirements, motives, preferences and any objections (which should have been overcome).
➢ Portray sincerity, empathy and a confidence that you are able to address their interests or meet their precise needs.
➢ Recognise closing signals.
➢ Apply a test close.
➢ Apply one or more closing techniques.
➢ Be silent after you have asked the closing question. Don't say another word until the other person has responded.

Two popular closing techniques are *assuming a close* and *direct close*.

Assuming a close

Here you proceed as if the other party is ready to accommodate what you seek, whether or not they have indicated it. With this type of close, the onus is on the other person to stop you if they aren't ready. The sequence is to pause, smile and ask such questions as:

➢ 'Incidentally, which is the best date for our next meeting?'
➢ 'Incidentally, which of your colleagues should I meet at our next meeting?'

Direct close

Here, you ask the other person directly—for example, whether they would like to continue to meet. Obviously, the risk is that they will decline, so don't use this method unless they have somehow indicated a definite readiness to accommodate what you seek.

A powerful analogy is the fly fisherman. Such people go to great lengths to equip themselves and to venture forth to cast and hopefully make a catch. In the final analysis, however, unless they get within range of the fish, and unless they cast the right type of fly across a patch of water the size of a table-top, they will fail to attain their objective. Closing is like this. You have to be equipped and prepared. You need to have tracked down leads to find prospects. And you have to find the right moment and place to cast that all-important fly (the close) with accuracy, in order to attain your objectives.

THE COMMUNICATION PROCESS

Selling yourself, influencing, finding allies and negotiating your way to success comprise basically a communication process and success at it depends on your communication skills. These skills can be learned and improved on, so as to upgrade the quality of communication and all subsequent contacts with your target audience.

What do we mean by communication? According to the dictionary:

> Communication is a process by which meanings are exchanged between individuals, through a common set of symbols.

The symbols take the form of speech, written messages, facial expressions, gestures and actions. Effective communication requires both a transmitter and a receiver. Simply 'explaining something' to a contact does not guarantee that communication has taken place.

In moving from you (the transmitter) to your contact (the receiver), or vice versa, there may be interference, or 'noise', which prevents the message from being properly understood. Some examples of 'noise' are:

➢ ambiguous words and phrases (such as 'We'll meet as soon as possible'; be more specific: 'We'll try to meet next Friday');
➢ speaking too quickly, or mumbling words;
➢ failing to clarify; you may know what you are talking about but your contact may not understand you;
➢ failing to use terms that are easily understood, and trying to impress with jargon;
➢ not taking into account the mood, attitude and corresponding attention span of the receiver, your contact, when delivering your information.

Effective communication implies the correct use of language and grammar, as well as tone of voice and volume. But it also implies the effective use and reading of body language (such as posture, facial expressions and gestures). Finally, effective communication implies active listening, as communication is a two-way process. Here are some rules for active listening.

➢ Be committed to concentrating on what your contacts are saying, rather than on formulating what you will say next.
➢ Take an active interest in what they are saying and express your interest through your responses, facial expressions and body language.

➢ Be willing to hear out your contacts fully. Never interrupt or try to take the words out of their mouths, as the complete story may throw more light on the situation.

➢ Try to prevent distraction by shutting out background noise and movement as much as possible. Focus on the contact's face and voice.

➢ As you listen, rather than interjecting your own thoughts, summarise what the contact is saying and pick out the key points.

➢ Practise your active listening skills at every opportunity. As with most skills, practice makes perfect!

Now take the opportunity to diagnose and prescribe ways and means by which you can further improve your communication performance at meetings (Chart 2.5).

CHART 2.5 Diagnose, then prescribe

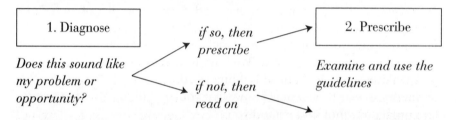

Diagnosis *Do you sometimes have difficulty getting the other party to open up, converse with you, or tell you what is on their mind? If so:*
Prescription *Ask questions.*

Effective personal selling requires effective communication, and questioning is a vital part of the communication process. The main purpose of questioning is to uncover the contact's interests, to confirm that your messages have been understood as you intended, and to encourage contact participation in the discussion process. It is through questioning that you find out the information necessary to help you do this. The trick is to know what you are looking for, and to ask the right questions in the right way.

The traditional method of personal selling spends a lot of time on small talk, but little on real information gathering. Professional personal selling shuns meaningless chit-chat, and focuses instead on drawing out the contact for the purpose of learning how best to address the contact's interests and needs. Most contacts today appreciate business networkers who, after a few brief opening statements, come right to the point and show some interest and concern for their needs by asking well-phrased, pertinent questions. The art of effective questioning is thus a crucial part of the personal selling process.

Diagnosis *Do you sometimes feel you are doing too much of the talking and telling? If so:*
Prescription *Question rather than inform.*

You can tell people things, or you can ask them questions. Which is preferable? Asking questions is always preferable because, when you inform someone about something, you are often pushing; when you ask them questions, you are pulling. When you say something, the other party may doubt it; when the other party says something, it is usually true in their minds. In summary, you should spend about twice as much time questioning as you spend informing.

In order to choose the correct type of question for the moment at hand, you must know what you are trying to achieve with your questions (uncover interests or needs, get the other party talking, zero in on a particular topic), and temper this with the other party's level of responsiveness at the time.

Don't ask complicated questions using technical jargon. The other party may be embarrassed to admit their ignorance, and thus may react in an abrupt or hostile way. In any case, straightforward questions, using language and terms that are easily understood, will be more likely to put the other party at ease and elicit an honest response. Also, it is better to present one idea at a time, gradually building as you go along, rather than confuse people with several questions at once.

Never ask others bluntly if they can help you, or if they have time. This puts them on the defensive and you may get an answer that is far from the truth. Instead, explain the reasons why it would help to have some idea of their interest in you or ability to spend some time with you, or to accommodate what you seek.

'Will your input be sufficient? I'm sure you understand—I really need to do my homework and market research fully' is better than 'Who's the best person to talk to around here?'. Most people will not object to such questions if you explain why you need to know.

In general, it is better to begin with fairly general questions and proceed to the more specific as you get a better idea of contact concerns and requirements. You may find, through effective questioning, that you have been trying to address an inappropriate topic—better to find out sooner than later!

Build on previous responses rather than jump around from one topic to another: stay with one issue until you are sure the other party has been satisfied. Organising your questions will help you to keep the meeting focused and thus maintain a sense of control, as you lead the other party through the stages discussed above—attention, interest, desire, commitment and action.

Diagnosis *Do you sometimes feel the conversation is not going your way, or that you need to somehow exert more control? If so:*

Prescription *Try closed questions.*

A closed question limits the contact's response in that it can usually be answered by a simple Yes/No. Closed questions are therefore also known as 'directive' questions. Some examples are:

➤ 'Are you happy with your present supplier?'
➤ 'Are you having any problems with the system you had installed last year?'
➤ 'Will you be needing to renegotiate contracts soon?'
➤ 'Do you feel the investment is too high?'
➤ 'Are you worried about the availability of top professional staff?'

Closed questions are not usually effective in drawing out the feelings and needs of the other party, but they can be used effectively to:

➤ steer the conversation towards a specific topic;
➤ uncover hidden queries or objections;
➤ control the time spent at the meeting;
➤ involve a contact who is unresponsive to open questions.

Diagnosis *Do you sometimes feel you haven't really identified the needs and interests of the other party, or that you have failed somehow to draw them out? If so:*

Prescription *Ask open-ended questions.*

Open-ended questions allow more freedom of response. They are therefore also known as 'non-directive'. Some contacts prefer this type of questioning, as they feel they are volunteering information rather than merely responding to your demands.

Open questioning, or probing, lets the other party express what is on their mind. It tends to bring needs and objections out into the open where they can be dealt with, rather than leaving them hidden where they continue to act as 'blocks' to accommodating what you seek.

Certain comments from the other party serve as signals that an open question should be used. For example:

Other party	'I really don't think that approach is suitable for our needs.'
You	'Why don't you tell me about your needs?'
Other party	'We are in a position to change course right now.'
You	'Why is that?'

Open questions that begin with:

> ➤ 'Tell me about . . .'
> ➤ 'What do you think of . . .'
> ➤ 'How do you feel about . . .'

give people a chance to open up, air their concerns, and ask a few questions of their own.

Most people engaged in personal selling use a combination of closed and open questions at meetings.

Diagnosis   *Do you get too many flat rejections? If so:*
Prescription   *Ask questions with options.*

A good way of ensuring positive responses is to ask questions with options. In other words, instead of:

You	'I'm in town today and wonder if I can meet you?'
Other party	'No.'
try	
You	'I'm in town today and wonder if I can meet you late morning or early afternoon?'
Other party	'Early afternoon.'
Instead of	
You	'When would you like to come and visit us?'
Other party	'I'll have to think about it.'
try	
You	'Would you like us to visit, say, next week or the week after next?'
Other party	'The week after next.'
Instead of	
You	'Would you like to join me at that luncheon?'
Other party	'No.'
try	
You	Would you like to join me at that luncheon or take in their function next month?'
Other party	'Next month.'

Diagnosis   *Do you find some meeting attendees give nothing away and remain sober-faced? If so:*
Prescription *Use 'engaging phraseology'.*

Engaging phraseology is designed to generate positive responses from another party or parties, and is based on such words as 'isn't', 'wouldn't', 'doesn't' and 'haven't'. For example:

➤ 'Quality of service is important to you, *isn't it?*'
➤ 'You would like improved professional input, *wouldn't you?*'
➤ 'Specialised input will be to your advantage, *won't it?*'
➤ 'Continuity of association makes sense, *doesn't it?*'
➤ 'They've been more evident in the industry, *haven't they?*'

Using engaging phraseology at the start of the question tends to be even more powerful:

➤ '*Isn't* quality of service important?'
➤ '*Wouldn't* you like improved professional input?'
➤ '*Won't* specialised input be to your advantage?'
➤ '*Doesn't* continuity of association make sense?'
➤ '*Haven't* they been more evident in the industry?'

Diagnosis   *Do you wish to improve your performance further in running meetings? If so:*
Prescription *Concentrate on these guidelines for chairing meetings.*

You may be asked to chair meetings, or this may be part of your ongoing duties. Bear in mind the following key guidelines:

➤ Chairing meetings requires good chairing ability, less so good speaking ability.
➤ Become knowledgeable about the speakers and the subject(s) to be addressed.
➤ Don't shatter the confidence of your speakers or meeting participants by actively demonstrating greater knowledge, by giving them too great a build-up before their speech, or by being too autocratic in directing them in what they will and won't say or discuss.
➤ Be fair, firm and amicable: the chairperson is the host and needs to treat speakers and meeting participants as guests. However, the chairperson controls the length of the meeting and doesn't let behaviour get out of hand. The chairperson is quite clear on why

the meeting is being held, and on the meeting's objectives and agenda.

➤ A good chairperson keeps their ego under control and doesn't try to steal the show.

➤ They keep everything under control and are good time managers.

➤ They empathise with speakers and meeting participants and don't show favouritism.

➤ They show interest, and are courteous and helpful to all attending the meeting.

➤ They thank all for their input when the meeting is closed.

➤ They show impartiality and encourage balanced input by all attendees.

➤ They remain dignified throughout the meeting and don't allow offensive behaviour.

➤ They make sure the meeting stays on track and disallow (in a courteous and positive manner) questions that are irrelevant.

Diagnosis   *Do you have difficulty closing in meetings—that is, getting the other party or parties to accommodate what you seek? If so:*

Prescription   *Try different closing techniques.*

➤ *Options.* With this common method of closing you give the other party a choice of two or three options. This forces them to make a decision—for example, not whether to assist you but whether to assist you regarding A, B or even C. Once they make such a choice, they have made a commitment to meet your needs. If they hedge, they will have to give reasons why a choice cannot be made, in which case you have an opportunity to expand further, based on their concerns.

➤ *Hidden close.* In the hidden close, you state and assume the decision to accommodate what you seek and then ask a question with two options, the question relating to a less significant aspect. For example: 'Well, it seems to me that it makes sense to continue meeting. Should we meet in each of our locations, or should I continue visiting you here?'.

➤ *Summary close.* With this technique you review the key benefits to the other party of helping you meet your objectives—you are appealing to logic here. This technique can be very effective, especially if you pause occasionally during the summary to elicit some form of agreement from them.

➤ *Emotional close.* It is a mistake to assume that most people make decisions about accommodating what you seek, based on logic.

While logic does play a major role in the decisions of some people, emotional factors appealing to pride, status and security can often provide the impetus to help you, even when logic dictates otherwise.

This type of close should be used carefully, as decisions made solely on emotional impulses can come back to haunt you later. Make sure that, in helping you meet your objectives, the other party's interest or needs are also satisfied. There should be a logical basis for helping you; an appeal to emotion can then be effective if the other party is hesitant about making the decision.

➤ *Silent close.* Stop talking, look at the other party and wait. This is most effective if done immediately following the presentation of a major benefit, after successfully answering an objection or after a visual presentation relating to the topic.

The length of the pause will depend on the other person's response. If they fidget, tense up or appear to be thinking things over carefully, don't break the silence—the signal is positive! If, however, they stare right back at you and don't change their body language at all, you have not been convincing enough and will need to expand further on your presentation.

MEETING IMPACT

Use Chart 2.6 to help you check how you communicate and the impact you create at meetings.

To use this tool, following a meeting, draw a line from the left of the chart (meeting start-up) to the right (meeting close-down) and place it vertically according to how you have been communicating at successive stages (dominant, conversational, questioning, active or passive). Then work out the % mix.

If 80% is not in the conversational, questioning and active bands, then you are letting yourself down at meetings and your influence is less favourable than it could be!

INFLUENCING IN GROUP PRESENTATIONS

It is interesting how far we have developed in communications. We can speak to people around the world and in space, and we can receive and project images over huge distances. We all treat long-distance telephone calls as a natural way of business and our personal life.

However, what happens when you have to stand up in front of an audience, particularly a senior one, and make a speech or presentation?

CHART 2.6 Meeting impact

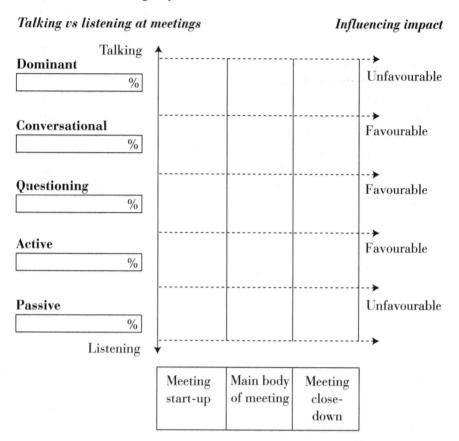

Talking vs listening at meetings   *Influencing impact*

Do you get a knot in your stomach? Does your voice rise an octave? Do you forget your words? How do you start? How do you perform as you get under way? How do you end your presentation? Here are some speaker traits you need to try to avoid!

➢ *Rambling on and on and going off in many different directions.* This speaker is not usually prepared and he often loses himself, as well as the audience, by moving from one subject to another without apparently noticing. The effect is disastrous as he fails to make his point successfully and the audience turns off completely.
➢ *Pacing backwards and forwards, like a lion in a cage.* This trait gives the speaker a thoroughly bored appearance. It is almost as though the time will pass more quickly if he walks to and fro.

> *'I . . . I . . . I . . .'* This speaker is constantly saying, '*I* did this, and
  I believe in that and *I* must tell you about the other thing that
  happened . . .'. She is pompous, sometimes arrogant, and certainly
  has a good opinion of herself. She puts the audience off quite early
  in her speech.
> *Lack of animation.* This presenter is expressionless, statuesque, blank-
  faced—and has a remarkable ability to put people to sleep after a
  good lunch.
> *Lack of sincerity.* This speaker is too contrived and too much of an
  actor to be convincing. She goes to the other extreme and tries to
  appeal to the audience's emotions, but without sincerity. She
  assumes that the audience will be fully behind her as she play-acts
  her role. The only trouble is, the audience senses that this is a
  well-rehearsed sham and they switch off.
> *Forced funniness.* How many funny presenters really are funny? One
  in 20 perhaps. The funny presenter often assumes he has to make
  his audience laugh and so he tells a joke, often resulting in laughter
  out of sympathy. Forced funniness can turn an audience off.
> *Difficult to hear.* The presenter who cannot be heard fails to realise
  she is speaking to an audience, and rambles on with her dissertation
  in a one-to-one affair with the lectern!

Most executives and managers suffer from some or all of these symptoms,
sometimes or even every time they make a presentation to a group. Such
apprehension and traits are often caused by concern about not being able
to remember your lines, or making a fool of yourself, or making a poor
presentation, or failing to meet your objectives, but mainly by inadequate
training and preparation.

Stand back from all this for a moment and do some 'imagineering'.
Dream a little! Suppose you were flying across the Pacific and the pilot
asked you to take over the controls, how would you react? Suppose you
attended a symphony concert and the conductor handed you the baton,
how would you react? Suppose you were in the operating theatre and the
surgeon asked you to take over an operation, how would you react?

You would probably get a knot in your stomach, you would get that
tight sensation around your collar and you would not know how or where
to start. You would definitely portray some strange and atypical traits as
you tried to grasp the fundamentals of your new and strange role. This
is because you are neither trained nor prepared to fly a plane, conduct
an orchestra or perform surgery. If you had been trained and prepared,
how would you have reacted? No problems—hand me the controls, music
maestro please, hand me the scalpel, nurse!

The secret to making successful speeches or presentations is to be both *trained* and *prepared*, particularly in the art of delivery, which is 80% of the group communication success formula.

Case Study

Most executives and managers find group presentations quite difficult, particularly to senior audiences, as did Demosthenes in ancient Greece, who was afflicted with a terrible speech impediment that caused him great difficulty early in his career. However, he persevered to overcome his impediment and practised his speeches by shouting at the surf and talking with small stones in his mouth; in this way, he coached himself to become the greatest orator of his time. His presentation 'delivery' became outstanding!

FIRST IMPRESSIONS COUNT

What happens to the audience when the speaker stands up or goes to the lectern? They stop, look, listen and form first impressions.

Here are some examples of first impressions. The first speaker immediately searches for a glass of water and gulps it down while eyeing the audience nervously. He coughs and loosens his collar. He has trouble getting out his notes and overheads, and drops something on the floor. His hands are shaking and, as if to stop them, he grasps the lectern with both hands and stares at the back of the room. He is obviously so *nervous* that the audience feels embarrassed or turns off completely.

The second speaker starts by not being sure where she should position herself for the speech—where she is sitting, at the table, or at the overhead projector. She scratches her head and looks blank and baffled. She 'ums' and 'ahs' and starts her speech by saying that she really cannot add much to the previous speakers. She is obviously *unprepared* and can turn the audience against her. Why should they bother to listen if she is unprepared? She is wasting their time.

The third speaker walks very slowly, even slinks up, to the lectern, looking very serious indeed and very *unhappy*. He scowls at the audience and starts off by saying they will have to bear with him as he does not normally speak in public. He seems as though he is about to take on a task he would far rather avoid. The audience can react by being reluctant too—reluctant to listen to him!

The fourth speaker has problems getting up off her chair—it is too close to the table. As she rises, she staggers forward as she gets her thigh caught against the table. Her glass of water rocks perilously and she makes a lunge to save it. A *shaky start* like this does not bode well for the rest of the speech, and the audience knows it.

The correct way to start and to create a good impression is to slide back your chair from the table and walk over to the lectern (if there is one) as though you are walking over to greet an ally whom you have not seen for a while. Then pause, look at the audience, smile and then start your presentation. Your audience is there to hear your speech. Make sure that your first impressions count and help them concentrate on your speech.

HOW TO DEVELOP SUCCESSFUL GROUP PRESENTATIONS

In planning a successful group presentation, there are several elements to be reviewed: administration, objectives, fact finding, assembling content, and format.

Administration
Review the following:

➤ date, time and location of speech;
➤ duration of speech and whether there will be time for audience questions;
➤ room size, shape and layout, and whether it will allow the use of visual aids;
➤ availability of visual aid equipment;
➤ speech subject and orientation: you may know the subject but are you aware of any preferred orientation—for example, theory versus practice or personal experience versus second-hand experience?
➤ the make-up of the audience in terms of age, sex, background, interests and reasons for attending the presentation;
➤ who the other speakers are and why you were chosen.

Objectives
Review the following:

➤ What information is to be imparted to the audience, and how can it best be imparted? Through a straight lecture? Using a Socratic approach (questioning the audience)? Through stories or anecdotes? Through audience involvement in case study, group discussion, individual exercise or simulation?
➤ How are you to excite the audience and provoke thought and

possibly action? By being enthusiastic yourself? By demonstrating a knowledge of relevant facts and figures? By demonstrating conviction? By being short and to the point? By asking the audience for response or action?

➤ How are you going to amuse the audience? Through limited use of humour? By keeping the speech short and easy-going? By appealing to their specific interests? By orienting your presentation to the specific event?

➤ How are you going to be convincing? By being logical? By appealing to their emotions? By quoting facts and figures authoritatively? By being precise? By quoting with accuracy? By articulating audience advantages?

Delivering information, exciting the audience, amusing them and being convincing are all important ingredients for successful speech making.

Fact finding
Being asked to speak on a selected subject or subjects requires the acquisition of information or facts. Fact finding can be conducted in many ways:

➤ *through desk research:* use of publications, books, periodicals and files at the office or at home;
➤ *through library research:* similarly, at the public library. Main branches can provide information on virtually any topic;
➤ *through computer databases:* you can access a wide variety of information on the Internet and other databases. By using keywords you can source abstracts and summaries from wide-ranging data sources;
➤ *by contacting people with the necessary knowledge:* informal or formal interviews, either over the telephone or in person, can provide very useful information which you may be able to use to amplify some of the bare bones or facts derived from other forms of non-personal research;
➤ *through careful analysis of all acquired information:* the raw information derived from all these sources needs to be refined through careful analysis in the context of audience needs and appeal.

Assembling content
Once the fact finding is refined and oriented towards the audience, the material has to be assembled in an order and format that can be presented. In terms of order, the following is offered as a guide and is somewhat similar to the steps for successful one-on-one meetings:

➢ How shall I start in a way that grasps audience *attention*?
➢ How shall I continue in a way that develops their *curiosity*?
➢ How can I continue in a way that enhances their *trust* of me and my presentation?
➢ How can I develop the *main thrust* of my speech?
➢ How can I end with *impact*?

Format

When considering the format of your speech, some of the key points are:

➢ The information provided must be to the point and relevant to the audience.
➢ The speech must progress logically from one part to the next.
➢ Time must be allocated suitably to each part of the presentation—for example, attention 10%, curiosity 10%, trust 10%, main thrust 60% and ending impact 10%.

However, in planning your time allocation, remember to allow five minutes for set-up time. Allow for questions too, which may account for 10–20 minutes, depending on the length and style of your presentation.

HOW TO GRASP THE AUDIENCE'S ATTENTION

You may have heard the expression: 'You win or lose the sale in the first 30 seconds!'.

The same applies to making a speech or presentation—you can win or lose your audience in the first 30 seconds. To improve the chances of successfully winning your audience in the first 30 seconds, you *must*, as stressed earlier, have done your homework and know who comprises your audience and what they are expecting, both as a group and as individuals. Also, in order to attract and keep audience attention, the way in which you 'open' the speech is vital. Some of the dos and don'ts are:

Don't:
➢ waiver—once you have taken your place at the lectern, and taken a few seconds to get yourself organised and to allow the audience to become quiet, move forward boldly to your opening;
➢ start negatively by using such statements as 'Public speaking is not my forte', 'I have not had time to prepare', 'Please bear with me', 'I am not very knowledgeable about this subject', 'I have been asked to speak against my will' or 'I am afraid you will find this topic unpalatable'.

Do:
➢ deep breathe well in advance of your speech: exhale deeply;
➢ move your chair away from the table before being introduced;
➢ make sure you have approached the lectern, or stood up at the table, in a positive, business-like fashion (like meeting an ally!);
➢ organise your notes, visual aids and microphone before you start speaking.

HOW TO BUILD CURIOSITY AND TRUST
Having grasped the audience's attention, the speaker's job is now to develop the audience's curiosity and trust. As noted before:

➢ *Attention* will only last so long, and relates to the audience's subconscious question, 'Is this interesting?'.
➢ *Curiosity* is the next phase in the sequence and relates to the audience's subconscious question, 'Might I learn something here? What has the speaker got up his sleeve?'.
➢ *Trust* is the next phase in the sequence and is linked to the audience's subconscious question, 'Can I trust what the speaker says? Is she someone of integrity?'.

The sequence of the speech can be likened to the ebb and flow of surf on the beach as the tide comes in. That tide has got to work its way up the beach, but in so doing the surf comes and goes, always moving higher up the beach. This is similar to audience interest: as the sequence of the speech unfolds, their interest ebbs and flows, but it must progress not only through the opening, curiosity and trust phases but also through the key issue and ending phases.

It is your job as speaker to control the audience's interest, just as it is the job of the moon's gravity to control the tides of the ocean! You have to get them up the beach. To do this, we now concentrate on the *curiosity* phase—the phase immediately following the opening of the speech, when the audience's attention has been grasped by your wonderful approach and opening statement! Here are some techniques.

➢ *Positive reactions.* It is often said that closing the sale is the culmination of a series of 'yes' responses from buyers. Get them and keep them in a positive frame of mind and they will close. This also applies to speakers and audiences, particularly during the early portion of the speech: you simply cannot afford to turn the audience off by provoking negative reactions.

➤ *'Confidential' information.* So-called 'confidential information—don't quote me' has an excellent effect on the audience and arouses considerable curiosity. Watch what information you give the audience, however. They are almost certain to quote you!

➤ *Visual aids.* We review these later, but they are useful tools for arousing curiosity and for use later in the speech.

➤ *Audience interests.* Whenever possible, relate to the personal interests of your audience, be these social, domestic, business or career. Work out in advance how your subject matter can relate to the personal interests of the audience, leaving your own interests until last, if you include them at all. 'You' followed by 'we' appeal is the name of the game.

For your audience to develop trust in you, the speaker, and in what you are saying, the following aspects need careful consideration.

➤ You must appear to be sincere and to be telling the truth.

➤ You must not appear to exaggerate; whatever you say must be believable.

➤ You must appear to show respect for the audience, by being punctual, by dressing suitably for the occasion and by making an effort in terms of content, delivery and manner.

➤ Verify your presentation with quantifiable evidence or support such as statistics and factual accounts, wherever possible.

➤ Try to demonstrate your expertise and experience, whether this be qualification, career, research studies, other speaking engagements or practical experience. This is best managed by the person introducing you, detailing your relevant experience in their introduction. You can then enlarge on certain aspects of your background that enhance the credibility of your presentation, as and when applicable. Keep these brief and to the point.

➤ Talk at the audience's level—never over the top of them and never down to them.

➤ Incorporate all the positive elements of voice, word, breath and eye control.

HOW TO DELIVER THE MAIN THRUST OF YOUR SPEECH

Speech making and presentations are a communication process. Effective presentation depends on the communication skills of the presenter, just as with professional and personal selling. These skills can be learned and improved on, so as to upgrade the quality of personal presentations and communicating with groups.

Effective presenters know that they must vary their approach and operating style, depending on their audience. This is quite natural. We don't act the same way with different kinds of people we meet or different family members; we are constantly adjusting our style, depending on the response we get. By understanding different operating styles, professional presenters adjust their presentations and overall style to elicit the most positive response. Audiences tend to prefer professional presenters whom they perceive to be most like themselves.

We all have enough facets to our personalities to downplay some traits and emphasise others in a particular situation, without appearing phoney. By identifying the operating styles of the majority or main members of the audience, you can adapt your own style to gain the most favourable reaction and response. The research for this is best undertaken in advance.

As a group, there can and will be differences—for example, a group of business directors will be a very different audience from that of a group of supervisors or shop-floor workers. You need to assess who are the key people in the audience and their individual operating style (addressed in greater detail in the next chapter):

➢ The *Responder/Initiator*. These people are assertive, enthusiastic and expressive and make quick decisions. They listen to you, but also tend to want to have their say. You need to *engage* in communication with these individuals to be most effective.
➢ The *Commander/Doer*. These people are assertive, goal-oriented, impatient for results and decisive. They dislike inaction or beating about the bush and prefer it if you stick to business, talk facts and come to the point quickly.
➢ The *Humanist/Empathiser*. This type is warm and friendly but a little hesitant to take risks and makes decisions very carefully. Here you will be more successful if you show interest and support, and provide reassurance rather than pressure in your presentation.
➢ The *Evaluator/Detailer*. This person is very organised, precise, analytical and cautious. There is a dislike of sloppiness, of failure to provide concrete facts and evidence, and of disregard for rules and regulations. You will increase your chances of success with this person if you are on time, provide guarantees and full details, and allow sufficient time to verify facts and make careful decisions.

➢ The *All-rounder.* This person has a flexible style and can get on with anyone providing they don't show extremes of behaviour. Showing versatility in your style, but using moderation throughout your presentation, will have the best impact on them.

➢ The *Idea Generator.* This person also has a flexible style but shows extremes and sometimes even inconsistencies in behaviour. He or she will need to be enthused and excited by both the content and delivery of your presentation in order to have the greatest effect on them. They tend to fly off in several directions at once and so need to be kept on track. Summarising your key points at the end of your presentation will be effective with these individuals.

A natural question is how to cope with different operating styles in the audience, as some of these styles seem to conflict. First, you need to identify who the key members of the audience are in terms of decision making, politics, power and influence; second, when developing eye contact with them, engage in a style of delivery that coincides with their own operating style.

If you haven't been able to identify the key members of the audience, or their operating styles, then the main thrust of your speech can be enhanced by ensuring, just like the salesperson, that you concentrate on presenting benefits (rather than features) along with verification (Chart 2.7).

Features are things that are important to you, the presenter. Benefits are things that are important to the audience. For example, in making a case about why the audience—a group of prospective customers—should do business with your firm, features you might consider using include: oldest firm in the business sector, most experienced staff, most technologically advanced products and services.

Converting these to benefits, they become: 'We represent your least risk purchase decision, as we have been in business for 15 years', 'Our

CHART 2.7   Features and benefits

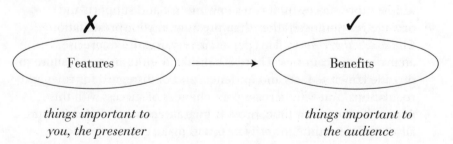

things important to
you, the presenter

things important to
the audience

highly experienced staff have the greatest capacity to understand and meet your precise needs'; 'Our products and services are designed to be cost-effective and quality-assured as a result of our state-of-the-art technology in production'.

Verification in a group presentation relates to providing validation, evidence or proof in the form of independent reports, testimonials, competitor comparisons, facts, statistics, case studies, demonstrations, anecdotes and examples. By building in such verifiers during the main thrust of your speech, you will become much more believable in the eyes of your audience.

ENDING WITH IMPACT

The football team starts the game with style. Their footwork, passing and team coordination are inspirational. They fail to score, however! This is the analogy of ending your speech or presentation without impact. No matter how good the speech has been, if you don't end with impact you won't have won over your audience. The ending needs to leave the audience inspired, motivated and, above all, in full accordance with what you have been saying. Ending with impact can be accomplished with the following techniques.

➢ *Act now*. This technique asks the audience to do something right way, to act. In fact, the audience is likely to act sooner rather than later after your speech if you ask them to do so. If you ask them to do something the following week, they will more than likely forget or procrastinate. 'Act now!' creates an excellent climax. Example: 'Register today and be assured of a place on the program!'.

➢ *Questioning*. Ending by asking the audience a question can also have excellent impact. The question best relates to the main thrust of your speech, or to your opening statements. The question should be phrased so that the audience focuses on the main issues you have raised. Example: 'What will you do about drinking and driving now?'.

➢ *Saying*. Quoting a well-known saying as an ending statement, one that directly relates to the main thrust of your speech or important elements of it, provides some speakers with good ending impact. Be careful not to use a saying that is less than totally relevant to your speech, nor one that goes over the head of the audience. A well-known saying from an authoritative source is by far the best. Example: 'All work and no play makes Jack a dull boy'.

➤ *Based on my experience.* This technique summarises a third-party factual experience that directly relates to the main thrust of your speech. Example: 'In England as far back as the 1930s with their Special Areas Act they attempted to diversify industry away from the major cities. They failed and in the main have continued to do so. It simply does not work'. With a factual example, the credibility of your speech and impact at the end are enhanced.

➤ *The accountant's ending.* You develop a 'balance sheet' by summarising the pluses and minuses of your argument, with the pluses far exceeding the minuses. Example: 'On the plus side, you have better prices, greater choice, better parking and higher levels of service. On the minus side, it will take you a few more minutes to get there. Isn't the choice obvious?'.

In summary, ending with impact is important if you are to leave the audience in a favourable frame of mind or motivated to follow your advice. The ending must leave them 'on a high'.

CHART 2.8   Ending with impact

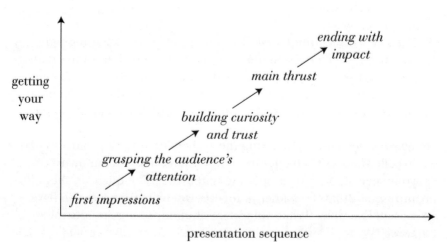

SPEECH AIDS

Several kinds of speech aids can be used in group presentations, according to specific requirements. The main ones are fully typed scripts and prompter cards.

Fully typed script

A full script is best used for formal occasions or for when you are 'going on record'. It can also be used when you have tight time constraints: a typed script will allow for an average of double the content compared to speaking from prompter cards.

When preparing a script, follow the sequence of: developing the speech, the start of the speech, curiosity and trust, the main thrust and ending with impact.

Use double-spaced typing and plenty of paragraphs, together with wide margins for making notes about first impressions, speaking style, and voice, eye and word control.

The most important delivery criterion is to eyeball the audience regularly. This will require a slower delivery than if you were simply reading a book out loud. Not only must you regularly eyeball the audience—you must also animate, using hands, facial expressions and supporting language. This is necessary because the audience may switch off if they simply see a statue reading a text they could have read themselves at home in half the time.

What in fact you are doing is acting out the text for them. Be animated. And don't *turn* pages—*slide* them across from one side of the lectern to the other as you finish each one, or slide them under your pad of pages if you are not using a lectern.

The advantages of the fully typed script relate to confidence that you are not going to forget your lines and that the intended content will be delivered accurately. The disadvantages relate to audience acceptance. You can appear to be formal, stilted or boring and the audience may react negatively: 'I could have read that—I didn't need him to read it to me'.

Prompter cards

Prompter cards can be used for any speech or presentation, providing you have the necessary notice to be able to develop them. The best prompter cards are of a size that fits comfortably in your hand—about 14 cm by 9 cm. They should be postcard weight for durability and ease of handling. Write on only one side of the card. Each card should contain enough information to relate to one important element of your speech. So the first step is to break down your speech into separate elements, each element addressing one idea or topic in full.

At the top of the card, write down the main lead-in sentence that addresses the element. Use bold letters to enhance legibility. Lower case often works best, but you can use upper case if you feel this is easier to read. Below this lead-in, note the various subelements that support or expand on the lead-in sentence. Again, use bold writing—felt tip pens are ideal. Each subelement should be in point or bullet form, to make it stand out from the rest.

In the left-hand margin of the card you can note when you need to show a visual aid, using the letters A, B, C etc., cross-indexed to the visual aids. Number the cards in sequence in the top right-hand corner in case you drop them. Use colour for highlighting key points.

For delivery purposes, just glance at your cards from time to time— don't read them. They are prompters only, not full scripts. They can be used at a lectern or at a table when standing or seated. Either lay them in front of you and slide them across as each one is finished with, or do the same in the palm of your hand, tucking each one behind the last one.

There is no need to hide the prompter cards—indeed, it would be wrong to do so—but don't rely on them to the extent that you are reading from them. Prompter cards are designed to be a brief synopsis of your speech, and are a marvellous prompting device to remind you what to say at any given time. Their advantages are far-reaching:

➢ They give you confidence that you will not forget your lines and that you will deliver all your intended content.
➢ They enhance your eye contact with the audience, allowing you to speak to them rather than just read a text.
➢ They allow you freedom to talk animatedly, rather than having to hold a typewritten speech, or to walk about and 'mix it' with the audience.
➢ They can be carried in a pocket or purse, and handled unobtrusively in the palm of the hand.
➢ They may be reused often, as they are durable.
➢ They can be used in front of both large and small audiences.

The disadvantage of prompter cards is that they do take time to prepare and are more effective if you also take time to practise with them.

Let us now look at how to prepare a speech or presentation, based on my 11-point plan (Chart 2.9).

An example of a presentation plan for a one-hour presentation is shown in Chart 2.10. This outline assumes you have one hour to make your presentation (including set-up and questions). The times noted will need to be changed for longer or shorter presentations.

CHART 2.9   Eleven-point plan for preparing group presentations

1. Try to get a good understanding of who the audience is and what they are expecting from you.
2. Develop your objectives: what are you trying to achieve with your presentation?
3. Collect appropriate information to attain these objectives.
4. Develop the structure and sequence of your presentation.
5. Develop the script or notes.
6. Review your script or notes to check they all coincide with your understanding of the audience and their expectations.
7. Develop your visual aids.
8. Check that they coincide with your understanding of the audience and their expectations.
9. Rehearse your presentation.
10. Deliver your presentation.
11. Critically appraise your performance—you should be seeking continuous improvement.

CHART 2.10   Presentation plan outline

(assumes one hour available)

Lapsed time (in minutes)	Stage	Notes
0—5	Set-up	
5—10	Attention	
10—15	Curiosity	
15—20	Trust	
20—40	Main thrust	
40—45	Ending impact	
45—60	Questions and close-down	

USE OF VISUALS IN GROUP PRESENTATIONS

Visual aids can help you make a better speech or presentation. The most popular alternatives include overhead transparencies and computer graphics, flip charts and whiteboards. Use of visuals is recommended whenever practicable because they increase audience retention rates (in other words, the amount they remember of your presentation) from 20–30% with words only to 40–50% with words and visuals. Retention rates are increased to 60–70% if you use words and visuals and also get the audience involved through discussions, questions, case studies or simulations. Naturally, visuals are not always appropriate—for example, with an after-dinner speech.

Visuals provide for greater impact, emphasis, clarity, understanding and interest. They help the audience to grasp complex issues, concepts and relationships more readily. They help you, the speaker, to stay organised and be more confident, and they help to ensure that you do not leave out important items.

However, don't forget that you might have prepared the greatest visuals or handouts but if you don't eyeball the audience and come across in a relaxed, genuine and confident manner—as at a dinner party—you simply won't have personal impact!

Overhead transparencies and computer graphics

There are many commercial firms that produce overhead transparencies—in colour, too, although these can be quite expensive. The alternative is to produce them yourself using a computer, graphics software and a colour printer. Transparent overlays can also be used to build up more complex charts and diagrams. For example, you could start with a map of China, then overlay it with the provincial borders, then overlay that with the provincial capitals and so on.

To point with transparencies, use a sheet of paper to gradually uncover the transparency and reveal an unfolding story, diagram or series of bullet points. You can also use a pen or pencil to point to particular items on your transparency or you can purchase special arrows for this. Never face the screen and talk at the same time, as this detracts from eyeball rapport with the audience.

In developing content for an overhead, make sure the text is bold and large. A standard font is usually too small—it has to be visible at the back of the room. Keep the overhead simple and precise—don't write too much on each one. Handwritten overheads must be legible and have a balanced format: using graph paper behind them when you write them up helps vertical and horizontal consistency. Number the overheads, as this helps to keep them in order and you can reference the number in your speech notes. Turn off the overhead projector when not using it to cut out the glare from the blank screen, which can be distracting.

Increasingly, presenters are replacing overhead transparencies with computer graphics which can be projected onto a screen through an adaptor. This makes for a highly professional presentation with great impact, but take care that the impact isn't being created by the technology rather than by the presenter. This can be the major strength or weakness of computer graphics—you be the judge!

Flip charts and whiteboards

Flip charts are usually large pads of paper on an easel or stand at the speaker's side. They offer a marvellous way of recording key points or features of your presentation, or audience comments, questions or replies. They can be written during your speech or presentation, or prepared beforehand.

One useful way to write them during the speech, and to remember what to include, is to pencil in the content in the top corner of the flip chart closest to you and then copy it when appropriate in full size on the flip chart. With complex diagrams you can prepare them in pencil (which will not be visible to the audience), then use a felt-tip pen to trace over the pencil guide—very impressive!

The same rules for content apply here as for overhead transparencies and computer graphics: boldness, clarity, simplicity and no verbiage. Use consistent letter styles and sizes and vary the colour occasionally for effect or emphasis. Felt-tip pens stand out most effectively. When writing on flip charts during your speech or presentation, avoid turning your back to the audience—and don't talk to the chart as you write!

If you decide to prepare them before the speech, use a blank sheet to cover the first chart, or intersperse blanks whenever you aren't referring to the flip chart. The height of the letters should be about 4 cm for every 12 m of maximum distance from the audience. If it is necessary to refer to more than one flip chart page at a time, you can tear them off the pad and attach them to the walls of the room using masking tape or 'blue-tack'.

An alternative to the flip chart is a whiteboard with special erasable markers, which again provides for impact, professionalism and ease of operation. Electronic whiteboards are particularly effective if you need a copy of what you have written.

THE CHALLENGES OF GROUP PRESENTATIONS

Group presentations, particularly to those senior audiences you are trying to influence, are never easy. You may experience some of the following challenges. If the diagnosis sounds like you, read the prescription. If not, read on!

Diagnosis *You would like to speak as clearly and articulately as top news-casters, who seem to be able to make the most of every word.*

Prescription *You may need an elocution lesson.*

Speakers are in the business of using words and their voices to get their message across. You will now find out what happens in an elocution lesson!

I will start with the vowels: A E I O U. Say these vowels as though in conversation and you will find that your mouth is only half-open, with little movement between saying each vowel. Now shout them in a pronounced fashion, moving your mouth, lips and tongue to really 'make a meal' of them. The effect is interesting—notice how different and 'pronounced' they sound by comparison with saying them conversationally. Good speakers go for a mid-way style of delivery, mid-way between conversational and pronounced, and in this way project their voices to the back of the room.

Let us move on to the consonants: B C D F G H J K L M N P Q R S T V W X Y Z. Again, say these conversationally and then shout them out in a pronounced way, moving your mouth, lips and tongue exaggeratedly. Now try the mid-way style of delivery as though projecting them to the back of the room.

Finally, practise the combination consonants: Br Ch Cl Dr Fr Gr Ng Pr Pl Sh Sl Th. Say them conversationally first, then shout them in a pronounced fashion as before. Now try the mid-way style though still projecting them.

In summary, good speakers aim for a mid-way style between conversational volume and pronounced shouting, and they aim to project their voices to be heard by those seated at the back of the room.

Diagnosis *You have an important speech coming up and you have to cover a lot of content accurately in quite a short time. You don't want to read it. What can you do?*

Prescription *Memorise it.*

This process can be used at any time, providing you have the time for memorising. It is best used for formal occasions or for when you are 'going on record'. It is also suitable for use with larger audiences—just as actors memorise their scripts.

In terms of preparation, the starting point is the fully typed script, as previously described. The learning-by-heart process then follows, which is best undertaken phrase by phrase, sentence by sentence, and paragraph by paragraph (as mentioned, this can take some time). One way of assisting memorisation is to tape the transcript and then recite the speech as the tape plays it back.

Don't deliver your memorised speech as though you are reading it. Animation is the key, along with developing and maintaining good eye contact with the audience.

The advantages of the memorised script relate mainly to accuracy of content—providing you have memorised it correctly. The disadvantages relate to the time taken to memorise the script, and the fact that the system is by no means infallible. Many a previously word-perfect speaker has forgotten all in the face of a large audience. Another disadvantage is that the speech can become a recital, stilted and formal.

Diagnosis   *You sometimes have difficulty, lack impact, or feel you are lacking something else as you start, or 'open', your presentation, speech or meeting.*

Prescription   *Use creative opening statements.*

- ➤ *Background.* Here the speaker starts with a rapid introduction to some element of the history of the subject. Brevity, relevance and appeal are all key ingredients. For example: 'Last August your board of directors asked me to undertake a preliminary analysis of the comparative productivity of your plant. After six months' work, I now have my preliminary results'.
- ➤ *The personal opener.* For example: 'I was just talking to Mr Saunders here at the head table and he mentioned to me that most of you would be interested to hear about . . .'. This is a very relaxed style of opening with good appeal to the audience and some impact.
- ➤ *The news-item opener.* For example: 'So the Liberals are in for another term—does this bode well for the poor?'. This can have good appeal, particularly if used with a question.
- ➤ *Provocative openers.* For example: 'Government programs of support to industry are ineffective. Firms simply do not bother to source them and utilise them—to their own misfortune'. This type of opener is particularly useful when you include your audience in the first apparently negative statement—they certainly sit up and listen! Try this form of opener with the after-dinner audience, or where the audience seems somewhat aloof or distant. Another example: 'Management training is useless, unless it is delivered in a specific

fashion that relates to the development of a competency, rather than simply the acquisition of knowledge'.

Diagnosis *You sometimes have difficulty closing your presentation, speech, meeting or personal selling endeavour? (By 'closing', I am referring to attaining your intended outcomes.)*

Prescription *Try asking, and test closing.*

Obvious as it may seem, many presenters fail to close because they forget to ask for what they seek, or don't know they are supposed to ask for it. Successful completion of a speech or presentation requires the presenter to initiate the closing stage. Very few audiences will actually ask you what you need, even if they are interested. No matter how involved the contact has been up to that point, it is up to you to initiate the close by asking for what you seek.

Test closing is also important and helps to offset the chance of a poor closing. One method of test closing is to offer several options:

> 'Which of the three approaches appears most to meet your needs?'
> 'The second.'
> 'So you would like to move forward into that approach?'
> 'Yes!'

Another method is to answer a question with a question 'boomerang':

> 'Are your colleagues available to meet now?'
> 'You would like to meet them now?'
> 'Yes!'

Yet another method is to make an assumption with an error (you may have made the error on purpose):

> 'And so it was the second approach you preferred?'
> 'No, the first!'
> 'Let me make a note about that.'

Diagnosis *You find it difficult to end your speech or presentation.*

Prescription *Understand what can go wrong and learn by these mistakes.*

Some of the greatest mistakes at the end of presentations are:

> ➤ *Fade-out.* Perhaps time is up, or the speaker has said all he wants to say. Fade-out can result in an abrupt end, or an end that literally fades out like a song that has no real ending—the recording studio

just turns the volume down to zero while the singers are still in full swing.

➤ *Grasping for lifelines.* Many speakers feel they have not done justice to their speech or presentation by the time they have to close. They try to throw in last-minute statements designed to rectify this situation. They go down fighting!

➤ *Off-topic.* Some speakers, having made their main points, tend to wander off topic during the closing seconds or minutes. It is as if they have become super-confident in front of the audience and decide to impart new content and ideas at the last minute, off the 'top of their head'.

➤ *Repeaters.* A repetition of your speech, even if considered useful for 'padding', is not the way to close. A summary of some of the key points or arguments is needed, but not too much repetition.

➤ *'Well, um, there may be some questions?'* Never be half-hearted about questions at the end of your speech. Decide beforehand whether or not you are going to invite questions. If you are, encourage the audience to ask them.

Diagnosis   *You have to make a really impressive presentation at a conference and you want to use visuals that are more impressive and professional than overheads. You don't have computer graphics. You don't know what to use.*

Prescription   *Try 35 millimetre slides.*

Thirty-five millimetre slides can be front- or rear-projected onto a screen— the latter requires less dimming of overhead lights. They can be operated by a remote control at the lectern. The projector should be turned off and/or placed out of sight when not in use, and you should practise using your slides in a way that enhances your professionalism.

The advantages of 35 millimetre slides are that they offer full colour and high impact, particularly when multiple projectors and screens are used. They can be very effective visual aids.

One disadvantage is that you cannot point to them easily to stress a point. You can point to an overhead slide in front of you, but with a 35 millimetre slide you are forced to move over to the screen and use a pointer, or a hand-held mini-laser light, which entails turning away from the audience.

Several companies offer 35 millimetre slide production services as well as 'do-it-yourself' kits for use with computer graphics.

Diagnosis   *Only half your audience arrives, and they all sit at the back of the room.*

Prescription   *Fill the room from the front.*

There is nothing worse than talking to empty chairs. Always encourage your audience to fill the auditorium, hall or room from the front. Assistants can help here, but don't be afraid to encourage your audience to do this from the lectern. This can help your nervous tension, too. This leads us to meeting room layouts.

The layout of meeting rooms is important in group presentations. Layout includes the seating arrangements and the positioning of such equipment as the projector, screen and lectern. Charts 2.11 and 2.12 show ways of organising these.

CHART 2.11   Meeting room layouts (a)

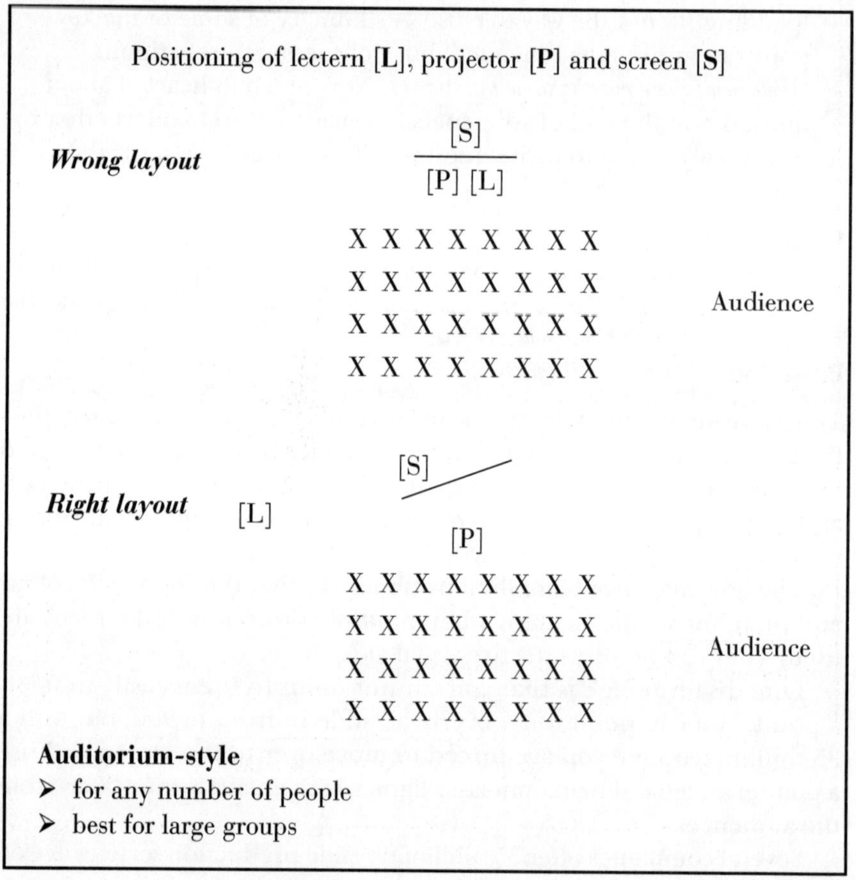

Positioning of lectern [L], projector [P] and screen [S]

Wrong layout

[S]
———
[P] [L]

X X X X X X X X
X X X X X X X X   Audience
X X X X X X X X
X X X X X X X X

Right layout   [L]

[S]   ╱
[P]

X X X X X X X X
X X X X X X X X
X X X X X X X X   Audience
X X X X X X X X

Auditorium-style
➢ for any number of people
➢ best for large groups

Diagnosis   *You feel that when you speak at meetings or presentations you come across in somewhat of a monotone and fail to inspire your audience.*
Prescription   *Use voice control.*

CHART 2.12   Meeting room layouts (b)

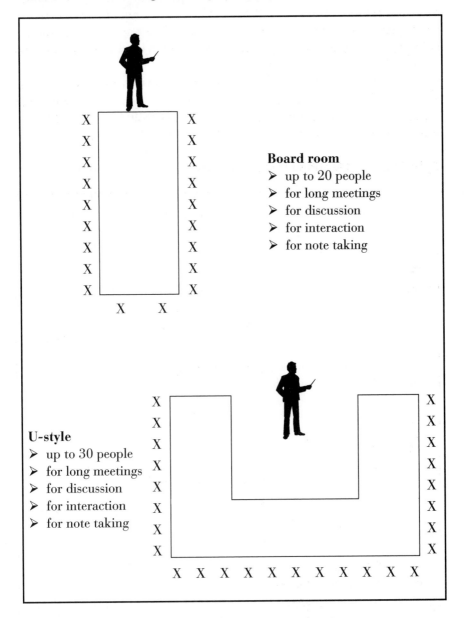

Vary your volume, sometimes loud, sometimes soft.
- Pause occasionally; as Ralph Richardson, the actor, once said, 'Acting is all about the pause'. You can pause for quite a long time with good effect.

- ➤ Vary your delivery from time to time by slowing down, speeding up, speaking more loudly or more softly.
- ➤ Emphasise key words.
- ➤ Deliver the bulk of your speech at your normal level or pitch—not too high, not too low.
- ➤ Occasionally, vary this level, for emphasis or variety, to keep the audience interested.
- ➤ Watch your quality of voice, or tone. Attempt to go for a rounded, almost musical tone—a resonant tone—rather than a rasping tone or a thin voice.
- ➤ Don't overact or sound false: your voice control must sound natural.

To practise voice control, read aloud from a book or newspaper on a regular basis. Take one element at a time that you wish to build into your speech making and practise it in this way by reading aloud regularly. When practising, remember to project your voice to those seated at the back of the room.

Diagnosis   *You sometimes feel you lack impact partway through your speech or presentation; you need somehow to liven it up and generate greater audience interest.*

Prescription   *Use creative continuity statements.*

There are many continuity statements that can enhance the main body of your speech or presentation. They include:

- ➤ *Anecdotes or stories*, factual or fictional, that relate directly to the subject as well as to audience needs and appeal. By bringing yourself into the story, the audience automatically becomes more interested in what it is you have to say. If you can make yourself the loser in the story, the audience will start to align themselves with you. If you are the winner, the audience may react negatively. The story must be well polished, and related in a way that arouses the attention of the audience. Relating it slowly usually has a better effect than telling it quickly. For example: 'When I was an apprentice welder, I worked in a plant headed up by a rather domineering type of manager. I was progressing quite well, until one day . . .'.
- ➤ *Quoting a well-known saying and giving its source.* This works well if the saying relates directly to the main thrust of your speech and if its source is an authoritative one. The best form of quotation is one that is short and to the point, and appeals to the emotions rather than logic. For example: ' "Inventiveness is 10 per cent inspiration and 90 per cent perspiration", Thomas Edison said'.

➤ *Asking the audience a question.* This can have dramatic impact, particularly if the answer to the question relates directly to the main thrust of your speech. The question should be framed so that the audience doesn't answer. You, the speaker, then proceed to answer it in a way that you know will appeal to the audience and grasp their attention. The problem with encouraging the audience to answer is that you might get a wrong or less than desirable answer, which could throw you off your stride. For example: 'As a manufacturing plant, how can we compete better against plants operating in lower labour cost countries?'.

➤ *'You' and 'we' appeal.* By building 'you' or 'we' into statements, audience involvement is enhanced from the outset. For example: 'You are here today to find out how Council's long-term transportation plan might affect your neighbourhood . . .'; 'We all want to see our neighbourhood's natural features preserved . . .'.

In summary, you select your continuity statements according to the main thrust of your speech, the type of audience and your personal style. These statements must be well rehearsed and well delivered and represent important opportunities for generating good audience impact.

Diagnosis   *You have a really difficult presentation coming up and it's a complex subject at which you're not an expert. You don't know what to do.*

Prescription *Use computer graphics or a video.*

Computer graphics and videos can make excellent visual aids, but videos can be expensive to prepare. There are many videos available for rental that address all kinds of subjects—for example, management topics and employee training. However, it is sometimes difficult to find one that relates to your particular speech or presentation.

When using computer graphics or videos, make sure that you have sufficient monitors for your audience: a rough guide is that one 51cm screen will be needed for each 20–25 viewers.

Diagnosis   *When you try to close your presentation, speech or meeting, you sometimes wish you had something tangible to which you could refer.*

Prescription *Use a closing aid.*

Closing aids include the tools needed to help you close, such as:

➤ *testimonials*—verification that others have found your input beneficial. Testimonials can be in writing from the satisfied contact, or even tape-recorded. The latter is far more powerful. Record it as though it is an interview: ask pertinent questions and lead the speaker into saying the sorts of things that will help you close;

➤ *paperwork*—reports, brochures or business cards. These, as needed, should all be at hand in a paper pad holder/folder. All paperwork must be kept clean and uncreased. The total package of paperwork must be out of the briefcase and instantly accessible—perhaps on your lap, under your arm, or on the desk or table in front of you— to allow you to move smoothly into the following sequence;

➤ *hardware*—the electronic organiser or diary. This must also be instantly accessible for logging follow-up meetings.

Diagnosis   *Sometimes you get put off in your speech or presentation by noises 'off'.*
Prescription   *Insist on no external interruptions.*

While you may want a participative and sometimes boisterous audience, you don't want outside noises such as waiters, or speakers next door, interrupting your speech. Don't try to overpower such distractions by raising your voice. Simply instruct an assistant to monitor and control all such interruptions. In the final analysis, it is better to stop or delay starting your speech until such interruptions cease.

Diagnosis   *You have heard presenters or speakers who do too much 'umming' or repeat annoying pet phrases too often. You think you do this.*
Prescription   *Keep 'repeaters' under control.*

Try to eliminate repeaters, such words and phrases as:

➤ Um   ➤ the point is
➤ Er   ➤ to be honest
➤ Ah   ➤ that reminds me
➤ Well   ➤ simply said
➤ Now   ➤ in plain language

These are the more common repeaters, but each of us has our pet repeaters, such as:

➤ the cough   ➤ and so on
➤ the nervous laugh   ➤ in other words
➤ huh   ➤ the question is

Diagnosis   *You often get caught out at conferences and find myself having to make impromptu speeches with almost no notice. You want to improve your performance.*

Prescription *Use notes on the 'back of envelopes'.*

This approach should be used only for impromptu speeches. Make sure you address, as always, the start of the speech (how you are going to open it), the development of curiosity and trust, the main thrust, and the ending—it must have impact and leave the audience on a high.

Sometimes there simply isn't time to make proper notes. Jot down what comes into your mind as you listen to another speaker, or as you are introduced. Go back over these notes and write the order of delivery beside them by noting (1), (2), (3) etc. With notes on the 'back of envelopes', make sure your writing is large and legible, and ensure the notes are complete enough to be useful.

Regarding delivery, don't worry or feel embarrassed about being seen to be using your notes—you have gone to the trouble of thinking through your speech for your audience (large or small) and this is a favour to them. Again, an animated delivery is the order of the day.

Advantages of back-of-envelope notes relate to speed and confidence. They can be prepared very quickly and help develop your confidence: you have a guide to follow and, providing the notes are complete, you will cover all you wanted to say.

The disadvantages relate to the limited time available to organise these notes. Legibility can be a problem also. Remember, 'back of envelope' refers to any suitable-sized cards or pieces of paper that will fit in a shirt, blouse or jacket pocket.

Diagnosis *You sometimes feel the audience is flat, uninvolved or, worse still, falling asleep.*
Prescription *Get the audience to participate.*

Getting the audience to participate helps them to:

➢ stay awake and interested;
➢ assimilate what you are attempting to present;
➢ retain what you are trying to present.

Such participation can be enhanced by use of:

➢ Socratic approach—asking questions of the audience;
➢ group discussions;
➢ role planning;
➢ simulation—case studies;
➢ individual exercises, self-help checklists;
➢ audience assistance with demonstrations.

Audience participation increases their retention of your speech or presentation to as much as 60–70% when used in conjunction with visuals and your spoken presentation.

Diagnosis *You sometimes have problems with choosing appropriate words and/or pronunciation the audience understands.*
Prescription *Watch for the pitfalls.*

Pitfalls regarding words used are:

➤ wrong use or choice of words;
➤ use of slang or technical jargon;
➤ wrong pronunciation;
➤ inadequate vocabulary (try expanding your vocabulary with *Roget's Thesaurus*);
➤ words difficult to understand;
➤ stereotyped, hackneyed phrases or clichés.

Diagnosis *You feel you lack the polish or professionalism of other speakers or presenters, who seem to 'have their act together' better than you.*
Prescription *Develop positive speaker traits.*

Good speakers:

➤ are punctual in terms of starting and finishing times;
➤ appear to be sincere, speak what they believe in and carry it out with conviction;
➤ are enthusiastic—otherwise, they are not likely to enthuse the audience;
➤ use tact and sensitivity, and orient their speech or presentation to the audience;
➤ allow their emotions to show, but never let them get out of control. Sorrow, anger and hatred are powerful emotions which can get out of control at the lectern;
➤ rarely criticise; if they do, they make the criticism constructive and try to keep it positive;
➤ offer praise where it is due;
➤ show they are not perfect and make the occasional mistake in their speech; they are human, too;
➤ make the audience feel they are important and appreciated;
➤ keep their ego under control—audience first, self second;
➤ use 'you' appeal—address audiences as 'you' to keep them involved and interested;

➢ use 'we' appeal—address the audience as 'we' when needing to gain their acceptance and approval;

➢ keep 'I' to a minimum.

Diagnosis   *You sometimes have problems gauging the other party's or the audience's reactions to your questions.*

Prescription   *Test the temperature.*

Contact or audience reactions can be classified in the following four ways:

1. *Hot.* This includes such contact responses as clearly positive statements about the topics under discussion, or agreement with what you are saying.
2. *Cold.* Here, the contact makes clearly negative statements about the topic in question, disagrees with what you are saying or otherwise responds in a deliberately negative way.
3. *Warm.* Reactions that are probably positive include smiling and nodding, leaning forward in the chair, or examining something you have shown them very closely. However, the prospect or contact *may* be reacting negatively.
4. *Cool.* Reactions that are probably negative include wandering attention, fidgeting, crossing the arms or moving away. However, the prospect or contact *may* be reacting positively. Be alert for these reactions, and adjust your questioning technique to them.

Diagnosis   *You sometimes find it difficult to grasp the audience's attention when you make a speech or presentation.*

Prescription   *Try these dos and don'ts.*

Do:

➢ make sure that the top half of your body, including your hands, starts in control and remains in control;

➢ take a second or two to look at the audience, sense their mood, empathise with them and *smile*;

➢ begin with confidence, which will be the case if you are well prepared;

➢ make the opening of your speech or presentation interesting and novel.

Don't:

➢ start in a stereotyped fashion: 'Thank you for inviting me to speak to you today' or 'I am honoured at the privilege of being able to address you' or 'May I say how delighted I am to be here today';

> start with too much emphasis, which may put the audience off—build up to your key issues and ending impact, rather than start too 'high' and end too 'low';
> be too lengthy in your opening remarks—up to a maximum of 10% of the available time is a rough guide.

Diagnosis   *You sometimes have problems answering difficult questions.*
Prescription   *Learn and deploy appropriate techniques.*

You can answer a difficult question with another question or a probing remark. For example:

> 'Please explain what you mean.'
> 'Why do you say that?'
> 'Why?'
> 'What for?'
> 'How?'

This gives you time to think about an answer. It also throws the questioner off guard and makes them think too.

Another technique is to agree with the critical questioner. For example: 'I think you're absolutely right in your contention but, if you take the (so and so) circumstances into consideration, I think you'll find . . .' or 'I agree with you, but we're not working in isolation and other factors have to be taken into consideration. For example . . .'.

This tends to quieten critical questioners and allows them to feel they have made a good point. It allows them to retain their self-esteem.

Another technique is the reversal. For example:

Questioner: 'If you develop that new industrial estate, it will adversely affect our parkland and leisure pursuits.'
Speaker: 'If we don't develop that industrial estate, there won't be enough jobs to allow people to enjoy their leisure pursuits.'

Stupid questions that are either too frivolous or too far off the subject to consider seriously may usefully be responded to by saying, 'You don't really want me to answer that, do you?' and then laughing it off.

When you really don't know the answer to a question, don't be afraid to say, 'I don't know, sorry!'—but don't say it too often. A little humility can win over the other party or an audience.

Diagnosis   *You have difficulties using microphones.*
Prescription   *Remember these guidelines.*

Do:

➤ try to test the microphone out before the meeting;
➤ check whether it has an on/off switch and that it is on before you speak. If in doubt, gently tap it and take your time;
➤ adjust the volume level so that you don't hear your own voice booming back at you;
➤ watch out for negative feedback or microphone whine. Lower the volume level, stand further back from the microphone and/or rearrange the speakers if you experience feedback;
➤ moderate your own speaking volume. Let the microphone do the work of projection for you;
➤ stand still in front of the microphone;
➤ stand about 50 cm from the microphone and ensure it is just below your mouth level;
➤ use a lapel microphone whenever possible—but remember, when it is switched on it will amplify every noise you make in its vicinity.

Don't:

➤ play with the microphone while speaking—hands off!
➤ fiddle with pens or papers near the microphone—these sounds may be amplified;
➤ speak too close to the microphone, as this will distort your voice;
➤ speak too far away from the microphone, as you won't be heard;
➤ continue speaking while you turn your head away from the microphone and move away to use a visual aid—you won't be heard;
➤ speak to the microphone. Speak to the audience, the object of your speech.

Diagnosis   *You have had problems with hecklers.*
Prescription   *Learn to handle them.*

The best approach with hecklers is to ignore them and let the audience take care of them. Be polite and hope the heckling will pass. The alternative is to answer a remark from a heckler with a remark that delights the audience. For example:

Heckler:	'You don't know what you're talking about.'
Speaker:	'That's why I'm up here and you're down there!'
Heckler:	'Boring!'
Speaker:	'Yes, you are!'
Heckler:	Abusive language.

Speaker:	'In future, please bleep. There are youngsters in the audience!'
Heckler:	Insult.
Speaker:	Either ignore it or go quiet, and then ask the insulter to repeat his remark. Most people will normally go quiet as the audience focuses their attention on them.

Diagnosis *You can't be bothered using visual aids with your presentations; you can't see their value, although people say they can be very effective.*

Prescription *Try using them for the following reasons.*

Visual aids are important tools to use in a speech or group presentation.

➤ They enhance audience understanding because they call on two senses—sound and sight.

➤ They enhance the organisation of your speech or presentation. You have to organise your thoughts in an orderly fashion before you can develop or use visuals.

➤ We are all visually oriented—sight plays an important role in our education, learning and communication.

➤ Visuals increase audience retention—from a low of 20–30% retention of a spoken speech or presentation to a high of 40–50% retention when visual aids are used.

Diagnosis *You sometimes have problems with your use of grammar.*

Prescription *Watch out for common mistakes.*

Good grammar is a prerequisite to successful speech making. Watch out for the following common mistakes:

➤ mixing tenses;

➤ using the wrong sequence of words and phrases, particularly adjectives and adverbs—they usually come in the order of time, manner and place;

➤ mixing plural and singular words in a sentence;

➤ using 'who' instead of 'whom';

➤ using 'neither . . . or', instead of 'neither . . . nor';

There are hundreds of books available to assist you with your grammar.

Diagnosis *You sometimes feel your appearance lets you down when making group presentations.*

Prescription *Follow these guidelines.*

The audience sees mainly the top half of a speaker's body. But the top half of the body can get out of control:

- ➤ tie knot slipped;
- ➤ jacket open and flapping, or with bulky objects in the pockets;
- ➤ hands on lapels, armpits or clutching the lectern;
- ➤ hands in the pockets, playing with keys or cash;
- ➤ hands pulling or scratching the ears, nose or chin.

Keep the top half of your body under control by:

- ➤ previously adjusting your tie or scarf, emptying your pockets and buttoning your jacket;
- ➤ keeping your hands in front of you, behind you, by your side, or even one hand in your pocket and one hand for gesticulating (particularly for informal presentations or speeches);
- ➤ staying balanced by placing your feet slightly apart with one foot angled slightly in front of the other.

Now that we have the top half of the body under control, keep it under control by *not*:

- ➤ coughing or blowing your nose—do this before you arrive at the lectern;
- ➤ looking at your watch;
- ➤ playing with pens or paperclips;
- ➤ swaying, slouching or leaning;
- ➤ looking around the room at anything but the audience.

Diagnosis   *You feel you are presenting to just a crowd, especially at large meetings, rather than personalising your presentation and developing rapport with individuals.*
Prescription   *Use eye control.*

Eye-to-eye contact, or eye control, is important in good speech making. Three golden rules apply here:

1. During your presentation or speech, speak only when you have direct eye contact with one of your audience or, in the case of large audiences, when you are apparently looking at the face of someone in the audience (even if you cannot focus on them).
2. Don't scan your audience rapidly while speaking; concentrate on individuals and give each one 5–10 seconds at a time.
3. Try to ensure you concentrate on each individual in the audience in this way during the speech. With large audiences this can be achieved by picking out an individual from each group around the room and looking at him or her. Those sitting in the vicinity of

these individuals will feel that you have been directing your words to each of them individually. This is a very powerful technique, because it personalises your presentation—you appear to be talking to each and every member of your audience.

Diagnosis *You feel that you need to end your sales pitch, speech or presentation with more impact.*

Prescription *Try these creative endings.*

➤ *Emotional ending.* Some people end very effectively by appealing to the emotions of the audience, rather than by citing facts and figures. For example: 'By funding this waterwell project, our club will not only be saving the village from certain disaster, but we will also be taking the lead in our district. Yet again, we will be the number one club in international service projects'.

➤ *Last chance ending.* This is where you make a convincing case that the audience has one last chance to act. A powerful ending, with considerable impact. For example: 'If we don't go ahead now, we will have missed our chance forever'.

➤ *Premium ending.* With this technique you keep one last selling point or benefit in reserve until the very end of your speech. This is designed to sway the audience over to you. It is a useful technique when you are speaking on a contentious issue. For example: 'Not only will all your stated requirements be satisfied, but we are also prepared to throw in a new purpose-designed community hall as part of the complex'.

➤ *Summarise.* A *brief* summary of the main elements of the speech can offer impact and reinforcement at the end of it. For example: 'We can afford it, we need it, we like it; and it will enhance our image as a community. We must go ahead'.

➤ *Options.* Some speakers leave two options before the audience, giving greater emphasis to the one the speaker supports. The danger is that the audience may select the other option. For example: 'We can build this year, when construction costs are at their lowest level, or we can delay building until the economy gets rolling again and construction costs go through the roof. We have the money. The choice is yours'.

Diagnosis *Your humour falls flat.*

Prescription *If you must use humour, follow these guidelines.*

When in doubt, don't try to be funny! If you feel you have to be funny, make sure you source your jokes and witticisms from such publications as the *Reader's Digest,* or other speakers or joke books, but always adapt the material to suit the speech. This is preferable to trying to make up your own jokes.

Always tell third-party jokes—jokes about yourself or your family can fall very flat and go over badly.

Don't give notice that you're about to tell a joke. Just get on with it. In other words, eliminate lead-ins such as:

'I told a marvellous tale last week . . .'
'I think this tale is relevant . . .'
'Stop me if you have been told the joke about . . .'
'One of the most amusing tales I've been told is . . .'

Many people have problems with foreign accents. Don't feel you have to include such accents in tales involving foreigners, unless you can mimic accents well. Never tell obscene jokes, or jokes that could be considered offensive to others. On informal occasions, you can certainly include the names of members of the audience in your jokes to good effect, but be sensitive.

Quoting from a publication or book is a good way to lead into a joke. This tends to give your story a topical flavour or air of integrity.

If you have trouble telling jokes, slow down your pace of delivery. This always helps. Always practise telling your jokes beforehand and always make sure that they relate to your speech.

Diagnosis *Your presentation or speech develops 'log-jams', doesn't go smoothly or appears unprepared.*
Prescription *Prepare thoroughly.*

Become familiar with your presentation or speech content, visual aids and related aspects. Practise your speech and rehearse it aloud, using your visual aids. The more prepared you are, the better will be your performance.

Diagnosis *You get nervous when having to speak in public or present to groups.*
Prescription *Take heart.*

Most public speakers suffer nerves from time to time. Take the approach that you are doing this for your family or your firm and that you will both benefit from a task that may cause you a little anguish. Remember the battle cry, 'For God and my country!'. Your battle cry may be, 'For my wife/husband and family!'. Go through the same animations as the warrior—literally clench your fists and go for it 'For the greater glory!'. Try it—it can work well.

INFLUENCING BY DEVELOPING WRITING EFFECTIVENESS

Writing has no goal other than to help readers understand and comply with your propositions, requests and ideas. The reader should never experience problems working out what you are trying to say. The first rule of any written information is to assist the reader to follow and understand what you are trying to communicate, and the guidelines below will help you attain this.

Giving your document 'person-appeal'

Check out these two statements:

> 'The package will be shipped express courier on Tuesday.'

> 'I will send you the package via express courier on Tuesday.'

The first sentence suggests a production line. The second has more person-appeal, as it tells you who will be involved. Include person-appeal wherever you can in your writing. Compare the following statements to see the effect of the person-appeal approach:

> 'An error was found when your invoice was compiled.'

> 'I found an error when I was compiling your invoice.'

Emphasise reader first, sender second

When you write, place yourself in the shoes of your audience. What might their first question be? How might the reader react to the write-up? What extra information might the reader seek? What information might raise doubts in the reader's mind? For example, a marketing manager reviewing a brief for the latest promotional campaign may be less concerned with costs and other financial matters if the writer emphasises the creativity of the promotions.

Be factual

Minimise unnecessary vagaries in your text. Listen to these two statements and assess which might be more effective in persuading you to accept the new approach.

> 'This latest approach can increase production and enhance your bottom line.'

> 'This latest approach can increase output by 15% without any extra staff expense, adding $90 000 to your margin in six months, according to our preliminary assessment.'

Write like a video camera

Try to visualise your subject as you write, just as though you were looking through the viewfinder of a video camera. Help your reader *see* your ideas, not just read your words. For example, 'Your restaurants are seas of happy faces' creates a graphic and realistic impression. 'You have a lot of customers in your restaurants' is an oblique and easily forgotten statement.

Simplify the reading

'Signpost' statements act as guidelines for your readers. They guide them to where your text is going. These statements are known as signposts because they reveal what is about to follow. They simplify reading, so your readers do not have to work out what you are trying to say. For example, 'Next I will summarise some possible disadvantages to our program and then why I believe you should accept it'.

Effective writing techniques

Some key techniques for communicating written messages effectively are:

➤ *Anecdotes.* 'Across the board we experienced great savings. For example, the technical division saved 15% against forecast by improved filing systems; dispatch saved 10% by recycling.'
➤ *Benchmarking.* 'Although personnel expenses increased 8% last year, in our business sector a 12% rise was more often reported.'
➤ *Metaphysics.* 'Our approach to monitoring operations follows the principle of the temperature gauge. It alerts the need for action if labour costs exceed expectations.'

Structure

Formal correspondence should never deviate from the theme that is being addressed at any one place in the text. For example, in a proposal for public relations, costs relating to investor relations might be addressed. In that same section, don't deviate by introducing an idea for better newsletters, unless this relates directly to the subject of those costs.

Structure relates to the sections of reports and needs proposals—paragraphs and sentences. All the paragraphs in one particular section should relate directly to the same subject. A paragraph needs to address just one topic. A sentence should include one single notion, not a range of concepts.

Establishing certainty

Writers strengthen their cases by establishing certainty in their texts. The best text is assertive and sounds credible. It makes direct assumptions rather than clouding the reader with uncertainties or ambiguities. Compare this ambiguous statement with the more credible statement that follows it:

> 'Our process may perhaps cause minor irritation.'

> 'Our process will cause some minor yet tolerable irritation, bearing in mind the benefits.'

Clarification

Probably the most annoying question for the reader to have to ask is: 'What are you referring to?'. Here is an anecdote demonstrating this: 'Our parts were sent in different packages without approved labelling and delivered by truck. We did not expect this'. What does 'this' refer to? Was the person writing the report concerned about the packaging, the labelling, the mode of delivery, or all three?

Statements that are unclear give the impression of muddled thinking. While some mistakes are mere hindrances to easily digested communication, failure to be accurate about what you are referring to can cause confusion.

ROB BALMER ON **INFLUENCING**

There is no better example of the need to apply the principles of 'influencing' outlined in this chapter than that of trying to get approval for a new initiative from a senior executive team.

After working through the 'influencing' module with Peter, I realised that I had all too often been taking the hard path to getting things approved. I tended to think that if the Managing Director was convinced, then I had the green light to proceed with my projects. I also tended to rely on my debating skills to 'argue the case' in senior team meetings, thinking that winning the argument was what it was all about. However, almost always it was a very hard slog to get things through. And even when I apparently had approval for a project, actually getting things done was very difficult and many 'hurdles' seemed to find their way into my path.

I realised I needed to do things differently. An excellent opportunity to try a new approach came two weeks before I was due to present to the senior leadership team seeking re-approval for a project that was quite a radical departure from the way we had traditionally gone to market. I say re-approval because this project had been approved previously, but new 'concerns' had been raised after a reshuffle of the senior team.

I spent a lot of time thinking about each member of the senior leadership team and identifying who was likely to have the biggest concerns with my project. I then arranged meetings with them individually before the main presentation. At these meetings, I discussed the project with each of them and identified the concerns they each had. I then worked through these concerns asking each of them to describe a solution that would overcome his or her concern and then finally to help me implement that solution. In every case, together we were able to overcome the concern.

By the time it came to the main presentation, not only were all of the concerns dealt with, but I had four or five extra supporters for my project who felt a sense of ownership of it and were prepared to show active support for it. Gaining approval was a foregone conclusion.

The best thing about this new approach was not that it made getting approval much easier, but that for the first time I truly felt that the entire senior team was 'on board' when the approval was given. My experience is that a project or initiative can go well down the path to implementation, often with significant expenditure, only to fail with the finishing post in sight due to the fact that not everyone was truly 'on board'. Attending to the principles of 'influencing' can ensure that everyone is 'on board' and that the project has a much greater chance of reaching a successful conclusion.

LEADERSHIP MYTHS	LEADERSHIP TRUTHS
➤ Power resides at the top of organisations.	➤ Power resides anywhere, and you'd better know who has it!
➤ Leadership is about what you know.	➤ It's also about *who* you know!
➤ Anyone can wing it at meetings.	➤ Your performance at meetings underpins your influence! Wing your influence?
➤ Meetings are all about telling and talking.	➤ Meetings are as much about astute questioning and active listening.
➤ Group presentations are all about great content.	➤ Great content is a given. It's the process of presentation delivery that really counts.

DON'T HIDE!

- ➢ If you are not selling your organisation externally, you may be seen as just a cost.
- ➢ It's often easier to spend time with low-yield allies—they may be your immediate colleagues. You have to develop and spend time with high-yield allies—and they may not even know you.
- ➢ If you don't close at meetings, you won't get the outcome you seek.
- ➢ The bottom line in active listening is that the Almighty gave you two ears and one mouth, and you should use them in this proportion.
- ➢ If you are not prepared to prepare your group presentations, be prepared to disappoint your audience.
- ➢ If you can't write well, why should anyone read your work?
- ➢ You may have prepared the greatest visuals or handouts, but if you don't eyeball the audience and come across in a relaxed, natural and confident manner, you simply won't have impact.

YOUR MONDAY REVIEW

1. Are we influencing key contacts outside our direct control to ensure they make optimal decisions affecting areas within our control?
2. Do we know where the power resides in the organisation?
3. Do we know and communicate with the right people, internally and externally?
4. Are we devoting sufficient time and effort to developing allies and alliances, through personal selling? In this, are we goal setting, prioritising and managing our time appropriately?
5. How's our meeting performance? Are we gaining attention, arousing interest, building desire, winning conviction, and getting action, our action, our sought outcomes, and are we remembering 'Thank you!'?
6. Are we closing at meetings, to attain the outcomes we seek?
7. Are we questioning and listening at meetings, to expand our influence?
8. Are we preparing sufficiently for group presentations: administration, objectives, fact finding, assembling content and format?
9. Are we focusing adequately on the process of group presentation delivery: first impressions, grasping the audience's attention, building curiosity and trust, delivering the main thrust of our speeches, and ending with impact?
10. Are we really acknowledging that it is the process of delivery that really counts, and preparing ourselves accordingly?
11. And, similarly, that it is the process of written communication (as well as the content) that really adds value in influencing?

CHAPTER 3

Synergising

Synergising is about leading peers and working with them to derive better decisions and outcomes for the total business!

KEYNOTES FROM THE COMMENTATORS

A major challenge facing executives today is the rapid creation of high-performance teams who can quickly respond to market challenges and continue to thrive and deliver under constantly changing environments. Ensure the only competition the organisation is dealing with is the external competition; in this fast-changing world, there is neither the time nor energy to lose focus by dealing with inefficiencies created by internal competition.

Lyn Cobley, Chief Executive Officer—tradingroom.com.au

(a joint venture between Fairfax and Macquarie Bank)

The variable organisation can include networks of virtual teams, some doing the business, some winning the business and some changing the business. Interchange of team members provides continuous learning and development. Knowledge is shared. And a good leader 'blends' their people in different ways according to different needs—and this can even mean hiring people you don't necessarily like—to optimise the blend.

Peter Scott, Chief Executive Officer MLC

Interpersonal relationships are the key. People, particularly younger people, need to *want* to work with you. The informal relationship structure counts as much as the formal organisational structure. You get things done through relationships; relationships are the glue!

David Hearn, Chief Executive Goodman Fielder

We've all heard of the **Silo Effect**—people at a similar level in the organisation working in separate functions, divisions or geographic locations and operating as though they exist in discrete 'silos'.

The trouble is that, in many cases, it is a combination of silos that meets customers' needs—for example, sales, production and finance. If silos in such instances are not operating in sync, the chances are that customers' needs will not be met optimally.

This raises the question as to which is the 'real' team (see Chart 3.1). Is it the sales team, the production team, the finance team or a cross-section of all the silos, which is the real team as far as the customer is concerned? Clearly, it's the last one.

Another good reason that we should be studying *synergising*—which by (my modified) definition means 'the power of one mind plus another mind equating three minds'—is that better decisions and outcomes are achieved.

Finally, Chart 3.2 shows that any series of silos, whether functions, divisions or locations, should operate not only as a *functional group* (where the emphasis is on each function to optimise functional results) but also as a *leadership team* (where the emphasis is on the total business and mutual accountability to optimise total business results). More of this later.

Now, change won't go away, it will only accelerate! And change creates new teams needing to get up to speed quickly and sustainably to yield benefits

CHART 3.1

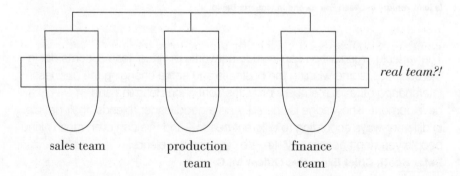

real team?!

sales team   production   finance
                      team   team

CHART 3.2

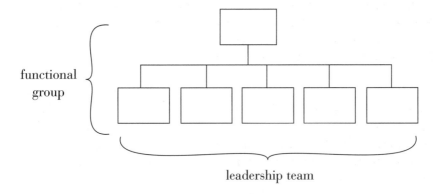

from the synergies and leverage they should create. To enable this, team members need to understand each other's behavioural styles and how their differences can be harmonised to create a star team, rather than just a team of stars.

Psychologists and behavioural scientists the world over agree that winning executive teams need to be balanced in their composition. In other words, teams generally perform best when the members between them represent all the main behavioural styles. But leading a team of clones can be a lot easier!

Leading a team of very different behavioural styles can sometimes see them 'clash' against each other like medieval knights jousting at a tournament, particularly when the team is working under pressure. This can become destructive rather than synergistic. Rather, teams need proactive input from each member and leader, contributed on the basis of mutual support, trust and cooperation.

Just as an organisation experiences different phases in its life cycle— start up, early and secondary growth, adolescence/turbulence and maturity—so teams can experience similar phases. The last two phases are often of particular concern because they are times when the team needs to regenerate, if not reinvent itself. Adolescence/turbulence often coincides with interpersonal friction among team members. Maturity can be associated with 'meetings for the sake of meetings' and not a lot of creative output.

Other forms of unsuccessful team makeup can include:

➤ all very clever people: disaster-prone;
➤ too many idea generators: good ideas produced but never taken up;
➤ idea generators and all-rounders: team looks brilliant but is always

beaten by better-balanced, broader-based teams that can accomplish things;

➤ fewer than six people: secondary roles/doubling up as needed;
➤ more than eight to ten people: difficult group dynamics and the possibility of imbalance.

Before going any further, what type of team do you participate in with your peers? For example:

➤ *a new or young team*—a collection of executives operating more or less independently, their main dependence being on the appointed leader for direction and support;
➤ *a divergent team*—affected adversely by a number of issues that it needs to resolve before team members can work together effectively;
➤ *a convergent team*—strong interpersonal relationships and alliances, but independent thinking is not particularly valued and the danger of cloning is high;
➤ *a synchronised team*—a highly developed team of independent team members. Combines star players with a star team. Often team decisions exceed what individual team members working by themselves would be able to achieve.

In summary, synergising requires high-performance teamwork, which is based on:

➤ conductive interpersonal relationships one-on-one;
➤ balanced team composition in terms of operating styles at the executive level;
➤ effective group dynamics, i.e. in-team behaviour;
➤ efficient processes.

OPERATING STYLE

As mentioned earlier, it is widely agreed that winning senior executive or management teams need a balanced composition, as it relates to the various operating styles of team members. In other words, teams generally perform best when the members represent between them all the main operating styles associated with human behaviour.

The gurus have developed countless models depicting differing personal styles, behaviour or personality. Drawing on much of this thinking and on my dealing with hundreds of executives for more than five years, I have been able to produce a new model that bridges conventional wisdom with my practical experience. The model first provides some primary guidelines on behaviour; second, it enables observers to determine their own and others' operating styles quickly and precisely; finally, it can be used in analysing team composition.

Case Study

Mary Hunter (not her real name) is operations manager in an airline catering and food service organisation in London. She is described by her colleagues as being highly 'hands-on' and action-oriented. She talks a lot to her staff, actively giving them instructions as they go about their work. She seems preoccupied with results and displays a strong output orientation. Mary exhibits highly *proactive* behaviour.

Case Study

Paul Wong (not his real name) is the employee relations manager in the sales and service centre of a major consumer electronics manufacturer in San Francisco. He is seen to be 'hands-off', believing that line managers and supervisors need to be the primary interface with hourly paid employees. Paul appears to be calm in nature, he is an excellent and active listener, and is regarded as extremely friendly and approachable by all. Paul evaluates situations with care and with special consideration of the human factor. He exhibits highly *receptive* behaviour.

Most of us are a mixture of proactiveness and receptiveness in the way we behave, and there are several different operating styles that blend proactiveness and receptiveness.

High proactiveness/low receptiveness

This style is somewhat like Mary Hunter, but perhaps not to her extreme extent. The label I give to this style is **Commander/Doer**, the key characteristics being hands-on, action, talking, results and, above all, an output orientation.

Commander/Doers direct others, often quite forcefully, and are people of action. They are always on the go and can never sit still. They put a lot of effort into things, can be very energetic and find it hard to relax. They have a down-to-earth attitude, relying on commonsense approaches. They prefer tangible, concrete objects to 'airy-fairy' ideas or feelings. They learn by doing rather than by reading. They are confident in meeting new circumstances or strange situations alone. Commander/Doers are happy to rely on their own capabilities in any environment or in tackling any matter.

High receptiveness/low proactiveness

This style is something like Paul Wong, but not so extreme. The label given to this style is **Empathiser/Humanist**, the key characteristics being hands-off, reflection, listening and, above all, a people orientation.

The Empathiser/Humanist is able to understand other people, their ideas, attitudes and behaviour, and is affected in mood or behaviour by what other people say or do. People of this style enjoy listening to others, are cooperative, and enjoy the company of others.

Empathiser/Humanists allow and encourage others to have their say; they believe in majority decisions, but not to the disadvantage of minorities. They dislike unduly forcing or asserting themselves over other people.

High proactiveness/high receptiveness

This is a combination of styles in the direction of both Mary's and Paul's style. We call this style **Responder/Initiator**, the key characteristics being a capacity both to get involved and to stand aside; to act and be reflective; to talk and listen; and to seek tangible results but also to be oriented towards people.

The Responder/Initiator tends to exhibit good levels of both proactive and receptive behaviour. People with this style of behaviour usually display great enthusiasm in working with others, being both active listeners and enthusiastic talkers. They sell themselves well and are usually good presenters.

Low proactiveness/low receptiveness

The label we give to this style is **Evaluator/Detailer**, the key characteristics being neither particularly hands-on, nor overly action-oriented, nor an active responder nor initiator. Such people tend to remain alone or detached, not engaging in much group or individual interaction. They tend to stay out of the limelight. They are often non-committal, yet invariably factual and analytical—classic planners and detailers, in fact.

The Evaluator/Detailer takes a lot of care over things, is sometimes seen as cautious, likes to do a job well and does not like sloppiness or a casual approach. People with this style take a consistently steady approach to all situations, are unflappable, are neither easily aroused or stimulated nor provoked, and are often thought of as cold and unemotional.

Evaluator/Detailers tackle things in a controlled way, are quite happy with their own company and are self-sufficient.

A mixture of low/high proactiveness and low/high receptiveness

This is the **Idea Generator**, who is a combination of the previous four styles. This person can dart nimbly from one operating style to another, often exhibiting extremes of behaviour and flashes of inspiration and creativity, seeing 'endless possibilities'.

Idea Generators are very concerned with the 'big picture', knowledge and theory, often forgetting practical application. However, they do jump in and apply themselves enthusiastically when committed to a course of action. People of this operating style are usually interested in the future and the longer term, perhaps more than the 'here and now'. They often change their minds or course of action and enjoy variety.

Idea Generators also have a preference for 'doing their own thing'; they do not always agree with other people, their wishes, ideas, attitudes or behaviour; and they enjoy freedom of choice.

A mixture of a reasonable degree of proactiveness and a reasonable degree of receptiveness

This is the **All-rounder**, who also occupies all four quadrants (see Chart 3.3) but seldom if ever shows extremes of any type of behaviour, exhibiting a balanced, yet flexible style. All-rounders often represent the stabilising factor in teams and can make good chairpersons. They can help the team reach consensus and are able to compromise. While not usually being seen as the life and soul of the party, they are quite popular and their opinions are often sought. They usually give others a fair hearing.

All-rounders are well able to identify with all the other styles and converse with them easily, providing extremes in behaviour are not evident, which can cause them some difficulties. Indeed, when others are exhibiting extremes in behaviour, All-rounders often act as moderators.

These six different operating styles are shown in Chart 3.3, which represents a model for assessing behaviour and operating style.

ASSESSING OPERATING STYLES

One way of assessing other people's operating styles is first to gauge their degree of proactiveness and receptiveness, in terms of the way they behave. How proactive and how receptive are they? This approach may

CHART 3.3   Operating styles

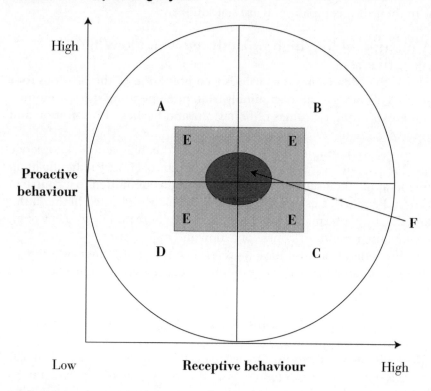

Code

A   Commander/Doer
B   Responder/Initiator
C   Empathiser/Humanist
D   Evaluator/Detailer
E   Idea Generator
F   All-rounder

lead you to operating style definition more easily. Anyone can display a combination of operating styles but will usually exhibit a main style with perhaps a subordinate style.

Operating styles can also vary depending on circumstances—for example, the main style of individuals working under stressful conditions may be very different from their style at home under more relaxed conditions. Clearly, for our purposes we need to concentrate on the work situation.

USE OF OPERATING STYLES

In seeking to develop good interpersonal relations and greater influence, you first need to be clear about your own communication style. By way of reminder, your operating style is likely to be one or more of the following:

> - *Commander/Doer:* usually directs other people and works energetically to get results.
> - *Responder/Initiator:* seeks to understand others, communicates very well and leads enthusiastically.
> - *Empathiser/Humanist:* people-oriented rather than production-oriented, with an amicable style.
> - *Evaluator/Detailer:* the analytical, logical and meticulous planner and organiser.
> - *Idea Generator:* the conceptual and creative thinker who can see endless possibilities and show extremes in behaviour.
> - *All-rounder:* the balanced individual who has a flexible style, yet doesn't show extremes in behaviour.

Next, you need to be aware of how your operating style affects the way you communicate, and what happens when you overuse your positive attributes.

The *Commander/Doer* often communicates rapidly and enthusiastically, exuding an air of confidence and a down-to-earth attitude. However, when overutilising these positive attributes, Commander/Doers can communicate too quickly, appearing somewhat shortsighted and too keen on action, rather than on taking longer-term or bigger-picture scenarios into consideration. They can also at times be overly blunt and uninterested in the social niceties.

If you are a *Responder/Initiator* or *All-rounder,* you have behavioural flexibility and should find it quite easy to adapt the way you communicate to meet the needs of other parties. The only caveat here is that All-rounders may come across as being a little flat or uninspiring at times, whereas the Responder/Initiator comes across as enthusiastic, sometimes too enthusiastic!

The *Empathiser/Humanist* probably reads the other party well and empathises with them. They usually come across in a friendly and courteous manner, often seeking the involvement of others through their use of questions, comments and examples. However, when overutilising these positive attributes, Empathiser/Humanists may become swayed by the mood and views of the other party and even lose control. They may also tend to harp on the historical perspective—'the way we used to do things'—and not come to the point very quickly. They may also be too anxious to please.

Evaluator/Detailers often communicate with accuracy and clarity and achieve their objectives in the time or space allocated. However, an overutilisation of these positive attributes may include a preference for being dogmatic or reading from a script, and failure to empathise with the other party. The delivery can sometimes be dull and monotonous, these individuals being preoccupied with content rather than *how* the communication comes across.

Idea Generators can communicate with plenty of creativity and bright ideas. However, when overutilising these positive attributes they can be hard to follow or understand and may be too theoretical. They can also be poor time managers or too long-winded in written communications, in each case having difficulty in emphasising the main point or ending with impact. They may also fail to read the other party or audience accurately, being more concerned with their own point of view.

In describing these operating styles, I have described the way they communicate and the caveats associated with overutilising such traits. Communication is a process and depends on the skills of the communicator. These skills can be learned and improved on, so as to upgrade the quality of communicating with individuals or groups.

In using operating styles, the third and final element is the way that effective communicators vary their approach and style, depending on the other party. This is a natural response. We don't act the same way with the different kinds of people we meet; we are constantly adjusting our style, depending on the response we get. By understanding different operating styles, professional communicators adjust their presentations and overall style to elicit the most positive response. People prefer communicators who are most like themselves.

We all have enough personality traits to downplay some facets and emphasise others without appearing phoney. By identifying the operating style of the other party, you can adapt your own style in order to gain the most favourable reaction and response. The research for this is best undertaken in advance.

➤ The *Commander/Doer.* These people are assertive, goal-oriented, impatient for results, and decisive. They dislike inaction or beating about the bush and prefer it if you stick to business, talk facts and come to the point quickly.
➤ The *Responder/Initiator.* These people are assertive, enthusiastic,

expressive and make quick decisions. They listen to you, but also tend to want to have their say. You need to 'engage' in communication with these individuals to be most effective.

➤ The *Empathiser/Humanist*. This type is warm and friendly, but a little hesitant to take risks and makes decisions very carefully. Here you will be more successful if you show interest and support, and provide reassurance rather than pressure in your presentation.

➤ The *Evaluator/Detailer*. This person is very organised, precise, analytical and cautious. There is a dislike of sloppiness, of failure to provide concrete facts and evidence, and of disregard for rules and regulations. You will increase your chances of success with this person if you are on time, provide guarantees and full details, and allow sufficient time to verify facts and make careful decisions.

➤ The *All-rounder*. This person has a flexible style and can get on with anyone providing they don't show extremes of behaviour. Showing versatility in your own style, but using moderation throughout your presentation, will have the best impact on the All-rounder.

➤ The *Idea Generator*. This person also has a flexible style but shows extremes and sometimes even inconsistencies in behaviour. Idea Generators need to be enthused and excited by both the content and delivery of your presentation in order for you to have the greatest effect on them. They tend to fly off in several directions at once and so need to be kept on track. Summarising your key points at the end of your presentation will be effective with these individuals.

TEAM COMPOSITION

The operating styles model (Chart 3.3) can also be used as a road map to plot the positions of the operating styles of others in your existing, future or most recent team. An example of a well-balanced executive team is shown in Chart 3.4.

Be careful not to assume that the team leader or chairperson automatically occupies the All-rounder or any other specific style position. Formal leaders can be of any operating style, providing the senior team has members who between them display all the six operating styles described, preferably as their main styles—if not, then as a combination of their main and subordinate styles.

Lower-level or specialised teams, however, may not need such a balanced composition and indeed may benefit from being unbalanced and biased towards one or more operating styles: for example, a sales team may need a bias towards Commander/Doers or Responder/Initiators.

CHART 3.4 Team composition

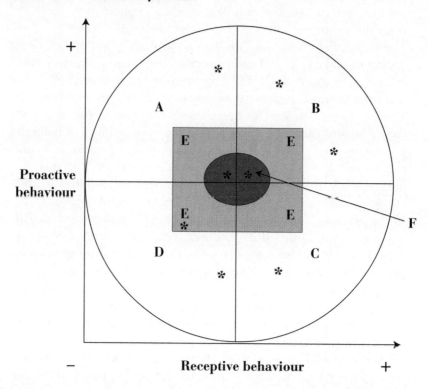

Code
A Commander/Doer
B Responder/Initiator
C Empathiser/Humanist
D Evaluator/Detailer
E Idea Generator
F All-rounder

* plotting of each
  team member's
  operating style,
  showing team
  composition

However, if a senior executive team is deficient in a balanced makeup, then in order to be fully effective it needs to make special arrangements to compensate for this deficiency. This may be done through new hires, secondment of others to team activities and team meetings or, not least of all, the team taking a deliberate stance to include all the missing operating style elements in discussions and relevant activities. This can be accomplished by appointing a 'champion' of the missing style to ensure due consideration to it.

By way of example, a team may lack an Idea Generator. Another team member may volunteer to champion this operating style and perhaps embark on a creative thinking training course to develop an understanding of how to use brainstorming techniques in the team setting. These techniques are deployed from time to time when significant matters are being addressed that require detailed and 'outside the square' assessment before resolution.

Clearly, with a well-balanced senior team, each member can be seen to make a valid and different contribution to team activities and meetings, enhancing the prospects of individual executives or managers and team success.

If you are the leader of the senior team, or about to become one, you now have the understanding and process to assess team makeup and to ensure that you lead and develop a well-balanced team that will succeed in its endeavours. In so doing, you will enhance the success prospects of your fellow executives or managers and yourself.

You may be asking yourself whether this theme of well-balanced senior team makeup is real or just hot air. We can assure you that, at the executive and managerial level, it is *real*. Studies and real-life examples have shown that well-balanced senior executive or management teams and their individual members succeed best!

However, sometimes even when team makeup *is* well balanced, some of these very different operating styles can clash, particularly when the team is working under pressure. This can cause difficulties in interpersonal relationships and become destructive rather than synergistic. There are two requirements in such cases:

➤ Share this information on team makeup, with a view to all team members knowing and recognising each other's main and perhaps subordinate operating style, and understanding the importance of a balanced makeup. The material in this chapter can be used to good effect in communicating and demonstrating this.

➤ Ensure that an All-rounder operating style is present and preferably is able to chair or intervene at meetings. This may be difficult when the leader or official chairperson is not the All-rounder—which is often the case. Under these circumstances, while the leader or chairperson may facilitate the execution of the agenda and ensure that priorities and objectives are attained, the All-rounder needs to be given sufficient 'air-time' to ensure that the strength in the style differences within the team is utilised positively and synergistically.

In his book *The 7 Habits of Highly Effective People*, Stephen Covey sums up synergy by saying that its essence lies in valuing the difference between people (or team members). The key to valuing these differences is to realise that all people see the world not as it is, but as they are. These differences in perceptions, when shared and understood, lead to new possibilities and new alternatives.

Clearly, clashes and poor interpersonal relationships are not what individual executive, manager or team success is about. Nor is team success about rook-like behaviour, where participants sit on the fence and wait and watch in which direction the flow is going, before going with the flow! The bottom line is that successful teamwork is all about 'fit'.

Successful teams need to avoid all these potential difficulties and be composed of mutually supportive 'henchmen', all doing their utmost to support their colleagues. As a team member or leader, by avoiding the pitfalls and using the approaches suggested regarding team makeup, you enhance success prospects for one and all!

IN-TEAM BEHAVIOUR

My conceptual model for in-team behaviour is shown in Chart 3.5, followed by definitions of the words used. I often get told off by my partners at The Stephenson Partnership about the use of such medieval terms, but I'm afraid I can't part with them. I claim that the use of metaphors and analogies is a legitimate and effective mode of enhancing adult learning.

CHART 3.5 In-team behaviour

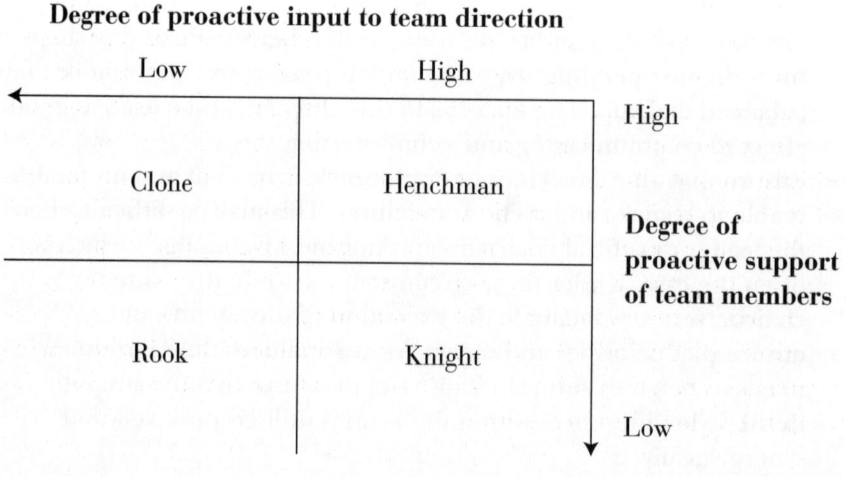

Degree of proactive input to team direction

	Low	High	
	Clone	Henchman	High
	Rook	Knight	**Degree of proactive support of team members**
			Low

Knights were originally of noble birth and are often thought of as medieval warriors wandering the land in search of chivalrous adventures. But knights also took part in pageants where they would joust by charging at each other with lances on horseback in an endeavour to dismount their combatant and win the tournament. A veritable 'I win/You lose' outcome! Knights in the team setting are very proactive in their input to team direction, but are usually somewhat or even very unsupportive of team members, and are often seen as internally competitive.

Clones, from a biological perspective, are genetically identical to one antecedent or, from the botanical perspective, are transplants from one original seedling. Clones in the work or team setting can result from the 'mirror-image' effect of hiring, where the comfort level of the hirer is increased if the hiree is of the same ilk. Clones in the team setting do not provide much proactive input to team direction, but they do tend to be very supportive of other team members, particularly the team leader, and usually go along with them.

Rooks, often mistaken for crows, are very common in Europe where they live in large colonies or rookeries. They tend to do their own thing in the rookery, often seeming at odds with the other birds. Ultimately, however, with reluctance and quite a lot of squawking, they will fly off with the others rather than be left alone. Rooks are really 'fence-sitters' and commit to a course of action only if it seems to be the way all the other birds in the rookery are heading. Rooks in the team setting are neither proactive in their input to team direction nor particularly supportive of other team members. They usually accept team consensus, however, if with some reluctance.

Henchmen (I apologise, but 'henchpeople' does not have quite the same impact!), historically, were squires or pages of honour and could always be trusted and relied on. Henchmen were also full of cunning and native wit and would often come up with good ideas on behalf of their colleagues. Also, whatever the needs of an individual or team, henchmen would endeavour to support and provide for them, enhancing the overall effectiveness of the group. Thus, henchmen are proactive both in terms of their input to team direction and in their support of team members. The 'evil' connotation of henchmen is a distortion—if the henchman is on your side, they are great people!

Teams need to be composed of henchmen. In today's fiercely competitive environment, there is little room for clones, knights and rooks, or for too much knight-like behaviour (although *some* can be catalytic and helpful).

DEALING WITH CONFLICT

All your good work on developing synergy can come undone when presented with a conflict situation. Chart 3.6 gives a great sequence for dealing with conflict effectively.

➤ *Get ready*
  - Deal with the conflict privately on neutral ground.
  - Open with the statement that you'd like to come out of the discussion with an 'I win/You win' result.
  - Review what you *do* agree on before discussing what you do *not* agree on.
  - Try to depersonalise the conflict by attacking the problem, not the person or people.
➤ *Establish the facts*
  - Restate your perception of the two sides of the conflict to check for accuracy.
  - Use active listening skills, particularly questions, to draw out the other party and help identify the real cause of the conflict, as opposed to just the symptoms.
  - Remain respectful and positive at all times.
➤ *Review the alternatives*
  - Once the central issue has been identified, jointly investigate alternative solutions and outcomes. Don't reject alternatives without hearing them out. Seek up to half a dozen alternatives: two or three are not enough.
  - Together, evaluate the alternatives, highlighting the pluses and minuses of each one.
  - Rank the alternatives according to overall merit and practicality and agree on the ranking.
➤ *Agree on next steps*
  - Restate the highest-ranking solution and the action plan to resolve it, with responsibilities and time frames. Be as specific as you can.
  - Agree on follow-up activities and dates to ensure that progress is being made. Be positive and provide praise when progress is made.

CHART 3.6   Dealing with conflict

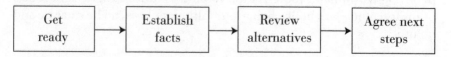

The best outcomes of conflict are when all parties feel they are the winners, or share in winning. 'I win/You lose' outcomes are to be avoided. If the other party seems intent on 'I win/You lose', don't be drawn into this. Stick to 'I win/You win' and challenge them as to why one party should win and the other lose. If this is really the case, you can't move forward effectively.

Another key element of dealing with conflict is to encourage active listening.

➤ Question, question, question, eliciting open-ended rather than yes/no answers.
➤ Listen, listen, listen!
➤ Use body language to show you are listening.
➤ Periodically paraphrase what the other party has said, to show you have heard it and to check you have heard it right.
➤ Don't interrupt the speaker.
➤ Active listening, as a habit, reduces the intensity and the occurrence of conflict.

Make sure you uncover the real problems as opposed to just the symptoms. Imagine you are a series of sieves, the mesh on each sieve becoming finer so that the last sieve lets through only the wheat germ. Your questions should be like this, probing further and further until the essence of the problem is uncovered. But probe in a way that is positive and supportive, pulling the other party along with you rather than pushing them. Summarise your understanding of the real problem, when you think you have uncovered it.

Finally, here's a range of other possibilities when handling conflict. You be the judge of their efficacy as you read them through.

➤ Withdraw?
➤ Just agree with the other party?
➤ Simply disagree?
➤ Argue?
➤ Constructively seek to move towards collaboration?
➤ Put yourself in the shoes of the other party to try to see it their way?
➤ Let them air their concerns fully—'vent' the issue—initially?
➤ When it gets too heated for too long (after the initial venting), reconvene at a later time/date?

TEAM PROCESSES

Just as businesses need processes in order to run efficiently, so teams need processes to ensure efficiency and effectiveness in teamwork. The following paragraphs describe powerful team processes. As you read through them, ask yourself the degree to which your own peer team coincides with the descriptions. What improvements to your teamwork should be made?

➢ The team has a compelling vision of the future and clearly defined and well-communicated statements of purpose. Plans are developed collaboratively and work is managed against goals or objectives. When priorities are revised, the need for change is discussed and agreed to by the team.

➢ Work is organised to support the team's functions. Roles, relationships and accountabilities are clear to everyone. Members are technically qualified to perform their jobs or have immediate plans for acquiring needed knowledge and skills.

➢ The values and principles used to support and manage the work of the team attend to both 'output' and 'human' needs. *Output needs* refer to activities required to accomplish work objectives, including such activities as problem solving, decision making and conflict management. *Human needs* refer to recognition, participation, appreciation, and general quality of team life.

➢ Interpersonal relationships are of high quality. Each team member interacts fully with every other team member. A high level of trust exists within the team, facilitating problem solving and making teamwork satisfying.

➢ The team does not compete inappropriately with other teams in the same organisation. 'I win/You lose' situations between teams do not exist, whereas 'I win/You win' situations do. The relationship between teams within the organisation is productive and satisfying.

➢ The team resembles a *leadership team*, whose members are highly committed to, and mutually accountable for, the team's reason for being, their approach to the job and total business performance. The team comprises no more than 12 people (ideally, no more than 8 to 10), with complementary capabilities and a strong commitment to each other. This is rather rare!

➢ The team resembles a *functional group*—people who operate more as functional heads, their leader assigning them priorities, establishing performance expectations, facilitating encouragement and motivation, consolidating functional results into total business results and holding each person accountable for their individual input. This is quite common.

➤ Team members operate flexibly somewhere between a *functional group* and a *leadership team*. They reserve leadership teamwork for major opportunities, threats or challenges. They balance their leadership team and functional responsibilities, rather than trying to mesh them together or operate as a single, all-purpose ongoing team. They learn not to trade one for the other, nor to compromise leadership team and functional performance.

➤ The team decides when to operate as a *leadership team*, selecting times and events judiciously, where real opportunities exist for collective leadership team input. They understand that addressing all business performance matters as a leadership team inevitably leads to frustration, even a sense of boredom. They recognise the need for different types of meetings: sometimes as a functional group with a full agenda and tight schedule to get through the business of the day; sometimes as a leadership team with a smaller agenda and looser schedule, tackling just a few key issues.

➤ When operating as a *leadership team*, the team pursues a common purpose, intent, performance goals and monitoring. They commit to a mutually agreed and acceptable approach to how they work, including shared values and team processes and procedures. They believe in, and practise, mutual accountability. They embrace and synchronise the diverse capabilities and operating styles of members, maximising synergy.

How would you describe the team processes in the peer team of which you are a member?

THE SPORTS COACHING ANALOGY

Early in my career I had the good fortune to be a sports coach, at a Cadet College at Hasan Abdal in Pakistan, where I was a volunteer teacher for 12 months as part of Britain's Voluntary Service Overseas Program. I coached various sports, including rugby, shooting, boxing, swimming and field hockey.

I believe there are some aspects of sports coaching which lend themselves to the business team setting and which form a useful checklist for follow-up use by team leaders, many of whom identify well with the sports coaching analogy.

➤ Business and sports success is won through *star teams*, not just a team of stars. Yet moulding a team of very different individuals into a world-class team requires as much focus on motivating and developing the *individual* as it does on the team. And individuals needs to be treated like individuals, and it requires a flexible tailored approach to bring out the best in each of them. In contrast, how many chief executives rely simply on team meetings to interact with their direct reports?

➤ *Individual motivation.* Whether in a sports team or business team, each individual responds to different stimuli in terms of their self-motivation. For some, it's a pat on the back; for others, it's the challenge of getting to the next level. Others are naturally competitive and, for them, benchmarking their own or team performance against others provides the stimulus to succeed. And the team leader needs to know the most appropriate stimulus to use with each individual, so that each of them attains and develops their best performance.

However, the overriding motivation of the team setting is camaraderie, team spirit and a mutually supportive and collegial atmosphere: 'We are in this together. Together we will win . . . or fail!'.

➤ *Building confidence.* Just like a professional sportsperson, any key person in an organisation will have times of failure, or will find it lonely and tough competing and performing at their best. Team leaders (like sports coaches) have to concentrate on building the confidence of team members to help them attain new levels of performance. To do this they have to create a motivational environment, in which each team member consistently enjoys incremental ongoing improvement. How many business team leaders do you know who are able to do this?

➤ *Respect* is earned if the team leader helps members to put their own interests last and the interests of the whole team first, yet at the same time recognises the achievements of individuals and directs credit to those deserving it.

Respect also comes about when individual or team failure is seen and treated as a learning experience rather than treated punitively. Failure plays an important role in team and individual development and should be used positively (assuming that failure is not overly recurrent).

➤ *Moulding the job* to fit the individual. Clearly, sportspeople are far better at some sports than others. Similarly, people at work will perform best when their roles as individuals and team members directly coincide with their interests, their motivational needs and capabilities, their job requirements, their values, their operating style, their leadership traits and their in-team behaviour.

If you are wondering, as a team leader, where to start, an 80% rule often seems to apply—80% of the responsibility for job moulding lies with the individual and, intuitively, if not planned, in 80% of individual cases there appears to be an 80% job fit. What the team leader does need to do is keep a watchful eye out for the 20% where job fit is less sure or, in the worst case, a straight bad match. Opening up some dialogue and putting the onus on the individual to think through job moulding options and potential will begin to lay strong foundations for enhancing job fit.

➤ *Goal setting and feedback.* Unless individual and team goals are mutually agreed, performance towards their attainment monitored, and supportive, motivational and/or corrective feedback provided, individual sportspeople or teams will never reach their full potential. Nor will business teams or their individual members.

As an executive coach, I often encounter huge gaps in establishing mutually held and understood expectations for results, and a void when it comes to the provision of real feedback by leaders in business. For the individual, feedback needs to be spontaneous and ongoing, as well as planned and periodic through more formal performance evaluation or appraisal processes. For the team it can be self-generated feedback, initiated by the leader: 'How do you people feel we are tracking? What's going well? What's going not so well? What do we need to modify or change?'. Responses by the team to such prompting—which, again, needs to be regular—can ensure team performance is enhanced and team development sustained.

➤ *Unique team players*—unique individuals working cohesively. Most successful sports coaches have sought, identified and worked with the uniqueness of each individual player, and galvanised them into a balanced and cohesive unit. This requires each person's willingness, indeed passion, to be a great team player as well as a great individual contributor.

Team leaders in business can learn these lessons from the sports analogy, because no single executive can have *all* the sought-after and ideal executive traits to run a company. But a team can, providing it comprises a range of unique characteristics in individuals who are team players.

➤ *Loss of key people.* Just as sports teams lose key players—often to the competition—so business teams encounter losses. This is perfectly natural, and to be expected rather than worried about. Teams need to realise that such a loss is a real opportunity to try out another player or team member. In this way, a potential negative can be turned into a positive, providing there is an adequate talent pool for succession.

The successor might not always be a perfect fit initially. Through coaching, that successor can invariably be developed to become a more perfect fit and performer.

➤ *Continuous improvement.* When sports teams become comfortable with success and rest on their laurels, complacency sets in and their performance starts to deteriorate. When business teams become complacent, results may be at risk. With the stewardship of their leaders, teams need continuously to seek new ways to improve their performance. In this, the spirit of the *malcontent* (the one who is never satisfied) can generate great profits when applied positively.

➤ *Team leadership.* Winning teams need effective leadership—and from behind, more than from the front, to create a sense of empowerment and shared leadership. Team leaders need to ensure that appropriate plans and strategies are in place—where and how the team is headed—and that the right environment is created wherein individuals and the team can thrive, with positive reinforcement and leadership by example. Building on team and individual strengths and attending to the weaker areas, with commitment to continuous improvement, are the keys to ongoing individual and team success.

➤ *Continuous development.* To attain continuous improvement in team and individual performance requires continuous coaching and development. Ask any athlete about the years of rigorous training they have to go through to realise their full potential. If the world-beating sports standards in Australia today applied to Australian business, I would probably not be writing this book!

And do not forget standards. Athletes know the times they have to beat; executives and teams also need stretch standards or benchmarks for them to attain their best, backed by continuous and rigorous training and development to help them get there.

ROB BALMER ON SYNERGISING

The best example of the strategies of synergising making a major difference to my business was in dealing with what I'll call the 'natural tensions' that existed between various functional departments.

We have all experienced these natural tensions. Here are some examples.

➢ The finance team gets upset that the sales team goes out and does crazy deals to get business and they (the finance team) then have to clean up the mess.

➢ The sales team gets upset with the finance department for putting what they see as unnecessary obstacles in the way of doing business.

➢ The marketing communications team gets upset with the product team for never getting the information about new products and pricing to them on time and changing things at the last minute.

➢ The supply chain team gets frustrated that the IT systems team can't get the system working the way they need it to handle the rapidly growing logistics challenges facing the business.

➢ The IT systems team gets upset with the supply chain team for continually changing their priorities and never being satisfied.

Every department was doing a fantastic job in isolation but, when it came to the overall picture, I felt like the referee in a World Championship wrestling match! When I sat down and talked it through with Peter Stephenson, I realised very quickly that what I had on my hands was a problem caused by my team not synergising. So I applied the principles outlined in this chapter to deal with these natural tensions.

The solution

➢ The team itself decided that we needed to restructure around the customer and not our internal functions.

➢ Three business units were formed and one member of each function became part of each business unit leadership team.

➢ Leadership team members were all made jointly responsible for ensuring the customer's needs were placed before all others.

➢ Individual team members were required to report back to their functional area to keep them informed of all relevant business unit activities and issues.

➢ Individual team members were required to keep the business unit informed of any issues arising in the functional area.

The result?

➤ complete elimination of communication issues
➤ better utilisation of diverse talents within each business unit
➤ customer the centre of everyone's attention
➤ complete elimination of all natural tensions

LEADERSHIP MYTHS	LEADERSHIP TRUTHS
➤ How you lead your team, your direct reports, is what really counts in leadership.	➤ How you engage in teamwork with your peers is also what really counts!
➤ You know how you come across to others, because you know yourself well.	➤ You probably come across differently to others than you would expect, particularly when you are under pressure!
➤ The best executive teams are those where team members get on really well with each other.	➤ The most effective executive teams are composed of members who exhibit a broad range of operating styles, not all of which naturally get on well together—and they can be the most challenging teams to lead and manage!
➤ Avoid conflict at all costs.	➤ Deal with conflict as a salesperson deals with sales objections: you can't overcome them until you have established what they are and where they reside.
➤ Planning is about strategy, followed by structure.	➤ It's also about leveraging people. By moulding their jobs to fit them best, you optimise strategy and structure.

DON'T HIDE!

➢ Unless your team is operating both as a functional group and as a leadership team—and knows when to operate in each mode—your team will underperform.

➢ The best way to develop interpersonal relationships is to act and communicate in a way that relates well to the other person's operating style. Behavioural flexibility is key.

➢ If team members are not behaving, in the main, like 'henchmen', how can the team succeed?

➢ If your team processes don't work, then neither will your teamwork.

➢ You'll lose good people. You'll hire good people. You'll develop good people. It's all about good people.

➢ Continuous improvement in team and individual performance requires continuous coaching and development—team leadership in action.

YOUR TUESDAY REVIEW

1. Are we suffering from too many silos and insufficient across-team interconnectivity?
2. Do we recognise and support the real teams, whose members may reside in different functional areas?
3. As peers, are we engaging optimally in teamwork?
4. Does our team operate both as a functional group and as a leadership team, and know when it's operating as each?
5. Are we avoiding unsuccessful forms of team makeup, and are we operating at, or pursuing, an appropriate stage of team development?
6. As peers, do we understand our own and each other's operating styles, and through this are we engaging in or developing strong interpersonal relationships?
7. As a team, do we comprise a broad and balanced range of operating styles and, if not, how are we compensating?
8. Do team members take a proactive stance both in contributing to team ideas and direction and in supporting other team members?
9. Do we recognise where conflict resides, do we know what it is, and are we dealing with it effectively?
10. Are we engaging in effective and efficient team processes, so that our teamwork and outcomes are optimised?
11. Do we engage in continuous improvement in team and individual performance, recognising that this requires continuous coaching and development—team leadership in action?
12. Are we using any of the lessons learned and techniques used in sports team coaching, in our business setting?

CHAPTER 4

Enabling

Enabling is about leading your people forward, and attaining superior results with and through them.

KEYNOTES FROM THE COMMENTATORS

Leaders, like any human beings, are vulnerable, and need to declare this. 'I don't know and I need your opinions' should be a stock phrase of executive leaders in working with their people. Also, executives should never underestimate the latent capacity of people in their organisations, so get out of their way and let them get on with it! We need to break the conditioning process resulting from top-down management, and get people to think, open up and contribute their ideas. Find out what your people have done in the past—at work and outside work—and you'll be surprised what a wealth of talent this represents, often untapped.

Peter Scott, Chief Executive Officer MLC

Executives have to respond to the increasing need in the new generation of employees for an environment of clear communication, empowerment, trust and their simple ability to question strategy and decisions! Maintaining balance between keeping up to date with the fast-changing external environment and remaining focused on the 'task at hand' so that initiatives are finalised also represents a challenge. Executives need to demonstrate the ability to maintain effectiveness in varying environments with different tasks, responsibilities and people. They need to have the ability to think outside accepted logic and find new and innovative solutions, combined with a talent to manage ambiguity.

Lyn Cobley, Chief Executive Officer—tradingroom.com.au
(a joint venture between Fairfax and Macquarie Bank)

Executive leaders need to connect to the future, whatever their roles in the company. Pursuing futures, concurrent with attaining required shorter-term results, requires a balanced focus. Additionally, our top-to-bottom review of operations—via internally appointed project teams—has enabled us to concentrate on the primary business drivers.

Peter Wilkinson, Chief Executive David Jones

Most executives have had some type of management training and development, and 'management' is one of the most written-about subjects in business texts the world over. In my experience, it is the basic management practices that can either make or break executives when it comes to maximising job performance and business results through 'enabling'.

However, with the corporate restructurings and downsizings that have flourished over the past few years, most executives find themselves having to 'do more, with less, faster'. This creates huge time management problems, often causing the basics of good management to be neglected.

We begin by describing a selection of management practices:

➢ primary business drivers
➢ external futures
➢ planning
➢ corporate communications
➢ organising
➢ monitoring
➢ decision making

➢ motivating
➢ delegating
➢ motivational delegation
➢ personal accountability and
➢ my new core management competence, 'Fast and simple!'.

PRIMARY BUSINESS DRIVERS

One of the biggest problems in business today is the breadth of responsibility held by most executives and managers, exacerbated by the stripping out of middle management positions. In days gone by, management science suggested that seven direct subordinates (each representing a discrete management function) was about an ideal span of control but it is not uncommon today to see senior executives with a dozen or even more direct reports.

Even if an executive or manager has a team smaller than this, compare today's breadth of responsibility with that of ten years ago in terms of such time-consuming (yet necessary) aspects as equal employment, age discrimination, unfair dismissal, protection of the environment, enterprise bargaining, occupational health and safety, quality accreditation, international lines of business focus versus geographic focus, and matrix reporting. The list seems endless. Senior people often feel they are spread too thin. Time and effort is dispersed across too broad a front. Primary business drivers are insufficiently attended to as other time-consuming aspects proliferate.

Executives and managers need to withstand being sucked into this vortex, determine what their principal business objective is and devote maximum time, effort and resources to the primary business drivers that will best deliver this objective.

Developing this further, what is your single most important business objective right now? You are allowed only one objective, the most important one! What are the first-level drivers of your principal business objective—in other words, the *two* main activities and result areas that will have the greatest impact on attaining your principal business objective? Which second-level drivers drive your first-level drivers? Which third-level drivers drive your second-level drivers? Which of all these drivers, if prioritised, can be most improved and will have the greatest impact on your principal business objective? Clearly, to answer such questions there has to be considerable decision-tree and/or financial analysis, or other form of evaluation.

My approach, which I refer to as the Profit Tree, leads to a better understanding of the *primary* business drivers, usually found at the second or third levels. These have the greatest impact on your principal business objective and, thus, on overall business results.

Case Study

Let us examine the case of an autonomous division of a large manufacturing and distribution company where I helped the general manager to develop a Profit Tree and determine his primary business drivers.

The principal business objective in this case was *return on total assets* expressed as a percentage, as supported by the two first-level drivers of *net pre-tax profit* and *assets employed in the business*. These two first-level drivers were supported by the second-level drivers of *sales*, *operating expenses*, *fixed assets* and *current assets*, which in turn were supported by a range of third-level drivers—a fairly classic Profit Tree for a company, in fact.

By developing a complete Profit Tree, the general manager was able to determine which drivers were 'primary'—in other words, which drivers he was able to improve most and which had the greatest impact on improving his principal business objective, and which he therefore needed to prioritise. These were:

➤ *sales*—increasing the domestic pricing differential, providing 'free' product in place of discounts for export sales;
➤ *variable expenses*—establishing a 'joint gain' productivity program;
➤ *fixed expenses*—reorganising and reducing staffing (via natural attrition);
➤ *fixed assets*—consolidating manufacturing and distribution and selling of excess equipment and facilities;
➤ *current assets*—reducing the debt-collection period, increasing/renegotiating supplier payment periods, improving the sell/make for the stock decision-making process.

In addition to enabling executives like this general manager to identify their primary business drivers and determine which to prioritise at any given time, the Profit Tree can also be turned upside down and superimposed on the organisation structure of the business, with relevant direct reports and their teams being held accountable for results in primary business driver areas, as well as in all other driver areas.

The general manager in this case did this with great success. He found that the inversion and superimposing of the Profit Tree on his organisation structure had a strongly unifying effect on his team—they all pulled together in the pursuit of maximising return on total assets, which they nearly doubled in three years!

Chart 4.1 shows the Profit Tree developed in the case study.

CHART 4.1   The Profit Tree I

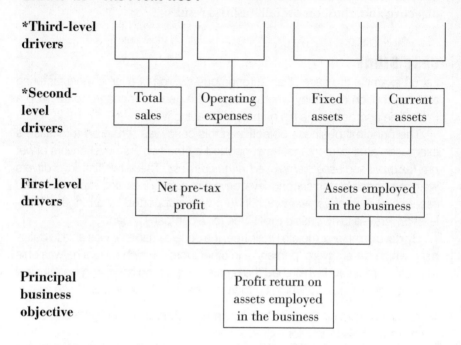

*Third-level drivers

*Second-level drivers

| Total sales | Operating expenses | Fixed assets | Current assets |

First-level drivers

| Net pre-tax profit | Assets employed in the business |

Principal business objective

| Profit return on assets employed in the business |

* homes of the primary business drivers

Case Study

Another example of primary business drivers involves the General Manager Sales and Marketing in a consumer products manufacturing and marketing company. He had inherited a new CEO who had initiated a broad range of process improvement programs, to the extent that wheels were spinning and results were suffering.

In helping the General Manager to prioritise, I decided to use the primary business drivers approach. We agreed that his principal business objective was substantially increasing profitable sales growth. The two first-level drivers were *increasing sales revenue* and *increasing margin*. These two first-level drivers were supported by the second-level drivers of selling more to existing grocery and route customers and increasing the number of new vending and route customers (for *increasing sales revenue*); selling more to the more profitable route customers and decreasing sales costs in the case of less profitable grocery customers (for *increasing margin*).

The third level of drivers comprised improved category management and competing more on the basis of quality of service (for *selling more to existing grocery and route customers*); exploiting underdeveloped channels and increased distribution in existing channels (for *increasing the number of new vending and route customers*); identifying and prioritising the more profitable customers as well as tailored growth plans for them (for *selling more to the more profitable route customers*); and better identification of cost drivers and a tailored plan to maximise returns (for *decreasing costs in the case of less profitable grocery customers*).

Having mapped out the Profit Tree in this way, further analysis indicated just three major strategies, three primary business drivers in fact, to be prioritised. These had previously been regarded as just three of the process improvement programs initiated by the new CEO, causing spinning wheels and slipping results. Yet, on further analysis, they were clearly seen to have a major and sustained impact on helping the General Manager Sales and Marketing and his 1000-strong permanent and part-time team to achieve more successfully their principal business objective of substantially increasing profitable sales growth. The three drivers were:

➢ maximising profitable sales revenue growth through existing grocery and route customers by selling more to them and increasing market share through advanced category management techniques and the acquisition of permanent secondary space;
➢ increasing margin by a better understanding of cost structures and by tailoring specific plans for high-volume and low-profit grocery customers— in other words, developing profit and loss statements for each major grocery customer and implementing margin improvement programs;
➢ increasing revenue by identifying new customers in existing vending and route channels and implementing appropriate service programs.

By concentrating on these three primary business drivers—having presented a convincing case based on the Profit Tree concept to the new CEO—results improved dramatically and the principal business objective was achieved.

Chart 4.2 summarises part of the Profit Tree in this case.

EXTERNAL FUTURES

The same reasons that prevent executives and managers from determining and concentrating on primary business drivers—too much to do, too much of an internal focus on time-consuming activities, being spread too thin—prevent many of the same individuals from being alert to the emerging changes outside their organisations.

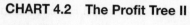

CHART 4.2   The Profit Tree II

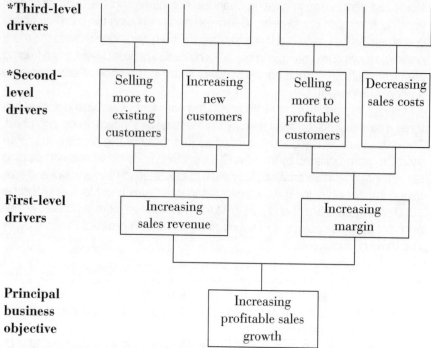

* homes of the primary business drivers

We can no longer assume that past trends will repeat themselves in a predictable cycle. It is highly likely that the future will bear little or no resemblance to the past. To assess external futures, we must look forward, not backwards, and try to get an idea of where future opportunities will be in the context of several external areas: *technological, economic, political, social, customers* and *competition.*

Technology

The rapid growth of technology is having, and will continue to have, a dramatic impact on executive management. What new kinds of businesses will new technologies create? Where will future business opportunities lie? Which sectors will experience growth in the years ahead? Which sectors will experience decline?

The impact of technological change must be viewed in relation to your own organisation and executive and managerial aspirations. For example, the growing trend towards automation in offices and factories has shifted the focus from manual to mental skills. Specialised knowledge, skills and decision-making abilities are more in demand than ever, and those organisations and individuals possessing and developing them will hold the power, as others come to depend on their expertise.

How can you make sure that you will be ready to respond to technological and other changes when they arrive? You can do this by keeping a close watch on the environment for 'signals'. The futures model shown in Chart 4.3 illustrates the stages of technological advance but is relevant to any aspect of external futures.

Technological advance begins with *innovation*, when a person or company develops some form of breakthrough or discovery. Next is the *media stage* when it is written up in publications, papers or other media (e.g. radio and TV announcements). This is the time to be alert and monitoring such indicators of future developments.

Next is the *material stage* when prototypes, models or pilot batches take the innovation concept to a more material form, often a test launch or limited initial release. Again, careful monitoring is needed. The next stage is when the material form becomes *refined, modified* or made more *effective*—in effect, produced and made available on a wider scale. The final stage is *widespread usage*—in other words, market acceptance, and by now it is history!

By monitoring at the media stage and then at the material stage, you may well be able to predict external futures, to your own and your company's advantage. Thus the impact of innovation can be determined years before it actually affects your business or yourself in any major way.

CHART 4.3 External futures model

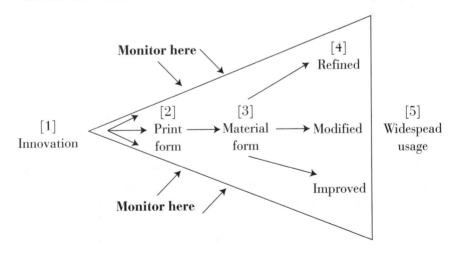

All it takes is to be aware of developments around you, keep up to date with your reading, talk to people who are involved with technology and other forms of innovation, and know what the predictions are and how they may affect your business plans or you. Constant monitoring is essential, in order to plan effectively to take advantage of future business and personal opportunities.

The economy

The economy certainly affects business performance, as some of us are painfully aware. For example, a prolonged recession causes many people who might otherwise upgrade their buying patterns and behaviour to stay put. It is precisely in times like these that contingency planning pays off, because it provides options not available to those who neglected to plan ahead. Knowing how to prepare for changing economic conditions will lessen the chances of your organisation or yourself being 'left out in the cold' when hard times hit, or when the economy swings upward again.

In the economic environment, we are looking at those factors that influence demand for your products or services, their supply from other sources and the competition for marketing them.

Too many executives ignore the fact of economic cycles in business planning. In good times the tendency is to reap the benefits of demand with little concern for the future. Then, when hard times hit and demand falls off, there is a struggle to develop new products and services that should have been developed earlier in anticipation of a downturn in the cycle. This all takes its toll in time, money and frustration.

Economic cycles and a variation in demand are facts of life.

Politics

In developing business plans, it is becoming more and more necessary to take into account political and legal implications. As we are all aware, the various levels of government are affecting our lives to an ever-increasing degree. For example, tax legislation has a great influence on personal lifestyles and business performance. It can also affect such business decisions as whether or not to develop and launch new products.

Society

Shifts in social attitudes, behaviour and values should be taken into account in business planning. Understanding social trends puts the executive or manager in a better position to take advantage of potential business opportunities. For example, we see an increasing number of dual-career marriages, where the career plans of one partner must take into account the career aspirations of the other. We also see a switching of the breadwinner/housekeeper roles, with more men tending families while women provide the family income.

Such social trends can affect your business performance but, with careful business planning and full consideration of the future, they should be seen as opportunities rather than threats.

Customers

The four external areas already mentioned also affect the lifeblood of any commercial organisation—its customers—and their requirements of your organisation. Being aware of external impacts and how they convert into customer demand is perhaps the single most important area relating to external futures.

Continuous customer monitoring and evaluation is needed, rather than an assumption that customers will continue to purchase your products or services in the same (or increasing) volume as in the past and through the same methods of distribution.

Competition

Competition is also affected by all these external factors, in terms of competitor responses to the changing marketplace and their reactions to your organisation as a competitor. Unless you are carefully tracking your competitors, it is only a matter of time before you get caught out.

Yet it is surprising how poor competitive intelligence can be, or how quickly it can become outdated. Continuous tracking is required both formally (perhaps via external specialists, who may be better placed to do this) and informally through the eyes and ears of customers, suppliers and staff.

PLANNING

Case Study

The best planner I have come across is Rosemary Langton (not her real name), Chief Executive of a regional airline in Europe. Running an organisation with complex logistics, customer and regulatory requirements, Rosemary has to be adept at planning, including objective setting and the strategies to accomplish them.

With her management team Rosemary specifies what is to be attained, and how, and takes into account the required physical, financial and human resources. She anticipates problems in progressing from planning to implementation. Rosemary personally monitors, controls and reviews monthly progress—on an 'exception' basis (taking particular notice of *over*performance which is celebrated and *under*performance which is rectified)—as each annual departmental plan is implemented, and ensures the update of plans according to progress, making any necessary changes. Objectives are quantified and address *what*, *when*, *where*, *why*, *how much*, *how often* and *by what means*. In establishing budgets, Rosemary ensures they are stretching, yet attainable.

Rather than being too rigid, Rosemary allows plans to be adjusted as they are implemented, according to prevailing or projected external circumstances: the economy, the market, competition and customers, all so volatile in the airline industry. She ensures departmental plans are complete and coincide with overall corporate goals and objectives. She also makes sure staff are involved in the planning processes so that they buy ownership of them and understand what is expected of them in terms of implementation.

When asked to comment on the key elements of successful business planning, Rosemary offered the following points:

➤ Be proactive rather than reactive—in other words, project and plan for external changes, rather than being caught on the back foot and having to react to them.

➤ Plans need to specify not only where the organisation is heading but also how it will get there. This includes a vision and a mission or purpose statement, objectives and goals, strategies, principles and policies, processes and methods.

➤ Planning should be ongoing, not a one-off or annual event. Continuous monitoring of performance (by 'exception') and external factors will require plans to be modified as they are implemented.

➤ Those involved in the planning process need to be good conceptualisers with a capacity to think about the future and unknown territory. They also need to be creative and to think unconventionally, 'outside the square'. An external perspective is also needed—an understanding of where the company currently resides in the industry and marketplace and where it plans to reside in the future.

➤ Successful planning requires top management commitment of the necessary time and resources for planning and this commitment needs to be communicated to all staff, who should feel involved in the planning process.

➤ The best plans consider both effectiveness and efficiency, the former focusing on outcomes and achievements, the latter on inputs and processes.

CORPORATE COMMUNICATIONS

Communication is such an important required competence of executives and leaders personally, as well as from a corporate perspective, that it is addressed in some way in every chapter. Here are some suggestions for effective corporate communications.

➢ The industrial age executive communicates top-down, mainly in that one direction; the information and knowledge age executive communicates both top-down *and* bottom-up—in fact, seeks to listen and understand *first*.

➢ Companies spend inordinate amounts of time, money and effort in developing vision; many spend little on communicating it. Hence, vision is often poorly understood and remains unattained.

➢ Executives need to be visible and always 'out there', listening to and interacting with employees at all levels. There has to be a *continuing* emphasis on communicating.

➢ Informal communication is often more powerful than formal means: lunch with the CEO has more impact than the corporate video.

➢ Even in this modern era, with its apparent transactional emphasis, employees actually want to 'belong'. Communicating with them continually facilitates a sense of belonging.

➢ Communicating with employees needs to be about such simple, often overlooked matters as: What's expected of me in my role? How am I performing? How can I improve my performance? How can I get help in this? How else can I help the department/business unit/organisation achieve its goals?

➢ At a more macro level, communicating lies at the heart of the following questions, often resulting in a communication gap: at the senior executive leadership level, 'Where are we headed, how and when will we get there?'; at the operating level, 'What does this mean to my department/business unit in terms of where we are headed, how and when we will get there?'.

➢ Often, communication from the top to the front line of the organisation breaks down somewhere in the middle. Some companies I have worked with refer to this as the 'concrete slab', or the 'layer of blancmange'. Unless middle management is completely at one with the intended communication loop, communication will falter and never get through to or back from the front line.

➢ While communication's effectiveness can be monitored via survey, do not underestimate the cost effectiveness of more informal approaches such as 'management by walking about' and asking questions. Make direct contact with the target audience: have they received the messages sent from the top?

➤ Corporate communications should be multi-media in order to convey and reinforce the message. Don't underestimate the potency of new technology, particularly for getting through to the younger generation (online chat facilities, web casting, and so forth). Multi-media should also include print, video, audio and, of course, face-to-face (group and one-on-one).

➤ The best corporate communications are two-way, and this needs to be prioritised, encouraged, rewarded (e.g. new ideas or suggestions) and made easy. Make it easy to hear from your employees; make it easy to get your messages through to them.

ORGANISING

Case Study

Harold Limmer (not his real name) served his time in the armed forces before moving into the private sector defence industry. He now heads up the sales, services and support group of a major aircraft weapons systems supplier. In advising Harold about future career directions I undertook a multi-level survey of his management practices and found that his peers, superiors and direct reports rated him highly in his organisational ability.

In terms of organisation, Harold ensures that all relevant parties understand the structure of reporting relationships, which are designed to organise people in the most effective, efficient and yet flexible manner to attain desired goals and objectives. Rather than the more rigid structure with which Harold was well acquainted during his career in the army, he ensures maximum flexibility and cross-fertilisation, relying heavily on multidisciplinary project teams and matrix management. However, with these approaches he has long since recognised that clarity of organisational and reporting relationships is a prerequisite for success.

The vital theme of coordination is enhanced by Harold ensuring that all parties understand who is responsible for what and who is accountable to whom, with those responsible and accountable having the necessary authority to attain their goals and objectives. Jobs are well defined but 'broad-banded' and flexible enough for individuals to adapt to changing operating conditions.

Harold makes sure that span of control—the number and types of job positions reporting to each line manager—is neither too broad (a common complaint today, causing the manager to be spread too thinly) nor too narrow (causing replication of work and effort). Also, he makes sure that people are clear about whom they need to liaise with and to whom they report, be this reporting in 'line' (to their line manager), liaising in 'functional capacity' (with any functional specialist who may be responsible for how the function is performed) or liaising within matrix-based teams, so often used in the sales and service environment.

Harold ensures that opportunities for delegation are maximised; that organisational arrangements maximise morale; and that teams comprise people with different operating styles rather than clones of the leader.

Finally, Harold's teams feel empowered, encouraged as far as possible to be self-directing, with a clear understanding of the role of the leader, who often acts as a resource and facilitator rather than a proactive 'micro top-down manager' of the old style. However, team members are also clear about their personal accountabilities.

MONITORING

Case Study

Georgina Reynolds (not her real name) heads up sales and customer service in one of Canada's largest telecommunications groups. I had the opportunity once of sitting in on a training session led by Georgina for new sales and service team leaders. This is what she had to say about monitoring, by way of introduction to a half-day training session on the subject, as part of a new supervisor's training program.

> Monitoring of progress ensures that goals and objectives are attained according to plan and is oriented towards *preventing* problems, rather than having to *solve* problems.
>
> Preventive monitoring helps your sales and customer service staff know in advance what is expected of them in terms of quality, quantity, time and cost. It also enables them to know their job parameters: scope of responsibility, authority and accountability; policies and procedures; availability of support and advice; relationships with others, in a way that offers them maximum freedom to achieve rather than confinement.
>
> Maintenance monitoring focuses on major result areas, signalling when progress to plan is adverse, major result areas being specific and including orders, units, errors, complaints, dollar volumes and dollar costs. As you are aware, each member of staff has up to nine major result areas in our organisation.

Preventive and maintenance monitoring takes the form of your on-the-job supervision; concentration on major result areas; systematic, periodic and random personal inspection; management by exception; and taking action when it is needed through your staff.

The individual performance standards for each major result area are established and agreed between you and your staff, coincide with overall corporate objectives and have to be specific. Our performance appraisal processes regularly monitor individual performance compared to these standards, identifying development needs and enhancing the further deployment of strengths.

Development needs of staff are quickly and effectively met through necessary counselling, coaching or training, which is your responsibility, backed by our training and development specialists.

DECISION MAKING

Case Study

I once had the opportunity to appraise the performance of several competing teams in a residential management course based on a rather complex computer-based business case study. I was particularly interested in comparing the decision-making approaches of the teams. The following is an extract from the final report the winning team wrote on what they had learned about decision making during the case study.

Decision making seems to be most effective when it is selecting a course of action from a variety of alternatives.

Decision making starts with fully defining and understanding the problem or opportunity and collecting all the available facts that may impact directly or indirectly on the decision. These facts need to be analysed, evaluated and interpreted in the context of the problem or opportunity.

A range of solutions to the problem or options for exploiting the opportunity is developed, and alternative potential decisions addressed. These are compared and ranked, the overall ranking determining the decision.

In defining a problem, the root causes as opposed to the symptoms need to be addressed: in collecting the facts, they have to be true and valid facts rather than guesses, opinions or lies.

In examining the possible solutions, creative, 'outside the square' thinking is encouraged, problems and opportunities are shared and all relevant parties are encouraged to contribute in the decision-making process.

It seems that a bottom-up as well as a top-down approach to decision making makes most sense, and we can see this approach as being particularly successful in the corporate setting.

DELEGATING

Case Study

Helen Spencer (not her real name) runs a large government department, having previously held a range of management positions in several government agencies. She is an excellent delegator, and she allowed me to interview her and develop the following guidelines based on her delegating techniques.

I believe that effective delegation is probably one of the most important management functions in running large organisations. All the other functional areas of planning, organising, monitoring and so forth can only be effective if the manager is a capable delegator.

I see delegation as a four-step approach: decide what needs to be delegated (and in this context 'more' rather than 'less' can and should be delegated in most cases); decide to whom the responsibility for such activities should be delegated; explain the reasons for and objectives of the delegated responsibility; and provide sufficient resources and authority for the responsibility to be carried through and for the required activities to be accomplished.

Based on my experience, some of the rules for effective delegation include:

- ➢ Only delegate if you are prepared to take some risks, which can be minimised through effective monitoring.
- ➢ Only delegate when you are prepared to put in sufficient time and effort to make delegation work successful.
- ➢ Delegate in those areas where you are conducting activities which do not use your greatest competencies and capabilities.
- ➢ Delegate to save time that can be used on activities which cannot be undertaken by direct reports.
- ➢ Delegate only when you have confidence in your direct reports to assume delegated responsibilities and accomplish required activities.
- ➢ Delegate to improve the involvement of your direct reports, which can enhance their motivation and personal performance.

> Delegate in order to develop your direct reports for increased responsibilities.
> Provide sufficient authority to the direct report to whom you are delegating and define the parameters of this authority.
> Establish priorities and time-lines for completion of tasks and for progress reports.
> Relinquish sufficient control for your direct reports to buy ownership of your delegation and to have freedom to act.

In my experience as a senior executive, manager and administrator, effective delegation throughout the organisation—particularly when connected to motivation—frees up the bottlenecks and allows executives to concentrate on higher-level matters, for which, after all, they are being paid an executive salary. Providing these guidelines are followed at all levels, the organisation can move forward with greater involvement, commitment, speed and effect.

MOTIVATING INDIVIDUALS

The key success ingredients of motivating people include:

> selecting and developing staff on the basis of a strong work ethic and high personal standards in terms of results;
> creating challenging jobs which build satisfaction, enjoyment and self-motivation;
> developing an external image and internal identity of the organisation, based on clearly articulated vision and values, with which employees can identify enthusiastically and in which they can visualise their own success;
> encouraging employees to be involved in goal setting (which buys their ownership of such goals and enhances their self-esteem), offering freedom and support in accomplishing such goals, especially where their own goals coincide with the goals of the organisation;
> creating a positive, active and mutually involving working environment with a sense of dynamism, progression and 'change for the best', with a commitment to excellence and winning, and encouraging a sense of self-direction and empowerment;
> creating an environment where personal power (which is earned) and influence (which is also earned) prevail, rather than formal authority (which is often mandated);
> praising in public, and counselling and taking action for poor

performance in private, both *at the time* such performance is recognised, and with consistency in terms of application across all direct reports;

➢ meeting the motivational needs of each individual as far as possible whether these are *material* (remuneration, safety and security), *structural* (degree and type of structure, bureaucracy and systems), *behavioural* (management style and interpersonal relationships) or *emotional* (trust, social, self-esteem, self-realisation);

➢ creating an environment where the style of executives and managers is based on integrity, is more democratic than autocratic, is consultative, participative and delegating.

A MOTIVATIONAL ORGANISATION

The key success ingredients of an organisational culture that is motivating include:

➢ a deliberate and continuous attempt to establish and develop an egalitarian climate wherein status differences are minimised;

➢ while reporting lines and authority are well understood, cooperation and a team-based ethos is even more apparent and promoted;

➢ open two-way communication prevails both laterally and vertically;

➢ job specifications and grades are broad-banded to maximise flexibility, cooperation and teamwork;

➢ spans of control are never so narrow as to impose a regime of very close top-down management and supervision;

➢ shared values and aligned goals are emphasised, as is group-based decision making;

➢ a climate of trust, fairness and cooperation prevails—employees trust each other and their managers (whom they perceive to be fair);

➢ an environment exists where mutually supportive teamwork helps people to synergise and have more effect *cooperatively* than they would have *independently*;

➢ the operational climate encourages personal development and advancement;

➢ the management style in the organisation maximises self-motivation, morale and productivity.

Case Study

I once worked for an international food group which was one of the most moti-vated work environments I can recall. In examining why motivation levels were so high, I am able to conclude the following:

➤ From the chief executive down, management style seemed to enhance the self-motivation of direct reports and others, the executives having created an operational climate of trust and integrity encouraging personal develop-ment and advancement. This was accomplished by open-plan offices (for everyone, including the chief executive) and continuous interaction between executives and staff.
➤ Management style was more democratic than autocratic, and was consul-tative, participative and delegating. This was based on the view that the leaders in the organisation certainly did not believe they had all the 'answers' to the opportunities and challenges confronting the company. Often, the best ideas came from the 'front line'.
➤ Employees were satisfied with their remuneration levels and were interested in, and satisfied with, the breadth and content of their jobs, finding them responsible and meaningful.
➤ Employees were recognised in public for a job well done, and were counselled in private when they were not attaining their standards of performance.
➤ Employees felt they were achieving their own goals as they achieved cor-porate goals. In other words, there was a strong alignment between the future of the individual and the future of the company. Employees also felt informed and involved in planning and decision making.
➤ Employees felt free to monitor themselves and to accomplish goals and objectives within defined parameters, and experienced a sense of self-direc-tion and empowerment in so doing.

MOTIVATIONAL DELEGATION

I have examined the principal causes of success and failure by execu-tives in the area of management practices, and I have been able to consolidate many of my findings into one core competence for effective staff management: *motivational delegation.*

Motivational delegation embraces two main themes: the individual executive delegating to direct reports effectively and creating a moti-vational environment, and the organisation creating a motivational environment.

Motivational delegation is summarised in Chart 4.4, which needs to

CHART 4.4 Motivational delegation model

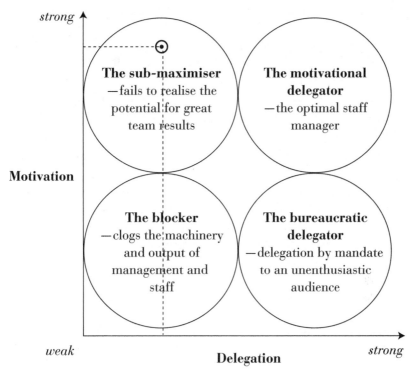

An example of plotting the relative strengths of motivation and delegation, the position-fix being shown by ⊙

be examined twice: first, in the context of delegation and *the individual executive or manager* creating a motivational environment; and second, in the context of delegation and *the organisation* creating a motivational environment.

Use this model to assess your performance in delegation and motivation. You will have to do this for 'motivation' twice, revealing the impact of your own motivating capabilities on motivational delegation, and then revealing the impact of your organisation's motivating capabilities on motivational delegation.

Plot your performance on the diagram by drawing two lines between the two positions, denoting your self-assessment of your performance on the vertical and horizontal lines, to form a square or rectangle (see Chart 4.4). Then draw a prominent dot or small circle on the corner furthest from the bottom left-hand corner of the diagram; this becomes your *position-fix*.

If you are not perceived as a motivational delegator, what needs to be attended to most—your *own* motivational capabilities, or the *organisation's*, or *both?*

Whether you include yourself or your organisation in this analysis, your direct reports will always perceive *you* as the source of delegation and the creator or otherwise of a motivational environment. This is why the labels and descriptors in the diagram refer to you! Don't take offence. If there is a problem, it may in fact be caused by the organisation. What will you do about it?

MODIFYING DELEGATION BEHAVIOUR

To maximise people and situations you need to modify your delegation behaviour. You can be more directive or 'hands-on' when a task is high priority and/or high impact, or when the capability and motivation of the individual is insufficient for them to use their discretion and decide how to accomplish the delegated task.

At the other end of the scale, where a task is low priority and/or low impact, or when the capability and motivation of the individual is adequate for them to use their discretion and decide how to proceed, you can 'abdicate' (be 'hands-off')—a real timesaver in today's flatter structures with broader spans of control and more complex reporting and communication lines.

'Abdicate? Sounds like heresy!' you may say, but study Chart 4.5 before you decide.

PERSONAL ACCOUNTABILITY

Whatever happened to personal accountability in organisations?

Back in the old days—the industrial age—accountability existed through the top-down 'managing the what' command and control approach. But in today's information and knowledge age when collaborative 360° facilitational leadership and teamwork are in vogue, it's easy for personal accountability to get diffused, even lost.

Let me provide a tight definition of accountability from the *Australian Paperback Dictionary*:

> **accountable** *adj.* 1. obliged to give a reckoning or explanation for one's actions etc; responsible. 2. able to be explained.
> **accountability** *n.*

In this definition, personal accountability relates to specific responsibilities and is about appropriate reporting to another person or people

CHART 4.5   Modifying delegation behaviour

Style of delegation	Priority of task *and/or*	Impact of task *and/or*	Capability of delegatee *and/or*	Motivation of delegatee	Degree of monitoring/ control required by delegator
Direct (hands-on)	High	High	Low	Low	High
Delegate (as Helen Spencer describes earlier)	Moderate	Moderate	Satisfactory	Satisfactory	Moderate
Abdicate (hands-off)	Low	Low	High	High	Low

regarding the status or change relating to such responsibilities, as a result of one's action or inaction. Here, I suggest exception reporting. As a leader you need to know quickly when results are 'over' so that you can celebrate success; also, when results are 'under' so that you can effect appropriate remedies. You don't need to know instantly when results are on track, as you will pick this up through normal financial or management reporting and, after all, this is what you and your people get paid for! It's a given.

In fact, personal accountability is one element of a potent management triad: responsibility, authority and accountability (see Chart 4.6).

> I am responsible for XYZ, I have the authority to act regarding XYZ, and I am personally accountable to my line manager for results relating to XYZ.

The bottom line about personal accountability is that all elements of the triad have to be in place to make it work. And, to make it work, certain distractors need to be avoided:

➢ too great an emphasis on the term 'empowerment' with too little emphasis on its *true* meaning, which *has* to include personal

CHART 4.6   The potent management triad

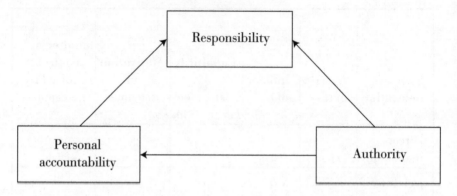

accountability. In fact, I refer to personal accountability as the flip-side of empowerment because, while it is an integral part of empowerment, it often remains hidden and does not get the attention it so deserves

➤ too much shared responsibility at any one level within the organisational hierarchy;
➤ too much emphasis on consensus;
➤ a too rigid, silo approach to life: 'Sales were to blame'; 'Production couldn't deliver';
➤ insufficient monitoring and control by managers and leaders;
➤ too much trust that direct reports will deliver;
➤ insufficient emphasis on primary business drivers: focus too diffused;
➤ too much tolerance of poor performance;
➤ insufficient candid feedback about an individual's performance— 'Say it as it is to the individual, not just to others!';
➤ not wanting to accept blame when things go wrong;
➤ a climate of fear and intimidation fostering reluctance to take responsibility.

What other distractors can you think of?

FAST AND SIMPLE!

A recurring theme in today's organisation, jam-packed as it is with communication and reporting lines, meetings to attend, things to accomplish, ever-changing priorities and competitive pressures, is how to move fast and keep things simple!

Actually, that's what this book is about in no small part. Consider the following:

➤ Developing and leveraging talent through leadership means employees should get the job done more quickly and less bureaucratically than if you micro-manage them according to the old industrial age paradigm (Chapter 1).

➤ Exhibiting greater emotional intelligence speeds up and simplifies interpersonal understanding and relationships; exhibiting more self-control makes interpersonal interactions run more smoothly (Chapter 1).

➤ Improved leading, upwards and externally, through influence, makes for better and faster decisions affecting your work-patch; time management and prioritisation in ally management enhance this even further (Chapter 2).

➤ Better meetings, group presentations and writing performance enable you to get your way faster, with fewer road-blocking objections (Chapter 2).

➤ Coming out of your silo more regularly and synergising with your peers leads to more effective decision making and outcomes for the total business; bottlenecks are reduced; mutual accountability towards business results is increased; everyone pulling together towards common goals improves efficiency and effectiveness (Chapter 3).

➤ Reaching out and tuning into the operating style or wavelength of others enhances interpersonal effectiveness and hastens communication receptiveness (Chapter 3).

➤ Conducive in-team behaviour lessens team friction, unjams the cogs and frees up the wheels (Chapter 3).

➤ Dealing with conflict better lessens log-jams (Chapter 3).

➤ Using the sports coaching analogy helps individuals and teams to excel further: they move faster and act more cohesively (Chapters 3, 4).

➤ By concentrating on the primary business drivers, there is faster, firmer traction and less wheel-spinning (Chapter 4).

➤ Exhibiting superior performance in all the other management practices areas—particularly, but not exclusively, motivational delegation and personal accountability (Chapter 4), drives 'Fast and simple!'.

➤ Exhibiting leadership traits appropriate to situations, priorities and people, backed by appropriate and continuous coaching (Chapter 4), also drives 'Fast and simple!'.

➢ Creating a more motivational environment for self and others—
through close job fit, atmospheric needs being largely met, coping
mechanisms and stress management techniques being applied when
not (all backed by proactive talent management)—translates self-
motivation into energy, and energy into results (Chapter 5).
➢ Career alignment of talent and dismissal avoidance further
enhances motivation (Chapter 5).
➢ Living the vision and walking the talk of fundamental values gives
employees the confidence to act and go that extra mile, making life
faster and simpler for the busy executive leader (Chapter 6).
➢ Effective change leadership allows the organisation to move like
liquid rather than sludge (Chapter 6).
➢ Best practice management of restructures turns that liquid into
liquid gold (Chapter 6).

My ultimate tool for facilitating 'Fast and simple!' thinking and practice
has to be Chart 4.7. You be the judge!

CHART 4.7   Fast and simple

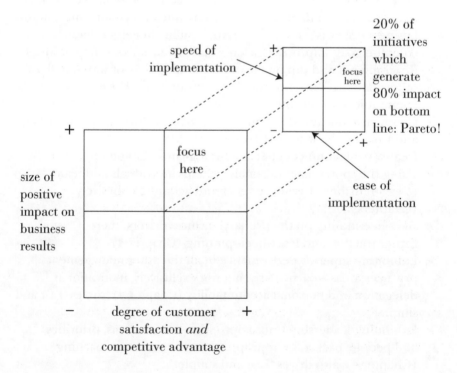

First, select those initiatives or tasks that have the greatest positive impact on business results, customer satisfaction and competitive advantage. Focus here!

Then select those that are quickest and easiest to implement. Focus here!

In all likelihood they'll turn out to be the 20% of initiatives or tasks that generate an 80% impact on the bottom line. Shouldn't Pareto be your focus?!

LEADERSHIP TRAITS

Determining ideal leadership traits was the quest of academics and authors throughout last century. As far back as 1916, H.L. Gantt wrote about industrial leadership and, in 1935, Ordway Tead wrote about the art of leadership. In the 1950s and 1960s there was a rush of further 'definitive' guidelines including *How to Identify Promotable Executives* by C. Wilson Randle, *Appraising Executive Performance* by Carl Heyel and *How to Select Executive Personnel* by Edith S. Sands. This continues to the present day, with a widening variety of writers endeavouring to define ideal leadership traits and related 'soft' competencies in such titles as *Real Change Leaders* by J. Katzenbach and *Roses and Rust: Redefining the Essence of Leadership* by D. Clancy and R. Webber.

Today, many executives and managers are seeking to digest, learn from and implement the findings and recommendations of David S. Karpin, who led an industry task force to report on leadership and management skills in Australia in the context of 'Renewing Australia's Managers to Meet the Challenges of the Asia-Pacific Century'. *Enterprising Nation*, or *The Karpin Report* as it is more often called, took three years to complete and proclaims itself as the 'most comprehensive insight ever into the way Australia prepares its managers for work and leadership'.

The book by Gary Hamel and C.K. Prahalad, *Competing for the Future*, is an international bestseller, and in the context of some of their work desirable leadership traits may be deduced as follows:

➢ *as an inspirational leader*—not being overly directive, putting the team before self, relating well to groups and individuals, and focusing on customers and people;
➢ *as a visionary strategist*—having a big-picture perspective, being less conforming, less structured, a creative problem solver, and using initiative in trying to create the future.

In reality, many organisations have not yet reached the point where they can specify *desirable* leadership traits, but they can often react negatively when *undesirable* traits are exhibited. These traits can be as germane as executives and managers being too production-oriented (rather than customer-oriented); too autocratic; not supporting equal employment or promotion; exhibiting racism, sexism, harassment or discrimination; being involved in unfair dismissal; making biased appointments; not engaging in adequate two-way communication; and not being prepared to delegate or change.

What seems to be lacking today is a simple conceptual model that can be understood and applied by individuals and organisations in their identification, pursuit and adoption of ideal leadership traits. We propose such a model shortly, but first a few examples of people displaying desirable and perhaps less desirable leadership traits: K.P. Singh, Kentaro Iwamoto, Marcel Pinot and Peter Hardwick (not their real names). Decide whether their traits are desirable or undesirable!

Examples of leadership traits

Case Study

K.P. Singh is a senior executive responsible for a significant sports footwear production plant and distributorship in Kuala Lumpur, Malaysia. He is well qualified with an MBA and a first degree in economics. He believes he is a specialist in sports footwear, emphasises low-cost production and tight centralised control, and involves himself personally in the detail of operations which he has divided into three strategic business units. He excels at administration, has good local knowledge and perspective, always conforms to head office directives and expects his subordinates to operate by the rule-book.

Although market demands change quite rapidly—sports footwear now being predominantly fashion items—Singh believes in the continuation of the status quo: develop and update the product according to customer needs, but produce and distribute it conventionally. Clearly, K.P. Singh is production-driven. When confronted by operational problems, he personally gets involved in solving them and he is seen as a logical problem solver.

Case Study

In Paris, Kentaro Iwamoto runs the French operations of a high-tech office equipment company. He is seen as being very considerate of his 3400 staff, displaying a caring attitude and relying very much on natural attrition rather than retrenchment for downsizing as the organisation flexes its way through the early 2000s. The firm pays its staff quite well and has the best employee sickness benefits, health insurance and personal disability and life cover in its industry.

However, Mr Iwamoto is also considered autocratic. He believes in discipline (he doesn't always seem to trust his staff), tight control and firm directive management. He has taken great pains to develop a formal and hierarchical organisation structure where jobs, reporting relationships, accountabilities and authority are all very clearly defined and rigidly adhered to. While he seeks to communicate with staff, he relies heavily on selectively transmitting information from the top down; the opportunities and processes for him to receive information from the bottom up are less evident.

As an individual he is fiercely competitive with his peers; he is often thought to be too self-promotional, putting himself rather than his team first when he visits his superiors in Japan for quarterly business reviews.

Case Study

Marcel Pinot works in London, UK, and is a senior executive in the publishing industry. He has lived in several countries and this seems to have equipped him with a global perspective and knowledge. He is considered by his industry peers to be a non-conformist, taking a highly customer-centred and entrepreneurial approach to the strategic development of his publishing 'mini-empire', although at the same time understanding, committing to and deploying the core competencies of his organisation as much as possible.

Taking a flexible approach and believing in decentralised control, Marcel and his team quickly respond to change and are considered to be pioneers and pathfinders in their industry. Personally, Marcel is financially astute, uses a lot of initiative and is perceived to be a creative problem solver with broad-based general management capabilities.

Case Study

Peter Hardwick runs a software development company in Vancouver. He is considered to be a natural and inspirational leader of people, whether employees or customers. Being both customer-oriented and keen to empower his employees, he has a track record of unparalleled software development success in his field; he is the first to market with true innovation, accomplished only by defining customer needs and relying on a committed team to convert concepts into real solutions.

When questioned at an industry conference about leadership styles, Hardwick emphasised his belief in a flat organisational hierarchy, open two-way communication, learning, people development and the need for leaders to relate well to both groups and individuals.

An article on his company in a business periodical reported an interview with several of his staff. They said he was trusting of employees, unstructured, certainly not directive, and always seemed to put the customer and his team first, rather than himself. They also applauded his creativity—his capacity to think outside the square—and his ability to enthuse others in innovative approaches and solutions.

These cases offer four very different sets of leadership traits but, in each case, a very successful person! Which traits are more desirable and which are less desirable? What are the common threads in each subset of traits? Of course, the degree of desirability or undesirability is defined by the orientation and perception of the beholder. Some of us do not trust staff; some believe in firm discipline, while others believe in a more hands-off or creative style.

Similarly with organisations—some companies have a culture where K.P. Singh would be perceived as exhibiting highly desirable leadership traits, while other organisations may prefer the traits exhibited by Marcel Pinot. Yet other organisations, particularly the larger and more decentralised, may identify well with a blend of three or even four different subsets of traits. Invariably, flexibility is sought in most executives and managers, rather than rigidity.

In the ideal setting, both individuals and their organisations must come to some agreement on what they mean by desirable leadership traits for executives to be successful. To do this, they need to develop a common language to describe this 'make or break' area of executive success.

DEFINING LEADERSHIP TRAITS

Two dimensions together define the major categories of leadership traits in the examples we have cited. The first dimension relates to the *degree of people orientation* versus the *degree of output orientation*. Clearly some executives are highly oriented towards output, tasks and production, whereas others are more oriented towards people, be they employees or customers. Some executives are a blend of the two, or verge towards one orientation or the other.

The second dimension relates to the *degree of control* versus the *degree of creativity*. Some executives are very dominant: they seek to be in control or impose controls on others, and they are likely to be intensive in their approach. Other executives think much more outside the square and are more interested in a hands-off and creative environment.

These two dimensions can be joined to form a matrix, as shown in Chart 4.8.

Increasingly, it seems, desirable leadership traits are perceived by employers as a dual orientation towards people and creativity, while not ignoring the need for visionary strategists too. This is because many organisations have been through a period of unprecedented restructuring and downsizing—managing the costs—when a production and control mentality was highly relevant.

Today, in this time of low inflation and high competition, many of these same organisations are seeking to regenerate and grow, perhaps into entirely new profitable areas, or by being very different from their competitors. This will only come about through an increased orientation towards people (both employees and customers) and creative approaches.

Having studied Chart 4.8 and the leadership trait descriptions, what main leadership traits do you believe you exhibit? I suggest you reality-check your conclusions, preferably with several people who know you well in the work setting.

Next, what desirable leadership traits are sought by the organisation, and what traits are considered undesirable? Is there a gap between the

CHART 4.8 Leadership traits

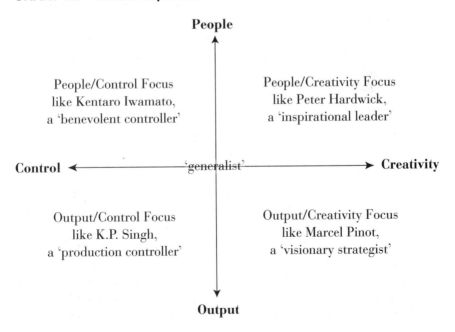

organisation's requirements and your own leadership traits? What are you going to do to narrow the gap?

Closing the Gap

If there is a gap between what is sought by the organisation and your own traits in your current role or in your future role, these are the alternatives:

➤ *Ignore it.* Hope that the gap will go unrecognised. However, in today's smaller and flatter organisational structures, every single cog has to be moving in harmony with every other cog. In the heavy machinery of old bureaucratic structures the occasional rusty cog could survive unnoticed; today every rusty cog is exposed and vulnerable.

➤ *Attack it.* Refuse to change and buck the trend, but beware! Organisations usually win out over individuals.

➤ *Change the organisation.* Try to change organisational requirements for leadership traits more towards your own traits—but how movable are mountains?

➤ *Change your attitude.* View the problem as an opportunity rather than a threat.

➤ *Change your traits,* so that they coincide more often with the expectations of your organisation.

➤ *Retreat.* Move to another part of the organisation or remove yourself altogether from the organisation.

THE NEED FOR FLEXIBILITY

In working with leadership traits, remember the need for flexibility. You probably have a natural 'centre of gravity' in terms of your more dominant/natural leadership traits. There may be a gap between this centre of gravity and the leadership traits sought by the organisation in your current or future job position: it's your decision as to what you do about such a gap. But the need for behavioural flexibility in leadership suggests that, anyway, you should move from your existing leadership trait centre of gravity and flex your leadership traits according to differing people and situations. Consider these questions:

➤ When should you exhibit more of an emphasis on output and control?

➤ When is it appropriate to focus more on people and control?

➤ When should you be emphasising output and creativity?

➤ When is it appropriate to focus more on people and creativity?

Just as you modify your delegation style according to the priority of task, impact of task, capability of delegatee and motivation of delegatee, so you also need to flex your leadership traits according to prevailing circumstances and the people you are leading.

The acid test is to ask yourself which of the following are going to serve your leadership interests best at any particular time: an orientation towards output or people? Towards control or creativity?

COACHING FOR RESULTS

Coaching direct reports for results requires a combination of both coaching and counselling. Counselling can be defined as a process entailing support, encouragement, questioning and listening by an executive *to help an individual define* and work through personal problems or organisational changes which affect job motivation or performance. Coaching is a similar process but also entails guidelines, examples, role plays, prebriefings and debriefings by the executive *to train and orient* an individual to the realities and demands of work and to help remove any barriers to optimum work performance or behaviour.

Counselling and coaching share many of the same characteristics. At times they may seem to overlap. However, as a guide, use *counselling* when there are personal problems or organisational changes affecting job performance or motivation. Use *coaching* when there is a lack of skill or knowledge about job responsibilities, or about desirable leadership, in-team or interpersonal behaviour.

PRINCIPLES OF COACHING

You should always be exceptionally well prepared for coaching sessions, clear about the ground to be covered and the outcomes sought.

But the key to coaching is to put the onus on the individual to make decisions and concentrate on what they are doing about their development, rather than you telling them what to do or how to do it. The ideal coaching approach combines the following five phases.

➤ The individual determines development areas, strategies, tactics and so forth with the coach's help and guidelines.
➤ The coach previews implementation steps via discussion, rehearsal, role play or other approaches.

➢ The individual then tests or implements modified practices or behaviours in the workplace.
➢ The coach debriefs by discussing how the implementation went.
➢ Both return to the first and subsequent phases of the sequence—in other words, it becomes a continuous process.

When approaching coaching sessions, consider the following points. What is your role as coach—judge, counsellor, supporter, manager, adviser? Clearly, at times you will be a counsellor when the individual needs a facilitator to unravel and manage an issue. *Never* be a manager or a judge! Offer plenty of support and advice, but be careful your paradigm doesn't clash with that of the individual when it comes to straight advice—it's better to be a supporter and, through a questioning approach, encourage the individual to determine appropriate outcomes.

Coaching is not telling or teaching but relies heavily on questioning and feedback; it creates an environment in which the individual can learn. Rely heavily on the formula given to us by the Almighty—we have two ears and one mouth and should use them in this proportion at all times!

How long should a coaching session be? We recommend one-hour sessions in a neutral meeting room or office (for confidentiality, greater session impact and fewer interruptions).

Other critical ingredients for coaching include:

➢ handing out any relevant guidelines or reading materials for subsequent discussion (at the next meeting);
➢ summarising and paraphrasing;
➢ active listening (nodding in agreement) and pausing;
➢ provision of clear, direct feedback embracing praise, support and challenge.

The oldest and still the most powerful coaching tactic for fostering critical thinking is *questioning*. Through questioning, we focus on getting individuals to work out their own appropriate solutions rather than providing the answers. The coach emulates an inquiring mind by continually probing into the subject with questions.

Coaches can question goals and purposes. They can probe into the nature of the question, problem or issue that is on the table. They can ask whether the individual has relevant data and information. They can consider alternative interpretations of the data and information. They can analyse key concepts and ideas. They can question assumptions that are made. They can ask individuals to draw out the implications and consequences of what they are saying. Coaches can consider alternative points of view.

A questioning approach is an appropriate entry point for coaching, which may usefully take the following sequence:

➢ background and current status;
➢ things that are going well at the organisation, department or individual level;
➢ things that lend themselves to improvement;
➢ the downsides if such improvements are not attained;
➢ the upsides of their attainment; the resultant needs for coaching, defined as specifically as possible.

But the most important element is to make sure the needs for coaching are carefully analysed, clearly articulated and then agreed between line manager and coachee.

In summary, a coach needs to:

➢ keep the meeting focused;
➢ keep the discussion relevant to the work setting;
➢ stimulate the session with probing questions;
➢ periodically summarise what has (and has not) been dealt with or resolved;
➢ draw the individual deeply into the dialogue.

ONGOING COACHING MEETINGS

In preparing for, planning and conducting ongoing coaching meetings, the following sequence can be adopted:

➢ counselling mode: an informal and questioning opening approach to see how things are going with the coachee—see the earlier section on counselling;
➢ meeting objectives and outcomes: what the coach and individual might seek to attain in the meeting;
➢ review general progress since last meeting;
➢ prebrief or debrief one or more new approaches to, say, performance improvement;
➢ agree on next meeting date;
➢ action items between now and then (individual and possibly coach);

> ➢ meeting summary and wrap-up;
> ➢ what the next meeting is intended to cover.

PERFORMANCE APPRAISAL

Formal performance appraisal processes and follow-up coaching are rarely correctly used. First, the paperwork associated with them is often used subjectively and becomes no more than a 'happy sheet' to be completed every year; second, when performance is assessed as below satisfactory, this is often inadequately communicated to the appraisee, who does not always 'hear' the bad news.

Third, individual development needs are often poorly identified and development plans inadequately defined or implemented. And, finally, if unsatisfactory performance is the case, formal warnings and supporting information are rarely adequately communicated or documented.

Yet the more objective use of performance appraisals and the real identification of, and attention to, development needs offers a range of advantages.

> ➢ Those being appraised know exactly what is expected of them.
> ➢ They have time and organisational support to develop their personal performance.
> ➢ They have early warning of potential outcomes if unable or unwilling to develop.

However, until the executives and managers involved in the performance appraisal process buy ownership of the need for performance improvement counselling and coaching, and are adequately trained in it and prepared to invest the time, it is unlikely that the full benefits of performance appraisal will be realised.

PERFORMANCE TURN-AROUND PROGRAMS

This unsatisfactory situation is often the case with performance improvement programs, which can usefully be applied following an unsatisfactory performance appraisal or at other times when an individual's performance is perceived as below satisfactory or deteriorating. Such programs are often given a time frame, anything from three to six months, and have a start and end date with specific objectives, action plans and review dates (usually monthly).

In addition to such ongoing reviews, regular discussion is needed between the individual and their manager about all key incidents, good and bad. The human resources function can usefully be involved, with a human relations executive present before, during and after reviews. The goals, of course, are to improve personal performance and prevent the situation deteriorating into a dismissal; this is invariably avoided when such processes are given the attention and priority they deserve.

If they do not result in improved performance to the extent required, the process can be extended or the individual may be transferred to another job position, demoted (what has happened to the demotion option? It is rarely seen these days) or dismissed. The key is that all concerned in the process understand and agree on the goals and the alternatives at the outset of the program.

Additional key elements of such programs include:

➤ regular feedback regarding progress, and regular coaching sessions—continual emphasis is needed;
➤ specific written objectives which spell out the results to be achieved, the extent of the desired achievements and the time frame;
➤ the results being sought, not just effort;
➤ mutual acceptance of the objectives to be attained, through joint establishment and agreement;
➤ a mutual understanding of what non-achievement may result in— for example, demotion or relocation (internal or external);
➤ fewer objectives rather than many—too many objectives may be received negatively by the incumbent, reducing their tolerance for the whole exercise or generating negative feedback;
➤ opportunities for the individual to have progress recognised, and to receive help with any required corrective action;
➤ written records regarding progress;
➤ a supportive approach throughout;
➤ when progress is not being realised, the restatement of possible outcomes and benefits of making progress, and possibly the establishment of new interim objectives.

THE SPORTS COACHING ANALOGY FOR ENABLING

As a final twist to this chapter, I would like you to consider this analogy and compare it with the way you operate.

➤ The sports coach puts in time one-on-one with each member of the team, helping them hone their techniques and further develop their capabilities and confidence. This 'putting in' by the coach earns respect and confidence ('credits') so that, when the coach has to be tough, whether at team coaching sessions or exhorting someone from the touchline (potentially incurring 'debits'), this is accepted by the individual team member on the receiving end because of the fertile ground already created.

➤ The sports coach knows how to conduct half-time meetings, taking a dominant leadership role, giving feedback, prioritising and directing individual team members in their different player positions—fast-paced and extremely businesslike.

➤ The sports coach knows when and how to conduct strategy meetings back at the clubhouse, taking a far less dominant leadership role, seeking more input and consensus, and promoting mutual accountability—'We can only win the next game, and the season, as a team'.

➤ And the sports coach knows when the team needs to socialise and develop camaraderie, often around the bar!

Are there any lessons in this for you, as an enabling leader?

ROB BALMER ON ENABLING

When I considered the different leadership styles identified in this chapter, I probably did what most people would do and quickly identified what I thought was the best leadership style to have. In my opinion, the Inspirational Leader was the best style because it most closely described the attributes that I consider most great leaders to have. This leadership style turned out to be the one that was my natural style, the one I am most comfortable operating in.

However, when I continued working through this 'Enabling' module and asked a number of those around me which style they felt best described the style I most often used to run my division, I was surprised to find that a number of my most senior managers (those who'd worked with me for some years) felt that my leadership style had changed from Inspirational Leader to Visionary Strategist. That is, they felt I had become more output-oriented and less people-oriented than I had been in the past. I was concerned by this when I first heard it as I had always considered myself a very 'people' person.

The most interesting information came when I followed up my initial approach to my staff with the question, 'Do you think that is the appropriate style for me to use?'. The answer was a unanimous 'Yes!'. I then asked 'Why?' and the consistent answer was that there were more than enough people-oriented managers in the team and it was important that someone was driving for results. So, without even realising I was doing it, I had flexed my leadership style to fill a role that was needed, even though this was not my natural style. The great thing about this exercise was not just understanding what my style was and how I was flexing it, but coming to the realisation that my team understood and agreed with the way I was flexing it. This, more than anything, made me feel good about the way I was 'enabling' my team.

But then I asked myself the question, 'What leadership style does my organisation want me to display?', and I realised there were some real issues I needed to be aware of.

When I joined the company in the early 1990s, it was still a relatively small operation in Australia. There were about 100 staff and the company was in a rapid growth phase. In this atmosphere, the leadership attributes most valued in the organisation were those of both the Inspirational Leader and Visionary Strategist. This was because the organisation was continually looking for new ways to grow and was regularly introducing new business units to the organisation.

Over the years the business became larger and larger through organic growth and acquisition. By the year 2000 the organisation had more than 3000 staff and was the market leader in Australia. Somewhere along the line, the focus of the organisation (in my opinion) changed from an aggressive emphasis on new opportunities and growth to protecting what we already had. This was not an official strategy, but it was certainly very obvious when one looked at the leadership style the organisation had begun emphasising.

In this new environment (some would call it more 'mature'), the emphasis of the organisation moved strongly from Creativity to Control on the horizontal axis of Peter's leadership style model. This meant that where once the Inspirational Leaders and Visionary Strategists had been strongly encouraged, now the Benevolent Controllers and Production Controllers came to the fore. I would therefore need to flex my leadership style further, particularly when dealing with groups outside my control who now had increased influence in the organisation.

Most organisations go through different phases in their development, and during these phases different things are encouraged. Particularly, the tendency to 'drift left' on the control versus creativity axis is something that more naturally right-inclined leaders need to be aware of, if they are to avoid a great deal of frustration and lack of effectiveness when dealing within the organisation.

LEADERSHIP MYTHS	LEADERSHIP TRUTHS
➢ You have to focus on quarterly results.	➢ If you're not focusing on external futures too, you won't be around long enough for quarterly results!
➢ Corporate communication is about keeping employees informed.	➢ It's also about hearing from and listening to employees!
➢ People can only motivate themselves.	➢ Leaders and organisations hold the key to individual motivation, by creating—or not—a strongly motivational environment where individuals can flourish.
➢ Never abdicate.	➢ Abdication, at one end of the spectrum, and direction at the other end are powerful and legitimate delegation styles—if you know when and how to deploy them!
➢ Personal accountability is all about taking responsibility and working with it for results.	➢ It's just as much about reporting on results to the individual delegating it, preferably by exception (when results are 'over', to celebrate success; or 'under', to effect a remedy).
➢ A consistent leadership style is best.	➢ Leadership style needs to flex according to different people, priorities and situations.

DON'T HIDE!
➢ If you don't have your antennae out, constantly monitoring, it's just a matter of time before you get caught out.
➢ Poor delegation is one of the greatest causes of bottlenecks, low morale and high staff turnover. It also represents—when connected to motivation—one of the greatest opportunities for positive leverage of human endeavour.

> Don't hide from your personal accountabilities, and don't let others around you hide from theirs.
> Coaching is one of the best ways to put leadership into action.
> Vary your coaching approaches to suit prevailing circumstances—but, above all, coach.

YOUR WEDNESDAY REVIEW

1. In thinking about enabling, how are we tracking in terms of the management practices of primary business drivers, external futures planning, corporate communications, organising, monitoring, decision making, motivating, delegating, motivational delegation, personal accountability and 'Fast and simple!'?
2. Are we pursuing our principal business objective well enough, by focusing on its primary business drivers (via Profit Tree analysis)?
3. Are we also focusing on external futures adequately: technology, the economy, politics, society and competition? Or are we too preoccupied with quarterly results and in danger of eventual derailment?
4. Through our corporate communications, are we hearing from and listening to employees as well as keeping employees informed?
5. Do we have our antennae out constantly rather than relying on too much ad-hoc monitoring?
6. Are we delegating well? Are we avoiding the bottlenecks, poor morale and high staff turnover of poor delegation? Are we maximising the potential for positive leverage of human endeavour, through delegating and connecting it to motivation?
7. Are we creating, both as individual leaders and as an organisation, a strongly motivational environment where individuals can flourish?
8. Are our people and ourselves accepting personal accountability sufficiently?
9. Are we pursuing 'Fast and simple!' in most of what we plan and do?
10. Are we flexing our leadership styles sufficiently to adapt to different people and situations? As leaders, do we know when to focus on output or people, control or creativity?
11. Are we putting leadership into action by doing enough coaching, and varying our coaching approaches to prevailing needs and circumstances?

CHAPTER 5

Energising

Energising is about creating a strongly motivational environment, for yourself and others.

KEYNOTES FROM THE COMMENTATORS

Job fit? Occupational interests? Capabilities? Well, I'm one of those people who realised very early on that my capability as a dancer, musician or actor simply did not match in any way my desire to work as a dancer, musician or actor! I envy people who are really good at their passion because, as Peter says, motivation is then unbounded. However, I do have capabilities as a strategic thinker, as a leader of people, as an organiser of work, as a coach and adviser to others and, on my good days, as a motivator and communicator. I like to think I have the capability of being a really good leader. So, for me, a career in business in various 'management' and leadership roles has in fact given me job fit, matching my interests and capabilities.

Meredith Hellicar, Company Director

The war for talent, exacerbated by changing demographics, is only going to get tougher, and requires that executives learn how to lead and manage human assets better. This requires a balanced yet flexible approach in order to attract and retain talent, the younger members of which may not engage naturally in strong company loyalty.

David Hearn, Chief Executive Goodman Fielder

A successful executive leader has personal balance in their lives and knows how to leverage their people (in a positive, non-exploitive sense). Successful executive leaders also believe in themselves as human beings. If it doesn't work out, have enough confidence to go and do it somewhere else. A successful executive leader takes risks and is fully prepared to do so.
Peter Scott, Chief Executive Officer MLC

In addition to the motivational delegation and leadership elements of 'enabling' in Chapter 4, which both favourably affect the energy levels in an organisation, this chapter on 'energising' addresses:

➤ *interests, motivational capabilities and values for job fit*: clearly, the better your job fits you, and similarly the jobs of your direct reports, the more your team and you will be motivated to perform—*energised*;
➤ *atmospheric needs*: the more you understand the ideal environment or 'atmosphere' in which you need to operate, and similarly your work colleagues, the more motivated all will be. Where the atmosphere is not ideal, the adoption of appropriate coping mechanisms will help people to remain *energised*;
➤ *talent management*: if an organisation can attract, develop, retain and motivate the talent it needs, this underpins a strongly motivated and *energised* environment.

JOB FIT

On my return, aged 18, from a year's voluntary service overseas as a teacher in Pakistan, the sponsors of my trip, Commercial Union, offered me a plum job as a graduate recruit (even before I had started my tertiary education!). The job lasted three months. I hated training to be an insurance underwriter despite the excellent career opportunities.

Later, in my late twenties, having pioneered the explosive fast food industry in the UK with a subsidiary of the Mars Bars Group, I inherited 150 more traditional industrial and retail catering outlets which needed serious attention in terms of operations and margin performance—that is, maintenance and development of the status quo. I hated it, reacted negatively and jumped ship to assume my first CEOship elsewhere.

And, on countless occasions over the past ten years or so, executives have come to me, or have been sent to me, who appear not to be fitting in or are reacting negatively to their role or their operating environment.

The lesson learned from all this, which forms an important element of our work as executive coaches, is that self-motivation—often assumed to 'be there' or taken for granted—is just as important in executive life as capability, if not more so. Motivation is the lifeblood of energy. And without energy, how can all these growth aspirations, personal and organisational, be achieved?

A large and reasonably well-understood element of motivation comes from an organisation's ability, and the ability of individual leaders, to create, nurture and develop a strongly motivational environment.

Based on our experience as executive coaches, and on conventional wisdom, is the belief that this comes about only by paying as much attention to the *people* side of the equation as to the *task*. It is coupled with great emphasis on results through effective delegation (which in our book suggests a clear understanding of when to abdicate, when to direct and when to delegate in a more balanced mode somewhere between these two extremes).

Elements that are less clear and less well understood in the context of motivation and energy are what we refer to as 'job fit' and 'atmospheric needs'.

Job fit is a *prerequisite* for job satisfaction, self-motivation, energy and personal performance. When in place, job fit creates a situation where you look forward to going to work and are perceived to be 'giving of your all' rather than coasting or 'going through the motions'.

Job fit depends on two very different components: the nature of the work itself, and the fit with certain personal characteristics. When these two components match, this generates outstanding fit, self-motivation, energy and personal performance.

The personal characteristics representing one side of the job fit formula include occupational interests and motivational capabilities. The nature of work, representing the other side of the formula, can be described in the form of a range of discrete career areas.

I work with twelve main occupational interest areas in job fit, including scientific, persuasive, practical and computational areas. Clearly, some interests relate more to certain career areas than to others, and a person's major occupational interests need to be represented in the job to enhance self-motivation, energy and personal performance.

Motivational capabilities are the other component of personal characteristics which need to be assessed in job fit ('motivational' means those capabilities we enjoy using). We may be born with them or we can develop them through learning and application. I use a range of ten capability areas in my work in job fit, including numeracy, spatial ability, creativity and social ability.

As with occupational interests, some capabilities relate more to certain career areas than to others, but they need to be represented in the job if self-motivation, energy and personal performance are to be maximised.

I now examine the job fit formula in greater detail (see Chart 5.1).

OCCUPATIONAL INTERESTS

On one side of the job fit formula is personal characteristics, which include occupational interests. The twelve main occupational interest areas are summarised below. (Note that these are *interests*, not necessarily *capabilities*, which are noted later.)

➢ *Scientific*: an interest in facts, particularly relating to the natural sciences; a desire to work out how things occur, why they occur and what results from them; an interest in finding things out, perhaps by using laboratory techniques or doing research; and analytical and investigatory activities.

➢ *Social*: an interest in people rather than things; an interest in listening to other people with a genuine concern for their troubles and problems; and an interest in supplying services that others need and will be happy to receive.

➢ *Persuasive*: an interest in meeting and convincing people, promoting your ideas, beliefs, projects or sales; an interest in influencing people in some way, their attitudes or behaviour; and an enjoyment in persuading people, in discussion, debate or argument.

➢ *Literary*: an enjoyment of writing and words; an interest in any activity that needs the use of imaginative verbal descriptions; a love

CHART 5.1   Job fit formula

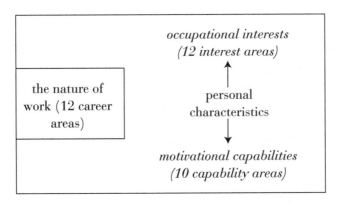

of books, reading or reciting; and an interest in writing or speaking originally and imaginatively.

➢ *Artistic*: an enjoyment of visual art, design or drama; an interest in colour and artistic activities with a desire to create something of imagination or beauty; and a keen interest in your surroundings or in some aspect of design.

➢ *Clerical*: an interest in administration, office or clerical work, often based on a routine requiring accuracy and precision; and an interest in recording and filing, coding and classifying, where detailed numerate, scientific or technical knowledge may not be needed to any great degree.

➢ *Practical*: being 'good with your hands'; an interest in repairing and making things; a preference for learning by doing rather than by reading; a liking for working with tools and materials rather than with words; and an interest in constructing or building things.

➢ *Musical*: an enjoyment of, or interest in, any type of music, playing musical instruments or singing; an enjoyment of listening to people play music; and a love of going to musical concerts, films or shows.

➢ *Computational*: an interest in working with figures; an interest in dealing with numbers and mathematical problems and concepts; an interest in using mental arithmetic or formulae; and an interest in proving or disproving things with figures.

➢ *Outside*: an interest in being or working outside, sometimes involving considerable physical activity and/or travel; a dislike of having to work inside the whole time, and of routine work or regularity; and an interest in animals, in growing crops or plants, or in moving from place to place.

➢ *Technical*: an interest in work that entails dealing with anything technical, such as machines, engines, tools, computers, or electrical and electronic equipment; a preference for operating anything technical; and an interest in how and why technical items work.

➢ *Medical*: an interest in medical and biological subjects; an interest in healing and caring for sick people; a desire to investigate the causes and relieve the effects of illness and disease; and an interest in various aspects of mental or physical health.

A person's major occupational interests need to be represented in the job to enhance self-motivation and personal performance.

MOTIVATIONAL CAPABILITIES

Motivational capabilities are those capabilities we enjoy using, whether we are born with them or develop them through learning and application. They also form part of personal characteristics and one side of the job fit formula. They can be summarised as follows.

> *Memory*: an ability to remember, to retain things in the mind and recall things from the past; a good memory may be better at remembering certain things—for example, faces rather than names.

> *Verbal comprehension*: an ability to understand accurately the meaning of words, both written and spoken; an ability to read and understand 'difficult' books or reports, and to differentiate between words with similar meanings; having an extensive vocabulary.

> *Numeracy*: an ability to understand and express ideas by way of numbers; an ability to understand mathematical concepts and numerical problems; and an ability to understand statistical tables, gambling or betting odds, and technical data.

> *Spatial ability*: an ability to see and understand shapes or objects in more than one dimension; an ability to understand complicated diagrams or technical drawings in three dimensions; a good sense of direction; and good at puzzles where you fit or disentangle complicated objects and shapes.

> *Perception*: an ability to perceive or notice things in detail, or to understand situations; an ability to notice quickly if something is wrong, or to pick up important details or information that others miss.

> *Fluency*: an ability to express your views or meaning in correct spoken words; a good communicator with an ability to argue or persuade; well able to make your meaning clear in discussion; and good self-expression.

> *Reasoning ability*: an ability to reason, to progress from the known to the unknown by using logic and drawing conclusions; an ability to solve problems, to see when people contradict themselves in a discussion or argument; and to resolve complex matters through logical reasoning.

> *Creativity*: an ability to produce a stream of new, useful or creative ideas; an ability to be inventive or creative and think of more than one way of looking at a problem or answering a question; and being good at art or design, or at creative problem solving, or at computer graphics.

➤ *Social ability*: an ability to get on well with other people from a wide range of backgrounds, beliefs and views; an ability to get other people to accept your views, to trust you, confide in you and to do things for you; and a capacity to mix with anyone socially.
➤ *Clerical speed and accuracy*: an ability to be quick and accurate with anything clerical: spotting typing mistakes, filing, cross-checking columns of figures, note taking; and good at office-type activities, typically undertaken in administration.

Motivational capabilities need to be represented in a job if self-motivation and personal performance are to be maximised.

CAREER AREAS
Twelve major career areas represent the other side of the job fit formula. Each career area relates more to certain occupational interests and motivational capabilities than to others. While these career areas represent an open field of choice for people at the start of their careers, it is surprising how people can resculpture their job content and/or make career changes later in order to maximise job fit and other criteria.

➤ *Practical careers* are for practically minded individuals who like to work with their hands, and this can often include outdoor work. This type of work often suits people who have a spatial ability. Typical careers include: the armed services; manufacturing and distribution; building, civil engineering and land services; agriculture, horticulture, forestry and parks, fisheries; clothing industry; metal and printing industries.
➤ *Technical careers* are for practical *and* technical individuals, sometimes with outside and/or medical interests and an interest in science. They often require a good memory, a capacity for thinking spatially, in three dimensions, and sometimes numeracy. Perception and reasoning ability are often required. Relevant career areas include: health and hospital services; science; engineering; management services; media services; metal and printing industries; building, civil engineering and land services; and agriculture, horticulture, forestry and fisheries.
➤ *Analytical careers* are for the computational and, sometimes, clerical-minded individual. Abilities include memory, numeracy, spatial skills, perception, reasoning and sometimes clerical speed and accuracy—often a 'detail' person. Analytical career areas can be

found in a range of business sectors and are often located in the management services functional areas of organisations.

➢ *Scientific careers* are for the scientifically minded and sometimes for those with social welfare, computational or medical interests. Ability requirements include a good memory, numeracy, spatial skills, perception, reasoning and creativity. Career areas include science, and health and hospital services.

➢ *Creative careers* are for the literary, artistic or musical individual, sometimes with persuasive or practical interests, often with spatial ability, perception, creativity, and sometimes verbal comprehension, fluency or social ability. Career areas include: creative art; fashion and design; entertainment and recreation; media and publications.

➢ *Careers in design* include artistic, technical and sometimes practical or computational interests. Requirements include a good memory, spatial ability, perception, reasoning, creativity and sometimes numeracy. Career areas include: creative art; fashion and design; technical design; media and publications; and building, architecture, civil engineering and land services.

➢ *People-oriented careers* are for the individual who has social welfare and sometimes persuasive, practical or medical interests. Perception, fluency, reasoning and social ability are often key requirements. Relevant career areas include: teaching and cultural activities; catering and personal services; health and hospital services; social work; human resources management; and transport, travel and materials handling.

➢ *Managerial careers* are for the more persuasive and sometimes social welfare-oriented individuals with good perception, fluency, reasoning and social ability. Career areas include: the armed services; management and administration; inspection; security and protective services; and transport, travel and materials handling.

➢ *Enterprising careers* are for individuals who are persuasive and sometimes social welfare-oriented. These people are perceptive, fluent, have good reasoning ability, are social and sometimes spatial and creative. Career areas include a marketing orientation in a wide variety of different businesses and sectors.

➢ *Entrepreneurial careers*—the entrepreneur is often a persuasive and practical individual who is perceptive, has good reasoning abilities and is sometimes fluent or creative. Careers include independent business and sales.

➢ *Administrative careers* are often for the individual with clerical and sometimes social welfare and computational interests, and require a good memory, verbal comprehension, perception, reasoning ability, clerical speed and accuracy, and sometimes numeracy and social ability. Careers in administration can be found across a wide range of business areas.

➤ *Professional services careers* often suit individuals with persuasive and sometimes clerical and computational interests and require a good memory, verbal comprehension, perception, fluency, reasoning, social ability and sometimes numeracy. Typical career areas include: law, finance and accounting; management or business consultancy.

Some of these career areas relate more to certain occupational interests, motivational capabilities and, in some cases, values than to others; ideally, your existing or new job will offer a good match in this regard.

In summary, a high level of job fit should enhance the prospects of feeling self-motivated in the work we do, enhancing personal performance. A low level of job fit will have the reverse effect and, if this is the case, you will need to consider your options.

Implications of poor job fit

We are amazed by how many executives we have found in jobs and work environments that do not fully accommodate their interests, motivational capabilities or values. Not only does this mean that, through lack of self-motivation, they often fail to perform at their personal best, but it also means that a large proportion of their lives—executives working some 100 000 hours in their careers—is unfulfilled.

One of the most exciting parts of my professional work is to help executives realign themselves in this context and to see them become self-motivated and perform at personal optimum, reaping the rewards of greater job satisfaction, improved personal performance and enhanced remuneration, at the same time being seen to be contributing more fully to their organisations.

JOB REQUIREMENTS AND VALUES

Job requirements and values—in other words, those needs and ideals that are important and virtually non-negotiable (particularly as the years unfold!) in the way we live and work—represent the last component of personal characteristics on the same side of the job fit formula. They cover a broad range, including the following job requirements.

➤ *Employment conditions*: high levels of salary, benefits and other elements of compensation; or security of employment and job stability; or an organisation where you can acquire a stake in the equity, or become a partner.

➤ *Prospects*: an organisation in which you can develop your career through promotions; or a job that requires and recognises qualifications.

➤ *Importance*: a job that has status and is respected; or a job in which you can lead or influence others.

➤ *Responsibility*: a job that helps others within the community; or a job within an organisation that has respect for the environment.

➤ *Fulfilment*: a job in which you feel you can achieve; or a job within a competitive environment; or a job within a challenging environment.

➤ *People orientation*: a job that interacts with people; or a working environment based on trust and integrity.

➤ *Autonomy*: a job offering independence and autonomy; or a work environment where you can be entrepreneurial or operate your own business.

➤ *Technical/functional*: a job that requires finely honed skills and competencies; or a job that involves research and development.

➤ *Lifestyle*: a job offering variety and change; or a job that allows you to balance work and home life; or a reasonably short working week.

Values relate more to our innate beliefs about the way we live and work and include such fundamentals as integrity, ethics, trust, fairness, service to others, professionalism, ethos of 'I win/You win', family orientation, personal health, freedom, environment and sense of purpose.

The degree to which our job requirements and values are met in our career depend not only on the job itself but also on the working environment, differing jobs and environments matching differing value sets.

You may have other job requirements and values, as this is not an exhaustive list.

ATMOSPHERIC NEEDS
Let me give you a simple analogy of atmospheric (motivational) needs. Compare two goldfish in their bowls: one has clean water and looks great; the other has dirty water—its atmosphere is polluted—and its response is to react negatively as it gulps for oxygen.

CHART 5.2   Atmospheric impact!

clean atmosphere   polluted atmosphere

The atmospheric needs of individual executives, in order to maximise their self-motivation and personal effectiveness, include a range of characteristics of the organisation, its culture and its management style:

➢ *material needs*: remuneration, safety and security;
➢ *structural needs*: degree and type of structure, bureaucracy and systems;
➢ *behavioural needs*: management style and interpersonal relationships;
➢ *emotional needs*: trust, social needs, esteem needs and sense of achievement.

Executives need to assess their own atmospheric needs and ensure they are appropriately accommodated in the organisation, if at all possible. If not, self-motivation and thereby performance are unlikely to be at optimum.

Atmospherics are a critical element of chemistry and fit and yet are often ignored in management or executive selection and development.

CHART 5.3   Atmospheric needs

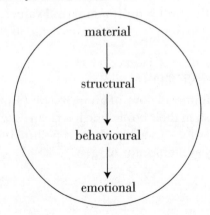

Usually, an orientation of 'Will the candidate fit in with us?' rather than 'Are we right for the candidate?' applies.

Material needs
Material needs relate to the base-level needs as described by the well-known behavioural scientist Abraham Maslow. They include all the basic needs for living and working:

➢ remuneration for food, clothing, shelter, health and education;
➢ safety and security at work;
➢ and even 'comfort' at work, whether in the office environment, cafeteria arrangements, style of car or fringe benefits.

Clearly, if the material needs of an individual are not satisfied, this may create, on the one hand, self-motivation to progress within the organisation and via promotion to improve material returns to a more acceptable level; or, as is often the case, it may cause dissatisfaction, poor morale and poor performance, potentially leading to a voluntary or involuntary separation.

Structural needs
Structural needs relate to the way the organisation is structured, including the degree of centralisation versus decentralisation and the levels of autonomy accorded. Other factors include:

➢ degree of bureaucracy and red tape versus a more free-wheeling environment;
➢ the complexity and intensity of management reporting and supporting systems;
➢ the degree and type of computer-based information versus paper-based, and requirements for computer literacy;
➢ rigidity or otherwise of policies, rules and regulations.

In terms of structure, the organisation may either meet the motivational needs of the individual or may be diametrically opposed to them, causing an adverse reaction, often stressful behaviour and apparent 'poor fit'.

Behavioural needs
Behavioural needs are more complex and can become something of a moving target because of the coming and going of the senior people in corporate life to whom an individual reports. For example, an executive may be hired by a chief executive who displays ideal behavioural

characteristics for the newly hired individual. However, chief executive job tenure now spans about three years and so there is a strong chance that any executive is likely to report to a new boss—it is simply a matter of time! That new boss may display very different behavioural characteristics from the original hirer, and those characteristics may not meet the motivational needs of the individual.

However, behavioural needs are met (or not met) not only by the senior executive to whom a person reports but also by the culture of the organisation, and so these needs and how they are satisfied are worth examining in detail. Behavioural needs fall into two main categories: *management style* and *interpersonal relationships*.

Management style

Management style encompasses such aspects as planning, organising, monitoring, decision making, motivating, delegating, adaptability, entrepreneurism, resilience and communication. These are summarised below in the context of assessing atmospherics.

> - *Planning*—the degree to which senior executives plan, set objectives, develop strategies, monitor, control and review the performance of direct reports; how 'top-down' or 'bottom-up' the planning processes are within the organisation; and how fixed or flexible plans are during implementation. Some executives are motivated and perform well in a highly planned environment, while others operate better in a more spontaneous setting.
> - *Organising*—in addition to the structural aspects of the organisation (addressed earlier), individual senior executives clearly have an impact on organising; for example, the degree of formality or informality in terms of team structure, reporting relationships, responsibility, accountability, authority, delegation and span of control. Some executives prefer a well-organised environment, others prefer a more informal or 'loose' setting.
> - *Monitoring*—the degree to which the monitoring of performance is preventive or maintenance; the number and specificity of major result areas and standards of performance; the form of monitoring, whether on-the-job supervision or hands-off, via reporting and information systems; and how individual development and learning needs are identified and addressed. Some executives perceive close and formalised monitoring as an unpalatable invasion of their autonomy, while others see this as the norm and need regular feedback on their performance.

➢ *Decision making*—the degree to which decision making involves
direct reports or is imposed; problems and opportunities are fully
defined or understood; a range of prospective solutions is
developed and assessed; root causes as opposed to symptoms are
tackled; and how much creative thinking 'outside the square' is
encouraged in the development of best possible decisions. Some
executives need an environment where decisions are made quickly,
where there is neither ambiguity nor 'shades of grey', others prefer
and operate better in a more reflective environment where there is
ample time for decision making, particularly when complex issues
are being handled.

➢ *Motivating*—the degree to which a motivational environment is
created; a climate encouraging personal development and
advancement; democratic rather than autocratic leadership; trust
and integrity; job interest and satisfaction; recognition of individual
or group contributions; alignment of personal and corporate goals;
and an egalitarian as opposed to status-based culture. Some
executives need and can survive only in a motivational environment,
others are more self-motivated.

➢ *Delegating*—the extent to which senior executives delegate in terms
of being clear about what and to whom responsibilities are
delegated; sufficient resources and authority being provided so that
the delegation can be carried through effectively; delegation to
maximise the skills and personal development of direct reports;
delegation to free up internal bottlenecks and allow senior
executives to concentrate on higher-level matters. Some executives
have an insatiable appetite for delegated responsibilities, while
others prefer to work to their own agenda and perceive an
environment where there is a lot of delegation as one where they
are continually on the receiving end of 'passing the buck', with
adverse effects on personal freedom, initiative and autonomy.

➢ *Adaptability*—the degree to which senior executives appreciate and
offer variety and change, adapt to changing circumstances rather
than resist them, and take a flexible management and leadership
style depending on the competence of direct reports and the
urgency of tasks. Some executives thrive on change, others resist it
to the hilt (and it can become the cause of their undoing!).

➢ *Entrepreneurism*—how far the organisation is prepared to experiment
with new ways of doing things, innovate in terms of products,
services, processes or systems, and display a certain amount of
daring in this (yet balanced by an appreciation and application of

risk management). Some executives need to work in a highly entrepreneurial environment, others fit best in slower-paced or more predictable settings, and perhaps in bureaucracies.

➢ *Resilience*—the degree of resilience in senior executives in the form of handling and managing stress, capacity to persevere when the going gets tough, seeing change as a way of life rather than a hindrance, and generally displaying that 'dogged streak' of perseverance at times of particular difficulty or uncertainty. Some executives fit best in a tough or resilient environment, others prefer a softer work setting.

➢ *Communication*—the degree to which people engage in open two-way communication, seek to understand the other party's point of view, minimise the physical and behavioural barriers that can so often detract from effective communication, and are considered approachable by direct reports. Some executives thrive on open two-way communication and actually need it to be effective, while others prefer a more traditional hierarchical setting and are more used to communication that is primarily top-down.

Executives need to be very clear about their needs regarding management style, whether in the senior executive to whom they report or from a management culture perspective across the organisation. If such needs are met, self-motivation and performance are invariably enhanced. If such needs are not met, difficulties arise and, in the extreme case, a negative stress reaction. Yet how many employers consider chemistry and fit from this perspective?

Interpersonal relationships

Interpersonal relationships is the element of behavioural needs, and executives need to be clear about their preferred operating styles of the senior executives to whom they report. Operating style may be one or a combination of the following (as addressed earlier):

➢ *Commander/Doer*—usually directs other people and works to get results.

➢ *Responder/Initiator*—seeks to understand others, communicates well and leads enthusiastically.

➢ *Empathiser/Humanist*—the people-oriented (rather than production-oriented) individual, with an amicable style.

➢ *Evaluator/Detailer*—the analytical, logical, meticulous planner and organiser.

> *Idea Generator*—the conceptual and creative thinker who can see endless possibilities and who often shows extremes in behaviour.
> *All-rounder*—the balanced individual who has a flexible style yet does not show extremes in behaviour.

We may have preferences about the operating styles of others and those to whom we report, yet we may not always be able to choose our bosses in organisational life. But even understanding that there are differences in operating style, and that these differences in the senior team setting are actually needed in order to provide a balanced team composition, all helps. In selecting a new role within your existing organisation or a new job outside it, there may be some extremes in operating style you would be better to avoid. *You* have to decide!

Although the initial focus in assessing the degree to which your behavioural needs are met is the senior executive to whom you report, and although this executive may change and be replaced by another, many of the elements of management style and interpersonal relationships also relate to the culture of the organisation, and so need to be assessed in this dual context: will my behavioural needs be met by the person to whom I report?; will they be met by the culture of the organisation?

Emotional needs

In considering the final category of needs, emotional needs, we revert to Maslow and the higher levels of his hierarchy of needs, which include trust, social needs, esteem needs and sense of personal achievement.

Trust relates to the organisation being seen as fair and reasonable in its approach to dealing with staff, to the belief that senior management is trustworthy, that results will be rewarded and that there will be no undeserved penalties or dismissals. *Social needs* encompass the theme of individuals feeling they 'belong' and are part of a group. *Esteem needs* are satisfied by executives being recognised as individuals, and for their contributions, capabilities and achievements. *Sense of personal achievement* describes the executive who feels a sense of high-level accomplishment in terms of attaining what has been striven for, which brings great personal satisfaction and self-confidence.

Most executives need an environment where their emotional needs can be met in one or more ways, and yet in today's era of organisational turbulence and uncertainty even large, apparently well-managed organisations seem to have lost the plot with many in their senior level ranks.

Trust has walked out of the door as a result of a hire-and-fire mentality. Social interaction has deteriorated as individuals in the group jockey for survival and the apparently fewer opportunities for promotion in today's flatter organisation structures.

Esteem needs may be only partly met as achievements go unrecognised, the pressures of 'doing more with less faster' leaving little time for such pleasantries, and a sense of achievement becomes an even more elusive butterfly.

Implications of an uncongenial atmosphere

During my work with more than 600 executives and other key people, I have estimated that more than 50% of unsuccessful executive career episodes are caused by the atmospherics of organisational life being at variance with the needs of the individual.

Executives should therefore:

➢ determine their main atmospheric needs from the various categories and items noted above;
➢ endeavour to position themselves in organisations, and under people, where their atmospheric needs are best attended to;
➢ judiciously select new roles or new employers with the same considerations in the forefront of their minds.

COPING MECHANISMS

When the atmospherics are seriously out of alignment with individual needs, prepare and implement a defensive strategy, which may include:

➢ *Attack it.* Dig in your heels and hold your ground until something works out.
➢ *Ignore it.* Pretend the conflict doesn't exist and keep up outward appearances.
➢ *Develop resilience through imagery.* The way I do this is to imagine I am wearing a suit of medieval armour. When the slings and arrows come my way, I do not let them through my defences. 'Ping!'—they bounce off. You really can develop resilience through imagery. Try it!
➢ *Change it.* Change the situation by persuading others to change or get your role or responsibilities revised.
➢ *Change your behaviour.* Speak up more or listen more, learn to say 'no' or 'yes' to demands, or work at a different pace.
➢ *Change your attitude.* View the problem positively as a challenge or an opportunity to remain alert.

➢ *Retreat.* Remove yourself from the conflict by transferring or resigning.

Of these seven possible reactions, the first two should be avoided as non-productive. They don't get rid of your negative reaction to a polluted atmosphere—your stress—which will continue to eat away at you. Each of the other five reactions will be appropriate in different situations.

There will be times when you should change your own behaviour, and other times when the only sensible thing to do to preserve your career and your sanity is to move on. Before leaving, however, examine the other alternative responses to see whether or not the conflict can be effectively handled in a less dramatic way.

Getting atmospherics right helps to create an 'I win/You win' situation for both the individual and the organisation. Getting it wrong can cause grief and lead to casualties—just like that gulping goldfish in the polluted goldfish bowl!

STRESS AND BURNOUT

We all experience stress to greater or lesser degree, and there is a tendency to regard stress as a negative force as it seems to be the cause of so many problems, both personal and professional. If not handled properly, stress can stunt career growth and development, but it can also be a very positive force in our lives, spurring us on to greater achievements.

The problem arises when the stress becomes excessive, or our ability to deal with it is limited. People differ in their opinion of what might be a stressful situation, as what produces stress in one person may not affect another at all. Stress is a very subjective thing, depending on the individual's capacity to 'roll with the punches', the work load taken on, the tendency to worry about things in general, or how much is expected of you.

Some people are able to cope with a great amount of stress and use it in a positive way as a motivator to achieve at a high level. However, prolonged exposure to stress in the work situation, coupled with an inability to deal with it, produces the occupational condition commonly known as 'burnout'.

Burnout has been described as exhaustion and cynicism that develops after repeated exposure to people in an intense, involved, stress-producing way, for a prolonged period of time.

How can you recognise whether you, a partner, a friend or co-executive is suffering from burnout? Symptoms will vary depending on the person's individual response to stress and on the extent of burnout being experienced. Common symptoms include:

- ➢ irritability with others at home or at work;
- ➢ often feeling tired and lacking in energy;
- ➢ feeling a lack of purpose or direction in life, or a longing to escape;
- ➢ a loss of, or low, confidence;
- ➢ indifference to work;
- ➢ easily becoming impatient with family and friends;
- ➢ increased use of alcohol or drugs.

These symptoms, brought on by work stress, illustrate a sense of 'uncaring'. Advanced burnout victims literally stop caring about the work they do or the lives they live. They stop caring about themselves and everyone around them.

In its most advanced stage burnout causes executives to stop even going through the motions of work—they stop working altogether. This is when, if nothing has been done to solve the problem up to this point, employers are forced to take action—all too often by firing the victim. Fortunately, most burnout cases do not get to this point. The victim seeks help in time, or is forced into seeking help by a worried partner or concerned employer. Obviously, the earlier the symptoms are recognised and dealt with, the better for all concerned.

Your idiosyncrasies

What about your idiosyncrasies? Do they suggest you are stress-prone, or stress-avoiding? Read over the following statements.

- ➢ I believe that if you miss the plane there will be another one soon— no need to worry about it.
- ➢ It doesn't worry me being late for a meeting.
- ➢ I like talking about matters other than the successes I have enjoyed.
- ➢ I really relax with a game of tennis or handball, by swimming or by participating in other sports.
- ➢ I really enjoy taking a holiday and just doing nothing.
- ➢ I couldn't care less if I lose in a game, even if I am really good at it.
- ➢ I enjoy working steadily without making any fuss about it.
- ➢ I never seem to feel hostile or angry with the world.
- ➢ I lead my life so that I am hardly ever rushed.
- ➢ I never feel impatient.

Now read over the following group of statements.

> My schedule is usually crowded and I find it hard to refuse people.
> I enjoy being ahead of others, especially others who are competitive.
> When I am doing something else, such as playing squash or cards, some of the best solutions to problems at work come to me.
> I usually feel guilty if I do not make good use of my time, and it's hard for me to relax and do nothing.
> I like to talk about things that are important to me; small talk bores me.
> Rather than wade through a whole book, I prefer reading book summaries.
> What really irritates me is a slow driver ahead.
> I am a fast eater.
> When I'm talking, I tend to accent key words.
> I always walk and move rapidly.

Which group of statements sounds more like you?

If the first group, then you tend to have stress-avoiding idiosyncrasies; if the second group, stress-prone idiosyncrasies. It has been determined that stress-prone idiosyncrasies are much more likely to cause heart disease, regardless of diet, weight and even smoking patterns. Stress-avoiding idiosyncrasies enable people to handle stress better and are more conducive to good health. So check your idiosyncrasies and see where you can perhaps modify them.

Stress management

As burnout is the result of prolonged exposure to stress, it follows that burnout can be prevented or controlled by learning how to handle stress more effectively. Even those who have not reached the burnout stage will benefit from an effective stress management program, of which there are five basic elements:

> *the supportive element*: being able to talk about it with a partner or close friend, and developing a support structure;
> *the physical element*: taking exercise regularly, reviewing diet, ensuring periods of relaxation, having a health checkup annually;
> *the behavioural element*: resolving conflicts, reviewing your behaviour, reordering your values;
> *the spiritual element*: prayer or meditation, confronting aging of self or family members and in some cases illness or even death,

developing a philosophy of life—What's it all about? Why am I here? What's my reason for being?

➤ *the organisational element*: identifying causes of stress, using group problem solving, improving work and home environment, managing time more effectively, allowing time for leisure pursuits.

TALENT MANAGEMENT

Research shows that the attraction and retention of key people is a growing issue which may become a key factor for companies competing successfully in the marketplace. Why do high performers leave?

> They feel underchallenged or undervalued; they see little opportunity for advancement; they do not receive enough recognition; they experience conflict; they are dissatisfied with their roles; they seek greater remuneration and benefits; they experience undue work pressure; they feel their worklife is out of balance; they get poached.

While organisations endeavour to address such issues and try to apply golden handcuffs to key people, this does not seem to be having the desired effect and the situation is deteriorating. The solution, in fact, starts with raising *talent management* to a boiling organisational imperative. This has to be the mindset, starting at the top.

Flowing from this is the relentless development of top talent—for example, placing people in new roles before they are ready; providing great feedback; recognising and attending to the size and scale of the retention problem by appointing 'talent-minders'; managing the unsatisfactory performers out; and, most importantly, providing coaching for continuing personal development and sense of career direction and attainment—an 'intrinsic' reward, generating the desired effect of *'If I'm developing, I'll stay'; 'If I can achieve my career goals here, I'll stay'.*

Case Study

A technically and functionally gifted executive missed a promotion because of poorly developed leadership skills. It was feared he might leave. A process combining executive coaching and career consulting turned around his people skills and enabled him to realign his career with the company, where he continues to be a first-class contributor with a good future ahead of him.

Coaching is particularly important when key people are appointed to new roles or hired externally. It can hasten them up the learning curve to success and win their early loyalty, by addressing a range of critical success factors we have identified from our research and experience relating to the assimilation of newly appointed executives. Coaching is also particularly important when the organisation is going through major change, including restructures and mergers. At such times external forces, including search companies, start raising doubts in the minds of the talent they target. They suggest greener pastures externally in place of organisational 'instability'—and the talent often gets poached.

Whenever coaching is offered—whether for personal development and/or career alignment with the organisation—it is, in effect, a statement that the organisation cares and that 'you are important to us'. As an extension of existing line management and human resources processes, it represents a powerful strategy for greater talent retention.

But, first, how great is the problem in your own organisation? Is it a growing problem? Why not review it? Quantify the costs of not attending further to talent retention, along with the financial benefits of so doing, and this may represent the start of an era that turns talent retention into a truly competitive advantage, rather than the threat that many organisations foresee.

Why talent management?

'Our number one problem is hiring, training and retaining employees', says the chief executive of an information technology and telecommunications company.

'We find it hard to attract highly talented people and we experience the loss of high performers, often to the competition', says the managing director of a major international corporation.

Time and again I hear such remarks and the situation appears to be deteriorating. There seems to be a severe and worsening shortage of available key people, and in many industry sectors and job functions a war is looming for talent that will probably become a key factor for organisations competing successfully in the marketplace.

In my experience, most companies are not well prepared to tackle this growing critical problem area, and even the apparently best-run companies are highly vulnerable. They seem to pay insufficient attention to the human factor, and continue to lead and manage their key people more like physical assets than human assets.

When you consider the costs of losing and replacing key people, it's really surprising that more executives do not pay greater attention to the subject of talent management. But then these costs often go unrecognised, as many financial management and reporting systems capture and categorise them inadequately.

First, there are the direct costs. These include the wasted training and development investment in the leaver, potentially to a competitor's advantage. Then there's the search or recruitment fee for the replacement and the costs associated with the six to twelve months' assimilation period of the new hire getting up to speed—some not making it, with the heavy associated induction turnover costs. And then there's the financial impact on business results during this whole process.

But it does not end there. The range of indirect costs during this process include: the impact on morale and productivity of co-workers; the potential decline in sustained customer contact, relationships and service; the potential decline in quality; the potential impact on management succession; and the potential loss of competitive edge.

The all-up cost? About twelve months' gross compensation per leaver, if not considerably more! Extrapolated, taking a population of say 200 key people, with average gross compensation costs of $100 000, at 20% turnover, this equates four million dollars annually!

Causes of the talent management problem

Now that I have your attention, what are the causes of the loss of talent?

Well, we have in Australia a strong economy, set to rebound. The demand for talented key people will keep growing. The supply is starting to decline because of the '13/17 factor': a projected 13–17% reduction in people in their mid-thirties to mid-forties over the next 13–17 years.

Compounding this, leaders and managers still display an orientation towards *results* only. People come second. How long is it going to take before they realise that optimal results come from putting *people* first. The age-old definition of managing is 'getting superior results through other people'. Why, after so long, is this still merely espoused in so many organisations, rather than put into action?

If you are an executive, manager or leader reading this, remember that *your key people deliver your results*. Optimal results will come about only if you treat your key people like valuable assets, and assets need to be continually maintained and developed in order to maximise ongoing returns from and through them.

And then there are the problems associated with the larger organisation. A more complicated economy and company structure needs talent with advanced capabilities in international business, ability to lead in a multicultural environment, literacy in information technology and telecommunications and outward-focused entrepreneurial competence.

It does not stop there. Executives need to be able to operate in wider, flatter spans of control where the number of direct reports, matrix reporting and communication lines are increasing. This places increased stress and strain on middle management positions particularly when higher standards are imposed from above—increased responsibility for making decisions, wider spans of control and higher performance hurdles generally; together with tougher requirements for leading and managing—more direct reports, continuous shedding of staff, and higher expectations for technical know-how in order to understand, monitor and add value to what's going on at operational levels.

Clearly, middle management roles—squeezed from above and below—are causing increased pressure for job holders, who themselves need ongoing maintenance and development. All too often, they appear not to get these from their line managers.

The problems and opportunities of size

There are more large-company problems! The growth in the availability of capital and more efficient financial markets have seen the advent of many smaller, faster-growth companies led by entrepreneurs, who depend for their success on the same motivated talent needed by larger companies. That motivated talent can find the smaller, fleeter-footed companies more attractive places to work.

Why? Well, the job offer may be very different, very attractive and certainly very challenging! For example, there are fewer risks that a big established company will fail; nothing is guaranteed with the entrepreneurial outfit.

Big established company employees are beginning to realise that their employer may no longer offer predictability in career paths. The entrepreneur places no value on predicting career paths at all—'You can add value wherever you can contribute, provided it's what we need and where we are headed. That will build your career. But we won't even try to predict it!'.

Case Study

A financial expert became dissatisfied with being 'pigeon-holed' as such, and was at risk of leaving the company. Through career consulting he was able to assess the transferability of his interests and capabilities into other functional areas. By demonstrating this potential he was able to move to a strategic marketing role within the company, where he has since excelled and developed his career.

In the big established company it is often difficult to be seen and recognised by top management unless you do well in a high-impact, high-visibility project or area of the company. In a smaller, entrepreneurial environment, everyone knows who is making the major contributions.

Big established companies tend to offer high base salaries, and staff may become eligible for options. In entrepreneurial and many smaller companies, you *can* become seriously rich—but only if the company succeeds!

In big established companies, management can be bureaucratic and even micro-managing. In entrepreneurial or smaller environments, management is usually far more freewheeling and hands-off.

And so the job offer in smaller and more entrepreneurial companies can be very enticing to the same talent that larger, more established organisations are finding harder to attract and retain.

Much of my work is with larger organisations, although entrepreneurial and smaller environments are also beginning to understand and reap the returns to be achieved from executive coaching and mentoring. Larger established company executives often ask how to offset the attraction and retention of talent challenge from the smaller and/or more entrepreneurial company.

Well, if you think about it, the larger more established environment offers many benefits. The size and scale of an individual's impact can be far larger. There is often a ready-made and greater depth and breadth of human resources for the purposes of developing into new areas of business endeavour, and the capital resource base is stronger to support such endeavours. The larger more established organisational environment usually offers a greater choice of experiences for the purposes of career development. Yes, the larger more established organisation *can* compete successfully for talent by understanding, promoting and using these competitive hiring and retention differentiators.

Why do high performers leave?

Why do high performers leave their companies? They feel they are inappropriately valued. They see insufficient opportunities for career development. They feel their work is insufficiently recognised. They do not see eye-to-eye with their line manager. They find many elements of their job dissatisfying or their organisation or work area lacking strategic vision or sense of purpose. They feel they are underrewarded in terms of salary or benefits.

Companies recognise much of this and try to respond accordingly: better remuneration, more responsibility, more recognition, more development and training, better-defined career development prospects and potential pathways, more flexible work arrangements, and more facilities at work (child day care, gym and so forth).

But for many organisations these attempts still seem not to have the desired effect. The symptoms may be addressed but the root-cause problems (and opportunities) often go unattended. And they need to be attended to from the top. Unless talent management ascends the list of strategic priorities and becomes a serious organisational imperative, the problems will remain largely unresolved and the opportunities unrealised.

Talent management strategies

Key people need personal attention, regularly. And to attract and retain key people, the organisation needs to design and develop great employment propositions—in other words, reasons for the bright, hard-working and ambitious person to want to come and work for you rather than for the leading or fastest-growing company in your sector.

Talent management requires top people being directly involved in the hiring of key staff, in raising the hurdle heights for performance, in being more explicit about expectations for results, in monitoring, in feedback and in performance coaching.

Explicitness is required at performance reviews; executives and managers really need to 'say it loud, and say it as it is' rather than tell the full story or complain to others after the performance review meeting.

And, in all of this, people at the top of organisations need to be very clear as to who are the *wealth developers, wealth sustainers, wealth investors* and *wealth eroders* (Chart 5.4).

The *wealth developers* are those who move with the flow and change with the times, whose performance is continually improving, who are seen as stars in their ascendancy and who may be seen as successors to senior management, provided they are seen to have development potential (not just outstanding performance in their current roles).

The *wealth sustainers* are those who are hot on the heels of the wealth developers, displaying sufficient resilience to cope with the vagaries of organisational life and its ever-increasing requirements for improved performance.

The *wealth investors* are those who have some way to go before becoming real assets, but who appear to offer the organisation potential. These individuals are important targets for encouragement, development and training to realise this potential. Perhaps they should be called investees, but they too are investing in their futures!

And then we have the *wealth eroders*. They appear not to be able to keep

CHART 5.4   Wealth contributors

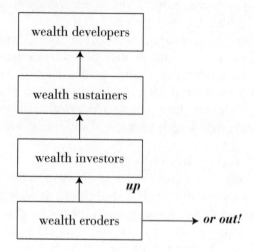

pace with change and, even though their performance may be seen to be adequate, it's often a real struggle to keep up. The investment in development and training here may be questionable, as the returns will likely be suboptimal.

And so, when it comes to segmenting the employee pool according to their capacity to develop or erode wealth, the bottom line in talent management is to focus on wealth developers, nurture wealth sustainers, develop wealth investors, and manage wealth eroders up or out via appropriate performance management processes.

Why manage them out? Well, measure the impact of a 10–20% below-par performance on co-workers, direct reports, teams and budgets. The bottom line impact can be huge and adverse. When managing out the wealth eroders, make sure it is undertaken on a voluntary basis rather than in the form of a dismissal. Executive coaching and career consulting can assist in this.

But if you see no way other than to fire the wealth eroders—and there are many other ways—be prepared to accept and suffer the consequences. The termination costs for senior people can often be 6–18 months' gross remuneration.

The role of company image
Why would a talented person want to work with your organisation? There are two main drivers: the first is your company's image as an employer; the second relates more to the work environment. Underpinning each of

these drivers, of course, is appropriate and competitive salary and benefits.

The first driver, company image, has to start with a thorough understanding of the types of people who are attracted to your organisation, and who tend to remain longer and be more motivated and productive.

Are they those who seek to attain career development opportunities in an environment perceived as successful? Are they those who are in it mainly for the money? Are they those who identify with the more intrinsic elements of what the company is trying to achieve and the challenges so created? Or are they those who are more interested in whole-life balance and who need flexibility in their work arrangements in order to accomplish this?

Organisations that are successful in talent management have identified the specific types of people they need to attract and retain for their specific family of jobs. Organisations that are less successful in talent management have simply not worked this out and take a shotgun approach to hiring and managing talent. The bottom line here is to work out who you are aiming for in terms of recruitment and retention, and to develop the company image as an employer accordingly.

The role of the work environment

Turning to the second driver, the work environment, the following factors can have a major impact on attracting and retaining motivated talent.

First, allow talented people more 'room to breathe' in their jobs. Out with micro-management and the 'controllersaurus' and in with breadth of role and scope of responsibility! Second, allow talent to grow in terms of decision-making responsibility and functional, technical or managerial leadership.

Next, don't overinvolve them in work that does not directly relate to the results they seek to generate, the results they have been hired to achieve and for which they are being paid. Also, talented people often want a job role that creates challenge and 'stretch' but does not defeat them.

Other important ingredients for ensuring that the work environment attracts and retains talent are variety and innovation—something new to work on, often—and 'great' co-workers, be they line managers, peers or direct reports. Successful people breed other successful people, and help an organisation to retain them.

No talent management process is complete without the talent having a comprehensive self-development program. Responsibility for the design, update and continuous pursuit of this program is theirs; it is yours if you are their line manager.

Ideally, self-development programs help the talent articulate and pursue the following aims:

> In the longer term, I seek to attain the following career objectives.
> In terms of self-development to attain these objectives, the following represent my priorities.
> I will seek to meet these self-development needs in the following ways and time frames.
> In the shorter term, I seek to attain the following job opportunities and subsequent career progress.
> In terms of self-development to attain these opportunities and progress, the following represent my priorities.
> I will seek to meet these self-development needs in the following ways and time frames.

However, the talent should not automatically assume that moving *up* the organisation to higher-level positions is the 'be-all-and-end-all' of self-development. They need also to be encouraged to consider 'central' and 'sideways' options.

A move centrally means expanding the professional boundaries of the existing job, thereby increasing a person's value to the organisation and becoming perceived as a greater 'centre of excellence'; with this central expansion often comes additional influence and even power. Talent should not underestimate the potential for central expansion!

A sideways move, offering new responsibilities, may be just what some talent need to meet their goals. It may not be possible to move upwards at the present time—this may have to be a longer-term objective. Upward promotion is always a tough proposition in today's smaller, flatter organisations.

A sideways move usually means a transfer to another area, to take up a position at the same level as the present one. This may be a viable option where the individual feels better suited to another functional or geographical area or department.

Turning to the role of compensation in all of this, the golden rule is that *money rarely motivates*, but it dissatisfies if it is inadequate. Nevertheless, it usually needs to be highly competitive and ideally offers opportunities for longer-term wealth generation for talent. Also, top performers need to earn considerably more than average performers, and know that this is the case. Considerably more? Try 20–30%—this may sound expensive but it's not if you work out the superb returns to be met from the extra investment.

The final ingredients relating to the work environment in the context of attracting and retaining talent encompass a highly proactive approach to talent development. This includes putting people in jobs *before* they are ready for them, treating and managing them as carefully as you would treat key customer accounts, moving wealth eroders out, and providing intrinsic rewards in the form of personalised coaching, career consulting and mentoring so that the following ethos prevails: 'If I'm developing personally, I'll stay'; 'If I can further my career here, I'll stay'.

Individual coaching input is particularly powerful with newly appointed key people to help them hasten up the learning curve and generate fast-track results. It also lessens the risks associated with induction turnover. Also, when the organisation is going through restructure, merger or major change, coaching helps people to adjust quickly if they are to be effective and timely change leaders of others, and more resistant to being poached.

In summary, the key ingredients in talent management appear to be:

> developing the organisation's image in the context of its values and culture; the fact that it is well managed, a place where exciting company challenges are pursued from a solid foundation of strong company performance and industry leadership, and where its cadre of key people represent outstanding talent.

Talent management is also about a work environment that offers freedom and autonomy, exciting challenges in its jobs, real potential for personal growth and career development, and line managers who are admired.

For many, it is also about great remuneration, differentiated according to performance, with those who perform enjoying high levels of total compensation. For others, it is about lifestyle. For others, it's about their age and stage of career and how the organisation can accommodate their career interests.

CAREER STAGES

In thinking about some of your talent, what stage of career are they at? What are the implications? How can they become more fully aligned with your organisation and make an even more valuable and motivated individual contribution, for longer?

Career strategies need different pointers at different ages. We now briefly trace the career journey from the 20-year-old to the 60-year-old, to see how young, middle-aged and senior people regard their jobs, careers

CHART 5.5   Career stages

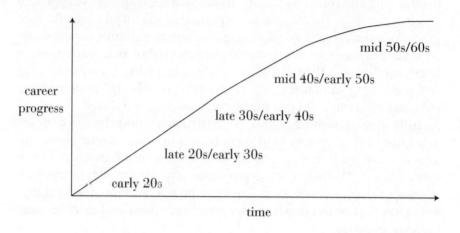

and the people they work with, and to help you assess the degree to which any of this is relevant in your own organisation.

Early twenties

Many young people today, unlike some of the 'flower children' of the 1960s, are highly ambitious and career-oriented. They pursue undergraduate and graduate degrees in droves. Many hold down jobs during the day and take courses at night to upgrade their knowledge and skills and thus further their careers. More than any other age group, people in their early twenties are anxious to get a job that will allow them to use their talents and educational background. Unfortunately, they must sometimes lower their expectations, at least to start out.

People in their twenties tend to be impatient with incompetence and are disappointed with what appears to them to be a lack of professionalism and with the rigid outlook displayed by some older people at work—which may or may not be a valid opinion.

Career advice to those in this age group includes: 'Learn your job thoroughly, particularly the base (and sometimes more boring) elements, and get to understand the organisational structure in your work environment. Do your share of the dirty work, work hard, seek help when needed. Communicate, get feedback, and develop career focus and goals. Be prepared to bide your time, as it may take a while to get where you want to be. Don't job-hop, but be prepared to move on in order to gain experience elsewhere'.

Late twenties and early thirties

People in their late twenties and early thirties are on the move more than any other age group. They are determined to find positions that will propel them to success. As a result, it is not unusual to find people in this age group making two or three job changes within a ten-year period. This involves a certain degree of risk but they can afford to take such risks, at least until they hit the really heavy financial responsibilities of their forties or fifties. They are, however, more careful and deliberate about job changes than people in their twenties.

People at this career stage become impatient with a job that does not allow them to get ahead fast enough. This period is also characterised by complete career shifts as values and goals are re-examined. Many people continue their formal education at this age through full-time or part-time study. Concurrent with this, if they manage to find a satisfying and well-paying position they tend to settle down for the long haul, at least until their market worth changes drastically.

People in their late twenties and early thirties like to be creative, utilise their talents, influence the organisation's direction and work with other motivated people. The main causes of job dissatisfaction at this age are lack of support from top management, lack of direction, poor communication, organisational politics and interpersonal problems. Many in this group switch jobs if they do not like or respect their manager or top management, or if they can find a position elsewhere offering a better chance for growth and success.

Career advice to people in their late twenties or early thirties includes: 'Understand the informal network in organisations and build relationships. Delegate properly and develop yourself to be able to fill the job above yours. Develop your direct reports too. Keep your sense of humour and stay physically fit, up-to-date, decisive and honest. Make contributions and, above all, be seen to get results'.

Late thirties and early forties

Many people in their late thirties and early forties are restless and looking for a chance to move up or on in their careers. They realise that there will be fewer and fewer opportunities later. Their approach to changing jobs is more cautious as they can no longer afford to take great risks, but they still often seek positions with more money or prestige. However, people in this age group feel that they can no longer switch jobs as often as before, as potential employers may look suspiciously at job-hoppers in this age group. They realise that their work record and reputation will be on the line more than when they were younger.

Many in this group feel that it is impossible for them to move, perhaps because they lack a formal education or fear a loss of financial security. Some may have been with the same organisation for 20 years or so in a specialty field, and feel trapped. Most have become fairly competent at their work, however, and have learned how to utilise the political network to get ahead. They value good communication skills, good health, a competent staff, teamwork and the ability to give praise and recognition where it is due.

Career advice to those in their late thirties and early forties includes: 'Develop a sense of personal security by ensuring that your skills and capabilities will remain in demand. If necessary, retrain or acquire new skills. Don't lie, double-deal, stagnate or become self centred at work. Don't be opinionated or a part of the rumour mill. Don't be ruled by money. Don't spend all your time in meetings. Ensure that sufficient quality time is spent with your partner, family and close friends; watch your health and weight, and get enough exercise'.

Mid forties through early fifties

Now we come to one of the most critical periods in anyone's career, the mid forties through early fifties age group. This is the time when all your past mistakes can catch up with you, and there is little time to rectify them. If you can survive this period you will sail through to retirement, but sometimes the period of the late forties through early fifties is when, in terms of a person's career, the roof seems to be falling in.

What do people in this age group have to worry about? There is an increased chance of sudden death, through heart attack or cancer, for both themselves and their partner. There is also the fear of finding oneself out on the street owing to a merger, acquisition, restructuring or divestment. The 50-year-old finds this much more devastating than younger age groups because of their perception (often inaccurate) of the reduced chances of their being re-employed. Unemployment hits this age group especially hard, as individuals are used to a certain comfortable standard of living and cannot believe that the job is not there any more.

Their job-search skills are rusty and, even if they find a position, they often find it difficult to adjust and start all over again. Fifty-year-olds who have allowed themselves to stagnate in their jobs, who have poor performance records or problems in the areas of chemistry and fit, will obviously feel the pressure of the axe more than those who are more successful performers. But sometimes, in today's economic turbulence, the good must leave along with the bad.

Fortunately, most organisations are willing to help the displaced employee find another job through the provision of outplacement services.

But key people in their mid forties through early fifties can survive this period with a little contingency planning, alertness to what is happening around them, a commitment to keeping up to date and competent work performance and fit.

As the wave of baby boomers enters the 'Big 5' years, it is horrifying to note the report from the Australian Bureau of Statistics, saying that nearly half of them are considered too old by prospective employers. For those in their mid fifties, nearly two-thirds have been reported as being considered too old. The trend appears to be deteriorating. In 1994 one-fifth of those in their mid forties to early fifties were unemployed, compared with less than 10% in 1970.

At the executive level the situation is potentially even more serious: unemployed at 50+ *may* mean the corporate career is over. If employed, how long is it likely to last? With chief executive job tenure now some three years, the impact on those next-in-line is profound, with three to five years the likely maximum tenure in any senior executive position.

Career advice to those in their mid forties through early fifties includes: 'Further develop a sense of personal security by contingency planning. Develop and promote UMDs (Unique Marketing Differentiators) relating to your competencies and capabilities—in other words, the unique and marketable strengths that differentiate you from your competition. Your UMDs need to coincide with demands within and outside your existing organisation; they represent your points of differentiation and competitive advantage compared with others.

'Remain aware of the political climate in your organisation and adapt to changing conditions. Keep abreast of developments in your field. Develop supportive social contacts and maintain a code of ethical behaviour, not blaming others for your mistakes and not taking all the credit for successes. Plan to continue working effectively until retirement, but be prepared with a plan of action should the axe fall anyway. Finally, consider and plan second-career options of consulting, contracting, non-executive directorships for senior people and so forth; in this regard, be clear about and further develop your UMDs!'.

Mid fifties through sixties

In spite of the myths about older workers, there is no real evidence that productivity decreases with increasing age. Many people remain active and productive throughout their later years. Although individuals in the mid fifties through sixties age group may be more prone to health problems, they usually take better care of themselves than do younger individuals.

As a group, people of this age have an excellent record. If they have made it this far, they have usually proved their competence. The ability to adapt and change does not depend on age; mature people are often quite flexible, while many younger people can be set in their ways and in their expectations. There is no adverse correlation between age and work performance, and there is often a positive correlation.

Issues of concern to individuals in this age group are time management, obsolescence, fatigue, and the speed of technological change. Many are bewildered by the developments in computing and telecommunications technology, and envy younger people who seem to cope better.

Career advice to people in their mid fifties through sixties includes: 'Discuss your career and retirement intentions with your employer, asking for input or advice when needed. Start planning retirement or second-career options if you have not already done so, and consider the alternatives for part-time work. Make decisions and be ready to say 'no'. Become involved in the community. Be honest, considerate and accessible, and keep a sense of humour. Above all, stay up to date, train your direct reports, delegate, and check your performance and fit continuously'.

CAREER ALIGNMENT OF TALENT

In the career environment today we see many smaller, flatter organisations, fewer middle management positions, apparently fewer promotional opportunities and continuing organisational change. It is no wonder that staff view their future careers with uncertainty. In many cases their commitment to the organisation, let alone trust, has been eroded, with significant impact on their job performance.

However, help is now at hand! Not only can greater attention to career development provide more clarity about individuals' future, greater sense of control over their destiny and thereby improved morale, but it should also be a fundamental element of performance management. It is often the missing link, as shown in Chart 5.6.

Conventional performance management systems start with what the organisation seeks in terms of skills, competencies and aptitudes and, through performance appraisal, leads to the identification of individual training and development needs. This is primarily an organisation-centred approach to performance management, often seen in organisations today, but so often failing to take full account of the interests, values, capabili-

CHART 5.6 The missing link

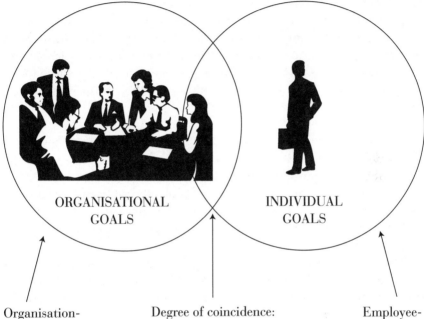

CONVENTIONAL PERFORMANCE MANAGEMENT SYSTEMS	THE OFTEN MISSING LINK
what the organisation seeks and resultant individual development needs	what the individual seeks and resultant organisational development implications

ORGANISATIONAL GOALS

INDIVIDUAL GOALS

Organisation-centred approach

Degree of coincidence: Bigger is Better!

Employee-centred approach

ties and preferences of the individual. By contrast, the *employee-centred approach*, often the missing link in performance management systems, takes great account of what the individual seeks, leading to implications for organisational development, training and management succession.

When both approaches are applied in an organisation, a greater degree of 'coincidence' exists between organisational and individual goals, leading to enhanced organisational and individual performance. Naturally, the greater the degree of coincidence the better. As executives and managers, what are we trying to achieve through greater career alignment?

First, we are trying to attain improved morale and sense of personal control and destiny by each individual. Second, we are seeking improved job performance and individual 'value' to the organisation in the case of each employee. Next, we are trying to redefine career progress—central progress (expanding the existing job) and horizontal progress (job rotation at the same level) as well as vertical progress (promotion), as the potential for the last of these is much reduced in many organisations.

Finally, by concentrating on individuals and their careers, we are trying to develop a sense of personal security in lieu of job security, or an ethos of lifetime employability, possibly with *several* employers, rather than life employment with *one* employer. We are trying to help individuals attain personal commitment to an outcome, which can include staying and progressing within the organisation (for most employees) or leaving the organisation voluntarily and developing a career elsewhere (perhaps for a small number of employees who cannot see their futures coinciding with that of the organisation).

IMPROVING TALENT MANAGEMENT

What might an organisation do to improve its talent management? First, study the real causes and demographics of talented people who leave, and talented people who stay. This knowledge should then drive further building and development of company image as an employer, and its work environment.

The outcome is likely to be a fair and flexible culture that helps make motivated talent want to stay, work lives that feel rich and rewarding, a sense of ongoing personal and career development potential, an open two-way communicative and collegial environment, all backed by an appropriate reward system.

The ethos must be to treat key people as though they are volunteers who do not have to come to work but who see the organisation as the type of place they *want* to go to, day after day—'A great place to work and grow!'.

But that great place to work and grow often needs to say goodbye to staff, and this is where all the other good work on talent management can come undone.

For example, I have come across many people whose dismissal—and the costs and trauma associated with it—might never have happened if some of the principles and practices in this book had been adopted. The irony is that often such 'failures' end up working very satisfactorily and effectively for the competition, or are hired back later as contractors or consultants. Also, many organisations downsize only to find that six months later they are in hiring mode again.

The anatomy of a 'firing' goes something like this. The individual's performance or fit becomes a concern and the boss perceives that 'things seem to be going a bit off the rails', without perhaps the boss or the individual really understanding the situation. Instead of talking about this in a constructive fashion, positions become polarised, two-way communication dries up, the situation goes from bad to worse, and . . . bang! . . . a dismissal is the outcome.

DISMISSAL AVOIDANCE

In addressing talent management, we need to examine dismissal avoidance strategies in more detail. To begin with, it is worth considering exactly what the more obvious reasons are for dismissals, from the employer's perspective (Chart 5.7).

Broadly speaking, employers categorise dismissals into four main groups.

CHART 5.7   Dismissal avoidance

Why dismissal?	Possible avoidance strategies
Economic	➤ natural attrition
	➤ salary freeze
	➤ lower base salary, higher incentive
	➤ shares offsetting pay cuts
	➤ early retirement
	➤ part-time work
	➤ job sharing
	➤ leave of absence
	➤ 'encouraged' holiday leave
	➤ study leave
	➤ secondments
	➤ voluntary redundancy
Capability	➤ internal redeployment
Self-motivation	➤ resignation
Not fitting in	➤ term contracts
	➤ performance appraisal
	➤ square-peg-in-round-hole counselling
	➤ mid-career counselling

> *Economic.* In the recession of the early 1990s in Australia, and in the economic 'correction' in the first half of 2000, while largely undifferentiated organisations continued to try to compete on the basis of low cost, staff at all levels became the target of an unprecedented volume of retrenchments. This has been exacerbated by international organisations seeking low-cost production and management, wherever this takes them worldwide. Economic rationalisation will continue into the foreseeable future for large and small organisations alike, as low cost continues for many to be the main competitive thrust. Genuine differentiation remains an elusive competitive concept for many companies.

> *Capability.* This relates to whether or not an employee has the necessary experience, competencies and, in some cases, qualifications to do the job. If the base capability is not there, the tenure of the employee is at extreme risk.

> *Self-motivation.* Capability is one thing, but putting into practice what you can do depends on the level of self-motivation through job fit and the degree to which the atmospherics of the organisation attend to the motivational needs of the individual.

> *Not fitting in.* If an executive or manager has difficulty with an employee who seems to have a personal chemistry or fit problem with the people and the organisation, then a replacement is usually sought rather than time and effort spent in trying to resolve the problem. One reason for this is that not many senior people are equipped with the necessary skills to deal with personal chemistry and fit problems.

However, the economic justification for firing 'misfits' has always been, and remains, highly doubtful, given all the costs associated with it. And, from a risk management perspective, how can you guarantee that a costly replacement will perform any better, particularly when you consider the inadequacies inherent in most hiring and selection procedures?

Dismissal for economic reasons

When considering alternatives to dismissals for economic reasons, natural attrition, or natural labour turnover, can be a very cost-effective approach to head-count reduction. This cost effectiveness comes from not having to pay separation packages, as a result of resignation rather than dismissal. This approach helps to minimise the trauma associated with dismissal which can be experienced not only by departees but also by the senior executives who have to dismiss them and the remaining executives, managers and staff who wonder when the axe may be wielded in their own direction. This takes their eyes off the job, affects their morale and self-motivation, and results in lost productivity and impaired job performance.

However, natural attrition may also have some drawbacks. The wrong staff (talent) may decide to leave. Better-performing employees are more readily employable elsewhere than those of less potential, who find it harder to secure alternative employment. At times of organisational difficulty or uncertainty, it is very often the talent that moves on first.

Also, people may move on of their own accord at the wrong time. With the rate and pace of change in the external environment creating the need for head-count reductions, savings are often needed fast—or so it seems to the board of directors and CEO. Waiting for natural attrition may just take too long for them. However, if they really did their sums and worked out the full costs of separation, lost motivation and productivity, and potentially adverse public and customer image at the time of major downsizings, they might be surprised to find that natural attrition can actually be a more cost-effective strategy.

But there is often more than meets the eye! Over the years many organisations have experienced the dreaded salary bracket creep, when salary bands at various levels—often fuelled by overzealous search and recruitment consultants whose fees are based on percentage of salary—have soared skywards, particularly costly at senior staff level. The savings resulting from removing, say, ten staff members, each with total annual compensation costs of $75 000, and not replacing them (relying instead on a flattening of the organisation structure and redistribution of their job content), is $750 000 annually. Very tempting, even if the costs of removing them are high.

However, this may not be as cost-effective as it may first appear. After such dismissals the new organisational structure can take a long time to recover, refire and really benefit from the savings. No wonder some dismissed staff members find themselves back at the organisation working on contract to help make this happen.

An alternative way to effect such savings, but at a reduced initial level, is to freeze the salaries of the employees in question, and even reduce their salaries following appropriate notice periods (having checked out the legal implications). But an across-the-board salary freeze or reduction may cause the talent to leave, and can damage morale and productivity over the longer term. Selective salary freezes or reductions may also be difficult to implement, but need to be considered as options.

The extent of this potential damage depends on how affected staff are managed at the time they are told about the change to their salary arrangements, and afterwards. For example, if they have been paid 'well over the top' as a result of salary bracket creep, they are probably earning well over the external market rate. This can be confirmed by compensation specialists, recruiters and career consultants, to whom access by affected staff should be encouraged, to check this out independently.

Other forms of pay cuts can also be used—for example, decreasing the base remuneration and increasing the incentive element which can be based on both organisational performance and personal results. Or pay cuts can be made in return for shares in the company.

Other strategies as alternatives to dismissal for economic reasons include early retirement, part-time work, job sharing, leave of absence, 'encouraged' holiday leave, study leave, secondments to other organisations and voluntary redundancy.

➢ *Early retirement and part-time work.* Offering incentives for early retirement can often be more cost-effective than dismissals, as can an offer to move to part-time work. There are many staff, perhaps in their fifties, who have a partner working full- or part-time, whose children are working and who have perhaps inherited some family assets. Such people might leap at the chance to work four or even three days per week, or seriously consider the early retirement option. Retirement counselling of the type offered by career consultants often facilitates this option.

➢ *Job sharing.* Taking the part-time strategy on a broader basis may create the opportunity for some jobs to be shared effectively. Job sharing will certainly not fit all organisations but may be suitable for the larger organisation with sizeable and homogeneous staff groups.

➢ *Leave of absence.* Leave of absence can also be offered, for study leave or a sabbatical. When offered in one company I recall, employees retained their benefits, received government unemployment payment and were 'rehired' when the fortunes of the company improved and they were needed again.

➢ *'Encouraged' holiday leave.* When business is slow, this may be the best time to encourage the taking of holiday leave.

➢ *Secondment.* Another approach is secondment to suppliers and customers, sometimes on a salary-sharing basis between the two companies. This offers the seconded employee the opportunity to develop new skills and understand more clearly the operations and needs of companies in the supply and distribution chain.

➤ *Voluntary redundancy.* The voluntary redundancy option offers humane, dignified and sensitive treatment to those affected, and can be offered across the board or selectively. Across-the-board offers for voluntary redundancy may mean that the best employees—those more readily employable elsewhere—put their hands up and leave, denuding the organisation of talent.

Selective voluntary redundancy may take several forms: one approach targets specific employees or areas of the organisation; another method involves a broader invitation for expressions of interest in voluntary redundancy with no guarantee it will be granted in every case. Selective offers may backfire, however, when those wishing to leave are asked to stay and therefore feel penalised.

The story can go like this: 'You mean to tell me that you are letting others go, with golden handshakes, who really have not performed well over the years, whereas in my case, and I'll remind you that all my performance appraisals have been rated "excellent", my reward is that I don't get a golden handshake and I have to stay and work even harder as a result of fewer people remaining in the organisation . . . this is totally unfair!'. Morale and performance can be adversely affected in such cases. Some companies have risk-managed these situations successfully by granting loyalty bonuses to key staff after restructuring when the organisation refires and attains new target levels of performance.

Despite the risks, voluntary redundancy has its place if carefully and sensitively planned and implemented, and has many advantages in the contexts of dismissal avoidance and enhancing sought-after employer status in the community.

Case Study

I was once called in to provide career counselling to an employee who had been led to believe, for six months, that his request for voluntary redundancy would be accepted; at the eleventh hour he found his request rejected. His reaction was to go on stress leave for two weeks and a resolve, on returning to work, to do the barest minimum 9.00 am to 5.00 pm, with the objective of triggering an involuntary redundancy at best, or a better worklife/homelife balance at the very least! Even a small loyalty bonus might have eased this situation—and, of course, he should never have been led to believe his request for voluntary redundancy would be granted in the first place.

In summary, because of the devastation that layoffs create, corporations should consider the range of alternatives. When layoffs are unavoidable, I have found that advance notification, severance pay, extended benefits, retraining programs, career coaching and outplacement counselling help employees the most, and also benefit the company.

Dismissal for other reasons

When considering alternatives to dismissals for reasons of capability, motivation and 'not fitting in', there is a range of alternatives: internal redeployment, allowing resignation rather than dismissal, term contracts, proper use of performance appraisal processes, performance improvement programs, 'square-peg-in-round-hole' counselling and mid-career counselling. Remember to get legal counsel first, as appropriate!

Internal redeployment is a humane and sensitive approach that may be very appropriate in many instances; invariably, it is preferable to dismissal. These instances can include:

➤ when the atmospherics in a certain part of the organisation do not attend to the motivational needs of the individual, whether those needs are material, structural, behavioural or emotional;
➤ when the individual exhibits leadership traits that are considered more desirable and relevant in other parts of the organisation;
➤ when the individual possesses a style that will add greater value to a team elsewhere in the organisation; the individual is perhaps too much of a clone in the existing team, or diametrically opposed to the current team leader in terms of operating style;
➤ where current job fit is poor—the interests, values and motivational capabilities of the individual are not represented in the current job;
➤ where career alignment is poor—where an individual's career path aspirations are better met by working elsewhere in the organisation;
➤ where the individual operates in a staff management capacity when a more functional or technical capacity may better suit the individual's strengths, or vice versa.

However, in reality, there may be limited opportunities for internal redeployment, as comparable level jobs may simply not be available (comparability means with the salary of the former job, at a reasonably nearby location and requiring a comparable skill-set), meaning that the potential internal redeployee may well be eligible for a separation package instead of being redeployed.

A major danger inherent in internal redeployment is the 'dead-wood transfer' syndrome, where an individual who is perceived to have poor capability, motivation or ability to fit in is transferred to another area of the organisation as a problem for someone else to manage!

Allowing an individual to resign rather than be dismissed may enhance self-esteem and dignity on the part of the departee, albeit somewhat superficially. For some departees, it is what others perceive that is important to them, and they may feel far better if they can be perceived as having resigned rather than as having been dismissed. From a re-employment perspective, a credible resignation is also better than a dismissal, but the emphasis has to be on the word 'credible'.

However, encouraging someone to resign rather than be dismissed may be fraught with legal dangers and can lead to cases of constructive dismissal and large payouts. A strategy to offset these risks is first to communicate to the individual at the termination interview that it is 'all over' and that the individual has to move on, career-wise.

Second, when it seems apparent the individual has accepted this information (be this at the first or a subsequent meeting) after a sufficient pause in the conversation to allow the dismissal message to sink in, ask how the individual would like this information communicated to other parties within and outside the organisation. Invariably, the conversation comes round to the concept of the departure being communicated as a resignation to other people, although the departee needs to understand clearly that this option is offered purely on the basis of meeting the best interests of the individual, and that the official behind-the-scenes line remains that of the organisation terminating the individual's employment.

It might be unwise to offer this option, however, if the performance of the individual has been very poor and is recognised by employees or customers as such. Under these circumstances, if a 'resignation' is allowed, there is a danger that management may be seen as lacking intestinal fortitude and going for the soft option.

Term contracts are becoming more popular in both public and private sectors, the term usually being between one and five years, although three years is often used. Such contracts offer the potential for non-renewal if the employing organisation is less than inspired by the performance of the contractee, and thus provide a cost-effective exit route and an incentive for the individual to perform if seeking contract renewal.

However, term contracts may not always seem attractive to potential new hires, who may favour the permanent employment option. The length of their terms can also pose problems if they underperform. Finally, payout arrangements can prove costly if the organisation needs to effect a termination prior to contract expiry.

Formal performance appraisal processes as noted earlier are rarely correctly used. The paperwork associated with them is often used subjectively. When performance is assessed at being below satisfactory, this is often inadequately communicated to the appraisee. Individual development needs and plans are often poorly defined. If unsatisfactory performance is the case, formal warnings and supporting information are rarely recorded.

A more objective use of performance appraisals, with identification of development needs and attention to them, offers a real alternative to dismissal, through rectification of performance problems before it becomes too late. The correct application of formal warnings in extreme and adverse cases is also advisable. The advantages of using these processes correctly include:

➤ the individual being appraised knows exactly what is expected;
➤ appraisees have time and organisational support to develop their personal performance;
➤ they have early warning of potential outcomes if unable or unwilling to develop;
➤ they can 'shape up' or 'ship out'—shipping out more often than not on a voluntary basis, usually knowing when the time will be for this to happen, and with time to seek alternative employment.

However, until the executives and managers involved in the performance appraisal process are adequately trained in performance improvement counselling and coaching, buy ownership of the need for it and are prepared to invest the time, it is unlikely that the full benefits of performance appraisal will be realised.

Such is the case with *performance improvement programs* which can usefully be applied following an unsatisfactory performance appraisal, as noted earlier.

'Square-peg-in-round-hole' counselling applies to those individuals who seem to be in the wrong job or somehow misaligned, with an adverse impact on attitude, morale or performance. It is also used when internal efforts to improve performance or fit issues have been exhausted and dismissal is a real possibility. The orientation for such counselling can be 'career management' when an individual's career is perceived to be in crisis and there is a need, somehow, to rekindle their motivational fires to optimise their contribution to the organisation. This is an important role for the career coach.

Case Study

An executive found herself in a role that failed to meet her motivational needs: she needed more autonomy than her rather conservative CEO would allow. Considered talent, she was offered job alternatives but it became apparent that she saw the CEO as a 'road-block'. Through career coaching she determined the time was opportune to leave the company and take a new career direction—far better than remain and allow her motivation to wane futher and performance potentially to deteriorate.

Mid-career counselling by an external specialist can also be useful applied at that critical mid-career period for people in their early or mid forties. Frequently, I find such individuals promoted beyond their capabilities, in performance plateau, experiencing chemistry and fit problems or indeed in mid-life crisis.

Whatever the cause, the notion of saving a valuable asset, where up to $1 million may have been invested in the development and training of, say, a 25-year-service employee, makes sound business sense. Such counselling can be difficult to accomplish internally because performance and fit issues are sensitive topics, particularly with senior, long-service, mature executives or managers. The problems can be exacerbated by underdeveloped communication and counselling skills, or insufficient time on the part of the senior executive who has to conduct the counselling.

THE ROLE OF CAREER COACHING IN TALENT MANAGEMENT

Career coaching exercises, whether with a square-peg or mid-career orientation, usually commence with a consultant undertaking familiarisation and a preliminary assessment with the line manager responsible for the problem individual, with a human resources executive also present. Symptoms and problems are addressed, the individual's career is reviewed and a strategy for introducing the external third party is developed jointly, in the context that the problem person needs to be in agreement and buy ownership of the career management program.

Once the program has been initiated, the early elements include self-assessment by the individual, with a personal, job and career focus. This can be complemented by confidential interviews with the individual's superior, peers, direct reports and sometimes customers, all with a job performance and future career options orientation. Fit issues, if they exist, are usually uncovered in this interview process, as are any other problems.

The desired outcome is to reach agreement with the individual regarding perceived problems and potential solutions. This may entail clarifying any ambiguities or uncertainties; improving understanding of, and communication with, others in the organisation; and identifying other development needs and appropriate resources, whether for technical, functional, management or personal development.

Career coaching programs of this nature culminate in action planning and implementation. Action planning involves a mutually agreed development program using the organisation's internal development and training resources wherever possible. Implementation of this is the responsibility of the individual, the line manager and the human resources representative—in other words, a shared responsibility—with the external career coach appearing periodically for progress reviews and always available for hot-line advice. At senior levels, the coach can continue to be used effectively for ongoing coaching in the key development areas ascribed.

The bottom line of such career coaching programs is to achieve some sort of outcome, whether improved performance or fit in the present job, modifications to the present job or reporting relationships, or successful redeployment within or outside the organisation—this last outcome via resignation or joint agreement rather than straight dismissal.

THE MAIN OPPORTUNITY

Apart from the fact that all these courses of action help organisations to manage their talent and avoid dismissals, they enable direct financial savings related to separation packages, recruitment fees, and new employee induction and assimilation.

However, the main opportunity for executives and managers deploying appropriate talent management strategies (including dismissal avoidance) is a high level of morale and performance, the further development of sought-after employer status by the organisation, and the attraction, retention and development of talented employees. This is the real opportunity. There is absolutely no reason why executives and managers cannot, and should not, prioritise talent management and dismissal avoidance principles and practices in their business operations. For those that do, the benefits are enormous.

Ask yourself the following question: 'Who are more important, customers or employees?'. Your answer initially may be customers, but without motivated, productive staff how can customer needs be fully met? The answer has to be both *customers and employees—equal in importance.*

ROB BALMER ON ENERGISING

Working through this 'Energising' module with my team, a common thread emerged when we sat down to determine our individual atmospheric needs. Almost every one of us rated as only 'average' the degree to which our atmospheric needs were being met within the organisation. I found this stunning! When I investigated further, I was amazed to find that the reason for this was the almost unanimous belief that other individuals, both within our division and from other departments, were having a huge energy-sapping effect.

Why were these people sapping our energy? We discussed it as a group and followed up with some more detailed analysis, and determined that the productivity of our entire division was being negatively affected by 30–40% due to the extra work caused by 'wealth eroders'. The cost of this poor productivity to the organisation could have been millions of dollars over time, but the cost to the energy level of my staff was perhaps of even greater significance to them and to me as we confronted the issue.

We collectively defined wealth eroders as being those individuals who were simply not doing the job they were hired to do, or who were having a significant negative impact on those around them in the process of doing their job. We were careful to ensure that we did not unfairly identify people as wealth eroders when the real problem was the processes they were forced to comply with. It came down to the fact that there were a few 'rotten apples', as we saw it, who were messing things up for many people around them.

How is it that these people are still around in the organisation? And how is it that just about every organisation accommodates many more of these wealth eroders than it should? It seems clear to me that the reason is the same for all organisations. It is the failure to manage up or out the wealth eroders, as part of a proper talent management program, to the same degree as the wealth developers are identified and developed.

Many organisations I have come across have tremendous development programs for the achievers among them—the people Peter calls 'wealth developers'. No doubt, these programs can have a tremendous positive impact on the energy of these achievers. However, if these same organisations had programs for effectively managing up or out the wealth eroders, they would have just as great an impact (maybe even greater) on the energy levels of their wealth developers. The combined effect of moving up, or removing, the wealth eroders and clearing the way for the wealth developers would be extremely potent.

Having completed this exercise with my team, my firm belief is that it will be those organisations with the courage to effectively manage up or out their wealth eroders that will win the ever-escalating talent retention war.

LEADERSHIP MYTHS	LEADERSHIP TRUTHS
➤ Job fit is all about individuals fitting into their jobs and the organisation structure.	➤ It's equally about jobs and the organisation structure fitting individuals!
➤ Self-motivation is a given.	➤ The organisational environment can make or break self-motivation.
➤ Good talent takes care of itself.	➤ If you don't manage your talent, it may take care of itself—with another employer!
➤ Talent management is all about fast promotion.	➤ Talent management is more about their continuous development within a stimulating environment.
➤ Career management is solely the individual's responsibility.	➤ if career management is left to individuals as their own responsibility, don't be surprised if they manage their careers elsewhere!

DON'T HIDE!
- ➤ Seek and deliver strong job fit: the organisation, your people and you will all be the beneficiaries.
- ➤ If you get overly stressed, it's within your control to do something about it.
- ➤ Wealth eroders have to move up quickly, or get out.
- ➤ Confront the career stage you and your people are at, and focus on appropriate career development strategies.
- ➤ Hire-and-fire, and slash-and-burn, can be costly indulgences that any sensible leader is wise to seek to avoid.
- ➤ Put candour on the table at employee performance reviews—while the employee is still in the room.

➤ Talent management should receive at least as much attention as management of the customer base.

YOUR THURSDAY REVIEW

1. Are we maximising the energising effect of appropriate motivational delegation and effective flexible leadership?

2. As an overview, are we maximising the energising effect of individuals enjoying good job fit, a strongly motivational organisational atmosphere and our continuing attention to talent management?

3. In job fit, are we trying to ensure individuals' interests and capabilities are matched by the nature of their jobs?

4. Are we meeting the motivational needs of our people—material, structural, behavioural and emotional—through a conducive atmosphere?

5. Are people coping when their atmospheric needs are not met, or only partially met, and are we helping them to cope?

6. Are we watching out for undue stress and encouraging the adoption of effective stress management approaches?

7. Are we recognising and attending to the growing war for talent? Are we managing talent effectively, rather than letting it sink or swim, realising that this greatly enhances our chances of both attracting and retaining talent?

8. Are we creating an environment where talent can develop continuously, quickly moving the wealth eroders up or out?

9. Are we addressing satisfactorily the roles of company image, of the work environment, of career management and alignment and of dismissal avoidance, in the context of all these criteria underpinning successful talent management?

10. Does talent management receive at least as much attention as management of the customer base?

CHAPTER 6

Trusting

Trusting is about leaders walking the talk: living the vision; and continuously upholding the fundamental values of the organisation!

KEYNOTES FROM THE COMMENTATORS

You get things done through trust. If people trust you they'll give of their all. This means walking the talk of a set of core values which don't move, thereby giving your people the confidence to act.

David Hearn, Chief Executive Goodman Fielder

Living vision—living at the front line, as well as in the minds and actions of managers—has a strongly unifying effect, and if you reward people in living the vision, chances are you will attain it. Adherence to strong value sets and standards, powerfully aligned to our stakeholders (customers, employees, suppliers and shareholders), is an integral element of our performance management processes. If people don't adhere to our fundamental values, we take notice and act.

Peter Wilkinson, Chief Executive David Jones

Do we walk the talk? Not enough. It needs constant underlying affirmation and renewal before we achieve true values-based leadership. But we know when we do, we'll have motivated and talented staff who feel energised *and* have a sense of trust in one another and in the firm itself. As a junior and middle level employee, my own happiest times have been when energy and trust abound.
Meredith Hellicar, Company Director

The variable organisation is here to stay: the cycle of downsizing followed by the recruitment of new skills, and moving people quickly into areas of new challenge or opportunity—this all means that fixed structures are gone forever. The challenge is inculcating this understanding and adaptability throughout the organisation. If executives are not aggressive drivers of change towards strategic opportunities, to make their company a leader, they will be eaten by the competition.
Peter Macdonald, Chief Executive Officer James Hardie Industries

'Right and wrong are not a matter of mere taste and opinion. People have this curious idea that they ought to behave in a certain way. They know the moral law', wrote C.S. Lewis.

Take any group of people and ask them to come up with a list of values for their organisation and the lists will look very similar, even across geographic, race, religious and sociodemographic boundaries.

But often these lists become just 'shopping lists', they lose their impact and are hung on the walls of office receptions or printed in annual reports, rather than being truly lived (not just espoused) from the top of the organisation. At times of particular pressure, expediency often prevails and values fly out of the window.

SHOPPING LISTS OF VALUES

What about the following shopping list, by way of an example? It comes from the Australian Public Service.

Case Study

The Service:

- ➤ is apolitical, performing its functions in an impartial and professional manner;
- ➤ is a public service in which employment decisions are based on merit;
- ➤ provides a workplace that is free from discrimination and recognises and utilises the diversity of the Australian community it serves;
- ➤ has the highest ethical standards;
- ➤ is openly accountable for its actions, within the framework of ministerial responsibility to the Government, the Parliament and the Australian public;
- ➤ is responsive to the Government in providing frank, honest, comprehensive, accurate and timely advice and in implementing the Government's policies and programs;
- ➤ delivers services fairly, effectively, impartially and courteously to the Australian public and is sensitive to the diversity of the Australian public;
- ➤ has leadership of the highest quality;
- ➤ establishes workplace relations that value communication, consultation, cooperation and input from employees on matters that affect their workplace;
- ➤ provides a fair, flexible, safe and rewarding workplace;
- ➤ focuses on achieving results and managing performance;
- ➤ promotes equity in employment;
- ➤ provides a reasonable opportunity to all eligible members of the community to apply for APS employment;
- ➤ is a career-based service to enhance the effectiveness and cohesion of Australia's democratic system of government; and
- ➤ provides a fair system of review of decisions taken in respect of APS employees.

We are not suggesting that this list of values is ignoble or not well intended. Every item has clearly been well thought out and is meritorious. But the problem is that it's a huge shopping list and overlaps into policy and operating principles and conduct—and the *Public Service Act 1999* (Commonwealth) also includes a Code of Conduct (not shown above).

Compare the APS values with those in the Aspirations Statement of Levi Strauss & Co.

Case Study

We all want a company that our people are proud of and committed to, where all employees have an opportunity to contribute, learn, grow and advance based on merit, not politics or background. We want our people to feel respected, treated fairly, listened to, and involved. Above all, we want satisfaction from accomplishments and friendships, balanced personal and professional lives, and to have fun in our endeavours.

When we describe the kind of Levi Strauss & Co. we want in the future, what we are talking about is building on the foundation we have inherited: affirming the best of our company's traditions, closing gaps that may exist between principles and practices, and updating some of our values to reflect contemporary circumstances.

What type of leadership is necessary to make our aspirations a reality?

New behaviours. Leadership that exemplifies directness, openness to influence, commitment to the success of others, willingness to acknowledge our own contributions to problems, personal accountability, teamwork, and trust. Not only must we model these behaviours but we must coach others to adopt them.

Diversity. Leadership that values a diverse work force (age, sex, ethnic group, etc.) at all levels of the organisation, diversity in experience, and diversity in perspectives. We have committed to taking full advantage of the rich backgrounds and ability of all our people and to promoting a greater diversity in positions of influence. Differing points of view will be sought; diversity will be valued and honesty rewarded, not suppressed.

Recognition. Leadership that provides greater recognition—both financial and psychic—for individuals and teams that contribute to our success. Recognition must be given to all who contribute: those who create and innovate and also those who continually support the day-to-day business requirements.

Ethical management practices. Leadership that epitomises the stated standards of ethical behaviour. We must provide clarity about our expectations and must enforce these standards through the corporation.

Communications. Leadership that is clear about company, unit, and individual goals and performance. People must know what is expected of them and receive timely, honest feedback on their performance and career aspirations.

Empowerment. Leadership that increases the authority and responsibility of those closest to our products and customers. By actively pushing responsibility, trust, and recognition into the organisation, we can harness and release the capabilities of all our people.

Notice how Levi's shorter list of values are first fundamental and far reaching and, second, described in such a way that they are more easily internalised and lived—more easily transferred into day-to-day organisational life without restricting organisational life; in fact, they allow leaders and staff freedom to make decisions that are in the best interests of the business.

Another example of a shorter list comes from Mars Inc., the $US12 billion confectionary and food empire run by John Mars and Forest Junior, where I spent the formative years of my management and leadership upbringing. Their list is referred to as 'The Five Principles of Mars' and is fully inculcated into all Mars operations worldwide, leaders and managers really 'walking this talk'! Their values are:

> ➤ *Quality*: the consumer is our boss, quality is our work and value for money is our goal.
> ➤ *Responsibility*: as individuals, we demand total responsibility from ourselves; as associates we support the responsibilities of others.
> ➤ *Mutuality*: a mutual benefit is a shared benefit; a shared benefit will endure.
> ➤ *Efficiency*: we use resources to the full, waste nothing and do only what we can do best.
> ➤ *Freedom*: we need freedom to shape our future; we need profit to remain free.

WHERE VISION AND VALUES FIT IN

Before we go any further, where do vision and values fit into the spectrum of moral law through day-to-day organisational life? Chart 6.1 is not exhaustive in its contents but suggests where vision and values might take their place.

> ➤ *Moral law* goes back to C.S. Lewis's statement that people behave in a certain way; right and wrong is not a mere matter of taste and opinion.
> ➤ *Living vision* articulates aspirational directions and goals (and they should be short, to the point and inspirational, like front-page news).
> ➤ *Fundamental values* comprise a short list of high-level values flowing from *moral law* and supporting *living vision*, as they relate to the needed and intended core culture of the organisation.

CHART 6.1   The vision and values continuum

> ➢ *Organisational policies* flow from *living vision* and *fundamental values,* and are then converted into *operating principles* and/or *codes of conduct*—often in the form of administration manuals/intranet sites.
> ➢ *Leadership and management* are then to uphold these principles/codes in the way they lead, manage and administer the affairs of the organisation in its *day-to-day life.*

But what happens in practice?

First, vision and values statements often comprise a mixture of vision, values, policies, principles and codes that weakens their impact and understanding, causing leaders, managers and their staff either to ignore them or to 'go back to the rule-book' for guidance as to what to do in any given circumstances.

Second, leadership and management simply ignore or fail to uphold organisational vision and values in practice. This is a result of pressures to perform, expediency and/or a belief that the finely printed shopping list of vision and values on the wall of reception is there to impress customers, new recruits and stakeholders, rather than reflecting the reality of pressured organisational life at the front line.

It is my conviction that if living vision and fundamental values are limited to a few core, high-level items that are truly inculcated into the behaviour of the leadership of the organisation, then you can *almost* do away with the lower-level elements of the vision and values continuum—'Get living vision and fundamental values right, and walk them, not just talk them'—and the rest will more or less take care of themselves.

LIVING VISION AND FUNDAMENTAL VALUES

When leaders uphold living vision and fundamental values, they behave reliably and instil trust in a way that frees up the creative energies within the organisation, rather than binding people to the rule-book (see Chart 6.2).

Living vision and fundamental values, firmly implanted in the centre of the organisation and lived (not just espoused) by leaders, cause reliable behaviour in the way people are led and managed, and results are pursued, yet maximise freedom to achieve, thereby unleashing the creative energies of the organisation.

Many organisations presume that, if there are leaders, there must be followers—'The business of leadership is leading the people in the business, the followers acting accordingly and getting on with their work'. But this ethos relates more to the industrial-age paradigm of managing top-down and 'controlling the what'.

In this era of knowledge, the information age, to be truly successful executives need to emulate collaborative, facilitational 360° leadership

CHART 6.2   Living vision and fundamental values

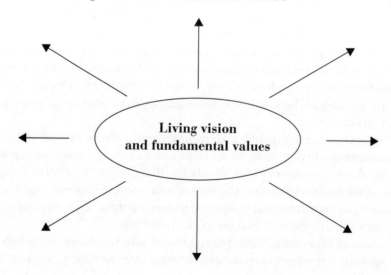

with a strong customer emphasis, and 'create the how' through and with people.

EMPLOYEES AS BUSINESS LEADERS

In redefining leadership, 'creating the how' can and should come from the front line, particularly but not exclusively at the customer interface. In other words, everyone in the organisation can and should become 'business leaders', *in their own jobs.*

The key to this is strongly held living vision and fundamental values— walked, not just talked—encouraging this to happen.

Compare the following statements:

> *Weak* vision and values create the need for more rules and controls, stifling creative energy and even encouraging employees to engage in safe pursuits—a formula for mediocrity.

> *Strong* living vision and fundamental values provide freedom to achieve, particularly if employees view themselves as business leaders in their own roles. Living vision and fundamental values, lived as well as espoused, creates reliable leadership behaviour and instils trust, giving employees confidence to go the extra mile and give of their all.

Chart 6.3 illustrates this.

There are many examples where, through strongly articulated living vision and fundamental values, employees perceive themselves, and operate, as business leaders in their own jobs, with confidence and two-way trust in their line managers:

➢ Take the case of the hotel chain where staff with heavy customer interface are given five-figure budgets to rectify customers' problems with no need to seek authorisation first. Thus, we have the CEO housekeeper, the CEO doorman and so forth!

➢ Take the case of the sizeable manufacturer where employees were shown—through Dupont-type analysis (or, in my jargon, 'primary business drivers of the profit tree')—precisely how they contributed to the bottom line. Results have since soared. What leverage, as the various business drivers are pursued by all, creating a veritable multiplier effect!

➢ Take the case of the hair salon that encourages its hair stylists to perceive themselves in the privileged role of touching people's lives,

CHART 6.3 Employees as business leaders in their own jobs

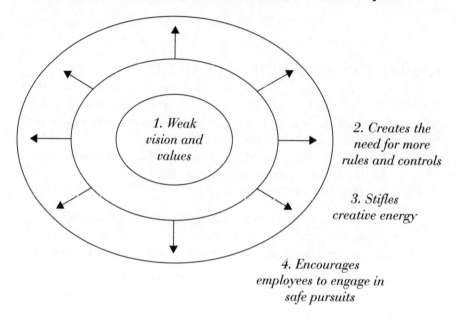

1. Weak vision and values

2. Creates the need for more rules and controls

3. Stifles creative energy

4. Encourages employees to engage in safe pursuits

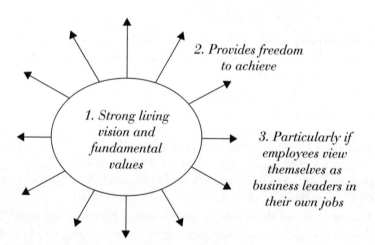

1. Strong living vision and fundamental values

2. Provides freedom to achieve

3. Particularly if employees view themselves as business leaders in their own jobs

4. Living vision and fundamental values, pursued as well as espoused, creates reliable behaviour and instils trust, giving employees confidence to give of their all from both emotional and physical perspectives, by making them look and feel better!

And we all know the impact of customer service, or lack of service, on the attraction, retention and development of customers and clients.

But none of this can be done without trust in the organisation, encouraged by the reliability of the behaviour of its executive leaders as they walk the talk of living vision and fundamental values in the pursuit of organisational goals.

And this creates both discipline and freedom: discipline, because 'I know and uphold our living vision and fundamental values'; freedom, because 'Knowing and upholding them I have freedom to act and achieve greatness as the CEO of my own job role'.

ACT AND ACHIEVE GREATNESS

As a pilot, you certainly need to have the confidence and freedom to act and achieve greatness as the CEO of your own job role. This only comes about through the way you are recruited, inducted, trained, developed and led.

I am reminded of the Royal Air Force in the UK as it was (maybe still is now) when I undertook a Flying Scholarship with them when I was sixteen. The squadron behind my training as a pilot had the fundamental values of 'Good faith, fortitude and steadfastness', supporting the living vision of 'Invincibility in the defence of the country'.

In selecting new recruits, applicants were interviewed by existing officers who had demonstrated a particular passion for this vision and these values. New recruits were inducted with an extensive emphasis on this vision and these values. They were encouraged to talk about previous experiences that were at variance with the vision and values—even if they had been at the centre of or had caused such experiences.

Initial training emphasised mutual accountability in upholding squadron vision and values—helping comrades on hugely taxing hikes and battle simulations, and in every other training event—under the watchful eyes of trainers who had been selected as trainers because of their outstanding performance, and who considered it an honour to have been chosen to conduct the training.

This meant that the whole process of hiring and induction was placed in the hands of the highest-calibre leaders. The aim was to inculcate vision and values in the lifeblood of the organisation, its new hires.

This is upside-down thinking for many organisations, which often add a session on vision and values during the induction process rather than base the whole induction process on them. For a more successful approach, the academically well-qualified trainers who run the induction course might convert their role to training exceptional company performers—particularly those with a zeal for the organisation's vision and values—to run the induction and initial training programs.

And perhaps such programs should be longer than they are, so that vision and values can be fully inculcated.

'Costly', you may say. But we see this as an investment. A top role model inducting and influencing a sizeable intake of new recruits presents an outstanding opportunity for positive human leverage, and is likely to generate substantial returns.

But initial training is just the start. Ongoing training, conferences and internal newsletters/intranet sites provide fertile ground for the reinforcement of vision and values, enhanced if the outcome of pursuing vision and values can be demonstrated in the form of accomplishments—results, customer compliments, staff who have gone 'that extra mile'.

FROM TALK TO WALK

How do we move from concept to reality in developing and implementing a living vision and fundamental values approach to maximising trust and employee effectiveness?

➤ First, where are we now? Do our executive leaders behave reliably in the way they lead, manage and behave, and consistently in terms of vision and values?

➤ Are we all acting in congruence on that spectrum and transition from industrial age to information age leadership?

➤ Do we talk about the vision and values we are trying to pursue and declare when we have failed to uphold them, as well as when we have succeeded?

➤ Do we train executive leaders, managers and others in how to pursue and uphold our vision and values? (If there are fewer living vision elements and fundamental values, derived from moral law and supporting company goals, the chances are employees will believe in them anyway, creating a fertile ground for such training.)

➤ Do we appraise and reward people according to the degree to which they uphold our vision and values as part of performance rewards?

➤ Do we ensure that major business decisions are made in the framework of vision and values, particularly but not exclusively at times of restructure, merger or downsizing, when people's livelihoods may be adversely affected? At such times are they treated fairly? Are early communications put in place and is this communication two-way?

➢ Walk the talk of vision and values in everything you do, say and tell!

In developing and implementing a living vision and fundamental values approach, where could we start in identifying and articulating what the living vision and fundamental values might be?

For vision, this will be company-specific but, for values, try using the elements of atmospheric needs in Chapter 5, on 'Energising'. They are grouped into material needs, structural needs, behavioural needs and emotional needs, representing categories of fundamental values that seem to apply across many geographic, race, religious and sociodemographic boundaries.

MORE TIPS FOR DEVELOPING TRUST

Having established living vision and fundamental values, and then walking them, not just talking them, here are some more tips for developing trust.

➢ 'Do unto others as you'd like them to do unto you!' is the one common principle across all religions.

➢ Go the extra mile in developing strong interpersonal relationships within the organisation, just as key account managers might endeavour to with their key accounts. Your colleagues and direct reports are your key accounts.

➢ Focus on the person that you're dealing with; put yourself in their shoes before committing to a course of action which affects them.

➢ Don't treat groups of people as groups—treat them as individuals. 'Don't treat me as one of a set or kind, treat me as a person!' Care for individuals, too.

➢ If you want to make money (and by now you should understand what trust has to do with making money!), lead and manage the people who make it or spend it for you—put the effort in there!

➢ Remain honourable at all times—don't rumour-monger, double-deal or talk behind people's backs.

➢ Behave like a person rather than a job title and don't be afraid to show your character, your 'signature' as a leader.

➢ Be in it for the long term with people—look at sustainable relationship development rather than seeking quick wins (some of them perhaps at other people's expense).

- ➤ Praise in public, criticise constructively in private (in person rather than in writing or by email).
- ➤ Help others to challenge their own assumptions; give them reasoning rather than conclusions; help them to make better decisions rather than simply impose your own judgments.
- ➤ Try to understand the other party first, rather than first try to be understood.
- ➤ Concentrate on always doing the right thing rather than just focusing on a specific outcome.
- ➤ Help others define problems and let them develop appropriate solutions.
- ➤ Keep your ego in check and see others at work as equals undertaking the same journey.
- ➤ Focus on others and listen twice as much as talk.
- ➤ Earn the right to provide advice, and ensure it is sought before providing it.
- ➤ Be credible: never tell lies, ever; maximise expression through body language as you communicate, with good eyeball retention; when you don't know the answer, say so; always do your homework; be relaxed; never show off; give away ideas.
- ➤ Be competent: you have to demonstrate competence in your role, producing great results; be seen as a true professional, capable on every dimension.
- ➤ Be reliable: reconfirm upcoming meetings, provide meeting goals, agendas, pre-circulation of reports and action-oriented minutes; be on time, don't keep people waiting; if you are behind schedule, notify other parties expecting to meet you, quickly; notify others of changes affecting them as quickly as possible; always deliver what's required on time, on budget and at the level of expected quality; never let others down; get back to people quickly.
- ➤ Be mutual: I win/You win; not 'them and us'; rather 'We are in this together'.
- ➤ Manage expectations by being clear about: what's expected and what's not; who is to do what (including yourself); parameters and working arrangements, e.g. time, manner, milestones, reviews; who receives what information; how reports and presentations are presented; what constitutes satisfactory and unsatisfactory performance; what constitutes success.

LEADERSHIP OF CHANGE

Leadership of change is an integral part of trust: leading change well will enhance it; leading it badly can destroy it.

'You have to be very conscious of the fact that change is going to accelerate', said John T. Ralph, former chief executive officer of CRA Limited, when interviewed about the book *Leadership, Australia's Top CEOs: Finding out what makes them the best*, by James C. Sarros and Oleh Butchatsky. 'You may think that we've had a lot of change in the last ten years, but there is going to be more in the next ten . . . You can't bring about change in an organisation if you don't have the people prepared to accept change and work to respond to it in a positive way!'

Besides knowing how to manage restructures, required competencies for the leadership of change include *adaptability*, certain elements of *entrepreneurism, resilience* and, above all, *open two-way communication*. Do you know executives and managers who display adaptability, entrepreneurism, resilience and skills in open two-way communication? How do your leadership of change competencies compare? What can you learn, and how should you adapt your behaviour, to become an outstanding leader of change?

Being an outstanding leader of change is inspiring others to embrace, cope with and excel at times of change. This requires not only being a leader of change yourself, but developing a culture and a set of business processes within the organisation that stimulate change and experimentation and celebrate risk taking, according to Professor Jerry Porras from Stanford Business School, co-author of *Built to Last: Successful Habits of Visionary Companies*.

Leadership of change is not about charismatic leadership. Rather, leadership of change embodies the capabilities described *and* ensures that the necessary organisational environment exists to seek out, embrace and exert maximum leverage of the impact of the changing external environment, for the organisation, its objectives and its people.

The following vignettes describe executives whom we believe display particular capabilities in the competency areas needed for leadership of change.

Case Study

One of the most *adaptable* executives we know is Fred Morely (not his real name), a senior executive in the information technology sector. When confronted by challenges at work, Fred is able to take a flexible approach to solutions rather than assuming 'business as usual'. He seeks variety and change at work rather than routine, and when experiencing new situations is curious and probing.

Although upholding corporate policy, Fred can be seen by colleagues as sometimes being non-conformist, adapting to changing circumstances rather than resisting them, comfortable with the unexpected and interested in the unconventional. Fred's management and leadership style changes according to the competence of the particular direct report and the urgency of the particular task, and is seen by direct reports as flexible rather than rigid in day to day operations.

In problem solving, Fred thinks 'outside the square' and actively seeks input from others when confronted by changes at work.

How would you rate your adaptability? Reality-check your thoughts with someone, preferably with several people you know well in the work setting. What might you choose to do more of/less of to develop your adaptability?

Case Study

We would describe Susan Rheingold (not her real name), marketing manager of a food service company, as an excellent example of an *entrepreneurial* executive. She is good at experimenting with new ways of doing things and is successful at innovation, whether in the form of new products, services, processes or systems. She displays a certain daring and tries out brand new concepts at work, taking the initiative and also accepting accountability for the results of the initiative, good or bad.

Displaying an independent style and acting autonomously, Susan is as good at development as she is at straight maintenance of ongoing operations. This includes taking risks when the rewards are high, but also understanding the possible benefits *and* adverse consequences of taking risks. Susan is good at managing risks and at applying appropriate preventive monitoring.

How would you rate your entrepreneurism? Check your perceptions with people who know you well in the work setting. What might you choose to do more of/less of to develop your entrepreneurism?

Case Study

John Baxter (not his real name) runs a medium-sized transport company. He can handle and manage stress: he avoids the negative impact of stress at work, leaves troubles at work rather than taking them home, and sleeps well and enjoys weekends rather than worrying about work.

Resilience also implies a capacity to persevere when the going gets rough. John is considered to be extremely tough and forges ahead at times of adversity, getting the desired results even when confronted by difficult work situations.

John confronts change as a way of life rather than as a hindrance, and accepts change positively. Even though the challenge may be extreme when given a job to do, he completes it and is seen as a good ally by colleagues when the going gets rough and when everyone is up against it. Resilient executives like John Baxter have a dogged streak of perseverance, particularly at times of change or uncertainty.

How would you rate your resilience? Reality-check your thoughts with someone, preferably with several people who know you well in the work setting. What might you choose to do more of/less of to develop your resilience?

Case Study

Val Neilson (not her real name) manages a major public hospital. One of the secrets of her success is that she engages in *open, two-way communication* with direct reports, peers and superiors, keeping them informed as and when necessary. This includes her understanding of the other party's point of view before responding, and *listening twice as much as talking* in interpersonal communication.

The physical barriers to effective communication are understood and minimised by Val—noise, outside interference, incoming phone calls and other interruptions—as are the behavioural barriers, the expectations of other parties which may be different from Val's own, influencing what they choose to hear. Val's written communications are usually planned and well thought out rather than 'dashed off' spontaneously. Similarly, her presentations to groups are well planned, with a clear objective of what is to be achieved with each particular audience.

At times of organisational change, Val communicates the changes to all affected parties, both in person and in writing, regularly: she has found that communicating changes once or twice is not enough at times of restructuring. She agrees with Robert Levering, a consultant with Arthur D. Little and co-author of the book *The 100 Best Companies to Work for in America*, that the better organisations encourage employees to ask difficult and even embarrassing questions. In his view, the human resources function should champion such mechanisms.

Finally, Val is seen as approachable by direct reports, encouraging questions and concerns and seeking to hear quickly about bad, as well as good, news.

How would you rate your two-way communication? Check your perceptions with people who know you well in the work setting. What might you choose to do more of/less of to develop your two-way communication skills?

The ultimate test in change leadership must be managing restructures! Managing restructures badly destroys trust. Managing them well enhances it. But so many restructures simply don't work out, and, usually, executives should take the blame.

RESTRUCTURING OFTEN FAILS

There is plenty of evidence that organisations do not attain their performance improvement objectives within an acceptable time frame after restructuring. *Corporate Downsizing, Job Elimination and Job Creation*, a survey in 1996 by the American Management Association of more than 1000 medium-sized and large companies in the United States, found that 70% of them experienced no immediate increase in productivity and fewer than half improved profitability the year after downsizing.

This was also found to be the case by Wayne F. Cascio of the University of Colorado at Denver, with his associates Clifford Young and James Morris, who examined whether changes in employment numbers affected company financial performance by studying more than 500 companies. Their findings showed that companies downsizing fared no better in terms of costs and profits, and that productivity improvement was often imaginary.

Other surveys, such as those conducted by the Australian Graduate School of Management and Professor Craig Littler of the University of Southern Queensland, point to the drawbacks of 'slash-and-burn' cost reduction and downsizing, which invariably lead to lower levels of morale and productivity. Richard D. Freeman of the London School of Economics suggests that this even puts at risk the longer-term viability of organisations, and *The Economist* in April 1996 labelled one adverse impact of

downsizing 'corporate amnesia', the result of throwing away the experience and knowledge that make organisations tick.

Going one step further, Dwight Gertz and Joao Baptista studied more
than 1000 large companies and concluded in their book, *Grow to be Great:
Breaking the Downsizing Cycle*, that managers must move beyond the current
rounds of downsizing, restructuring and re-engineering and that they
must grow to be great, arguing and demonstrating that growth opportunities are everywhere and across all business sectors, even in stable industries and companies 'too big to grow'.

David M. Gordon on the other hand, in his book *Fat and Mean: The
Corporate Squeeze of Working Americans and the Myth of Managerial Downsizing*,
says that downsizing at the executive and managerial level has not gone
far enough; most companies have gone only halfway, being 'mean' but
far from 'lean'. Indeed, most American companies employ more
managers and supervisors than ever before.

However, restructuring can work well provided it is meticulously con-
ceived and even more meticulously implemented. But first of all, let us
examine some of the causes of the failure of restructuring.

Why restructuring fails

The common causes are usually cited as low morale and poor productivity. We take a different stance. Based on eleven years of Australian
empirical research relating to more than 70 significant organisational
restructures, I see the cause invariably as poor change leadership by the
organisation's executives. It's not that executives don't know how to lead
at times of change—more that they need to adjust to change quickly if
they are to be effective and timely change leaders of others.

Therefore, in addition to the more conventionally recognised needs
of a clearly articulated and shared vision, clearly defined objectives and
a rationale for major change, I believe that five key factors also prevail
in restructures.

1. *Faster progress.* Some companies find that it takes executives in new
   roles or reporting relationships after a restructure or merger nine
   months to become 'profitable'—that is, to perform at an acceptable
   level. Some perceive that over 40% of them are not performing at
   their personal optimum within the first year, and a significant
   proportion leave within 20 months. The negative leverage on staff
   can be punitive.
2. *Faster synergy.* Restructures create new teams. Any newly constituted
   executive team needs to get up to speed quickly and surely to

generate the much-needed synergy and positive leverage it can produce. But what often develops is a sense of guardedness and even mistrust. Self-interest and power plays can predominate, and business imperatives assume lesser priority.

3. *Delivering change.* The bell-shaped curve is alive and well when it comes to an executive population's competence range in terms of change leadership. Some executives are natural change agents, others are more effective dealing with the known. The much-needed change leadership competencies include managing restructures, adaptability, entrepreneurism (innovation balanced by risk management), resilience and open two-way communication.

4. *Misalignment.* Restructures leave some executives in roles or reporting relationships where their comfort levels, motivation, capability and performance deteriorate. Several feel they have lost out, or their future promotional prospects are shot. Until any such misalignment is fully addressed, the negative leverage effect takes hold and progress stalls.

5. *Talent retention.* At times of major change, executives and managers often find they are spending their time working with problem areas that include lower-performing staff. Higher-performing employees, the talent—who often adapt to change more quickly—are left to fend for themselves. This can be the ideal time to poach them, just when the organisation needs them most!

Executive coaching adds great value in attending to the factors highlighted above and greatly enhances chances of success.

Executive assimilation coaching helps executives with new roles or reporting relationships, significantly reducing the time it takes for them to get up to speed after restructuring, and lessening the risks of early turnover.

Team coaching for newly constituted executive teams fast-tracks the development of team processes, and in particular interpersonal relationships—the base ingredients for effective teamwork.

Executive coaching is also able to help executives develop advanced change leadership competencies. Career coaching is a powerful way to address 'square pegs in round holes', invariably generating win-win outcomes through a sense of mutual realignment.

And finally, through executive coaching and/or career coaching—seen as intrinsic rewards and a statement that the organisation really cares—talented key people are less vulnerable to the poachers.

Let's now see just how bad it can get when it comes to a major restructuring, if such coaching support interventions are not put in place!

ANATOMY OF A RESTRUCTURING — WORST CASE SCENARIO

Two-thirds of restructures are estimated not to achieve the objectives of restructuring within the desired time frame. In his book *The Unwritten Rules of the Game,* Peter Scott-Morgan verifies this from a detailed survey of 350 major companies across the United States. Almost every company turned out to be in the throes of a major change initiative, often to reduce overhead costs, streamline the organisation or increase sales, and typically driven by a change of leadership, change in business direction, financial pressures or competitive pressures. However, only 17% were really satisfied with their initiatives and 40% were positively unsatisfied. What goes wrong?

Case Study

A food factory wanted to relocate some of its production lines to a new factory in another state. Two years earlier, the accounting and administration departments had moved from the site to head office, an exercise that was far harder and took far longer to implement than senior management had believed possible. Management might have learned some lessons from this, but they obviously had not, for the relocation of the production lines turned out to be even more unsatisfactory, for *all* parties.

The problems started when employees noticed that managers were going missing. For some reason, weekly and daily routines began to change as managers attended extra meetings, some of them off-site. During breaks and in the canteen, employees from production, warehousing and distribution compared notes. Yes, senior managers across the company seemed to be involved in some sort of planning exercise. Could it be another restructure or, worse, a closure?

The signals were certainly there that something 'big' was going on. The factory started to miss a beat or two as the signals drove speculation. With unsettled minds on the shop floor, productivity dipped. Managers seemed not to notice. Meanwhile, a group of supervisors were heard to be talking in the canteen about the earlier centralisation of accounting and administration, and how it had never really worked out.

By the day of the announcement of the relocation of the production lines, speculation was so intense that when employees were assembled to hear the news there was an air of inevitability and bad omen. The upcoming changes were announced and employees learned that the decommissioning and relocation of the three production lines would be phased in over the next 12 months, and production moved to a newer factory in Queensland. The critical point made by management was the need for continuing productivity, quality and output, as consumer demand for the product lines affected was increasing. The news was received with anger and scepticism. Not only were people going to lose their jobs, but the plan for a running handover to the new factory clearly wouldn't work.

This prophecy by the sceptics became a reality as productivity dropped and quality problems soared during the transitionary period. It was clear that building the required stock levels by the time of the handover to the new factory was going to be an insurmountable challenge.

Eventually, what the company had to do was invest in brand new production lines in Queensland instead of phasing in the relocation of the more modern process and packaging equipment from the existing factory. This was at enormous extra cost, and the whole exercise took more than two years to complete.

This worst case scenario is summarised in Chart 6.4.

ANATOMY OF A RESTRUCTURING—BEST CASE SCENARIO

Case Study

An insurance company decided to contract out its information technology department and call centre (inbound and outbound telemarketing and customer service). Rather than rush this exercise, even though cost savings and other benefits appeared significant, the company decided to take a well-planned approach in order to minimise disruption, employee resistance and the potentially adverse impact on customer service if things went wrong during the changeover. Coaching support was provided and it appeared to pay dividends.

Six months before initiating the contract-out option, management became more proactive in its communication with staff. Briefings were conducted on the 'changing face of the insurance sector' and information was shared about responses by competitors to these changes. Communication was two-way at these briefings—feedback, questions and ideas were encouraged. Managers were encouraged to become more available to staff and a more open, positive and communicative environment developed. In this way, development opportunities for the company were regularly discussed, as was the need to move forward in response to external change.

CHART 6.4   Worst case scenario

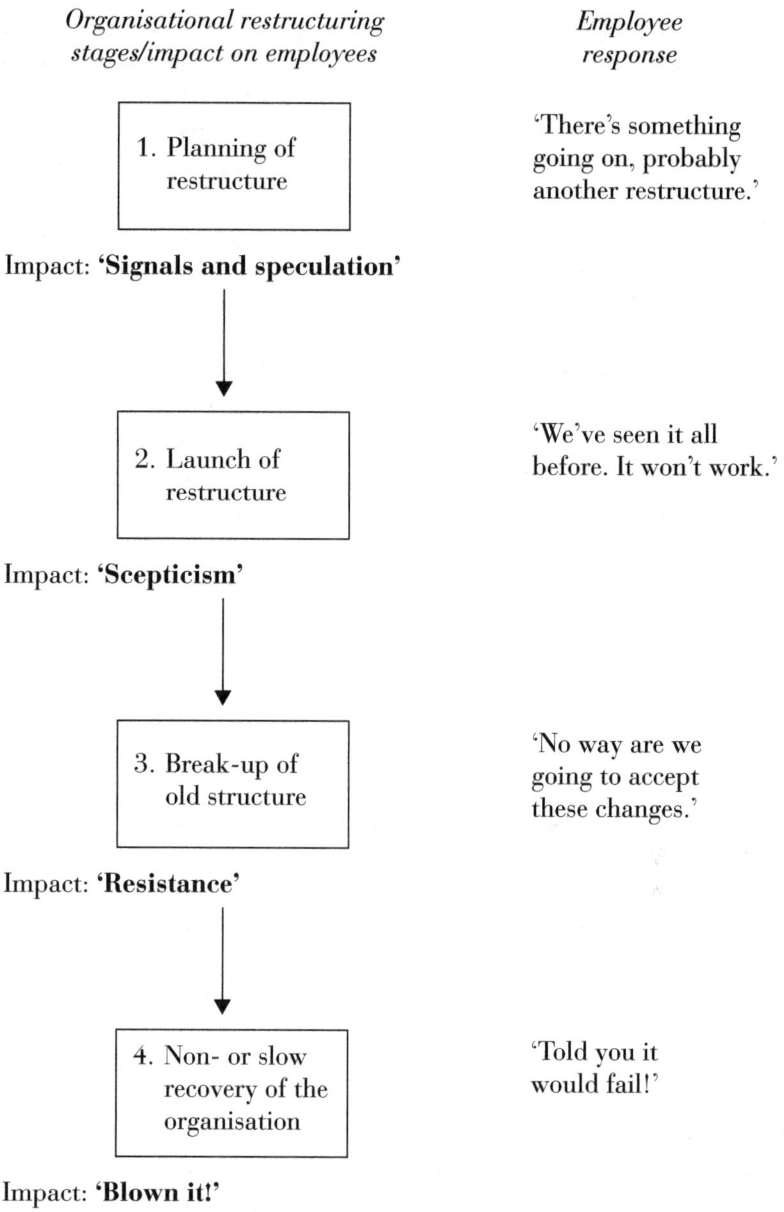

*Organisational restructuring
stages/impact on employees*

*Employee
response*

```
┌─────────────────────┐
│  1. Planning of      │      'There's something
│     restructure      │      going on, probably
└─────────────────────┘      another restructure.'
```

Impact: **'Signals and speculation'**

$\downarrow$

```
┌─────────────────────┐
│  2. Launch of        │      'We've seen it all
│     restructure      │      before. It won't work.'
└─────────────────────┘
```

Impact: **'Scepticism'**

$\downarrow$

```
┌─────────────────────┐
│  3. Break-up of      │      'No way are we
│     old structure    │      going to accept
└─────────────────────┘      these changes.'
```

Impact: **'Resistance'**

$\downarrow$

```
┌─────────────────────┐
│  4. Non- or slow     │      'Told you it
│     recovery of the  │      would fail!'
│     organisation     │
└─────────────────────┘
```

Impact: **'Blown it!'**

By the time the contract-out plans were announced, the organisational environment was so receptive to the news that even those directly affected seemed to accept the decision as being right for the company. What helped were the painstaking efforts by senior management to describe how this change tied in with the vision of the company, and the values and principles that drove how the exercise would be implemented, including extremely fair separation arrangements for those who would have to leave the organisation (some of them joining the two external contractors).

In the words of Jack Welch, CEO of General Electric, quoted in the book *Control your Destiny or Someone Else Will* (Tichy & Sherman), 'Companies need overarching themes to create change. If it's just someone pushing a gimmick or program, without an ovorarching theme, you can't get through the wall'.

At the insurance company, from initiation onwards, the exercise was a success. All staff seemed clear about their changing goals and roles, and a 'can-do' atmosphere prevailed. As progress was made, staff not only cooperated but also took the initiative, and necessary modifications were made on the run in order to facilitate the changes. In this, managers seemed to be leading more from behind, staff often seeking and implementing their own solutions.

As the new information technology and call centre arrangements settled into place, everyone felt themselves to be winners. Morale and productivity were at new heights, bottom-line results flourished, and the size of annual salary increases recognised the efforts made by all and was funded by the cost savings.

The anatomy of a successful restructuring is summarised in Chart 6.5.

How does your organisation's performance and/or your own performance compare with the worst and best case examples? What needs to be done better next time you restructure? How and where should coaching support be provided? Any improvements will clearly enhance the further development of trust.

BEST PRACTICE IN DOWNSIZING AND REBUILDING

Time and again, thunderbolt 'slash-and-burn' staff cuts have not resulted in the desired cost reduction or other goals. The reasons often relate to the trauma caused by such draconian measures and the negative impact on remaining staff in terms of reduced morale and productivity.

More enlightened organisations seek to attain any necessary headcount reductions in two ways. First, they do so by improving their forward planning and relying on natural attrition, internal redeployment to other

CHART 6.5   Best case scenario

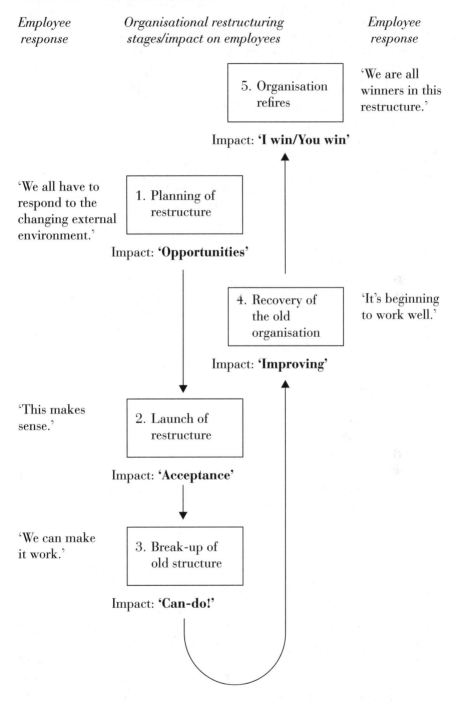

Employee response

Organisational restructuring stages/impact on employees

Employee response

5. Organisation refires

Impact: **'I win/You win'**

'We are all winners in this restructure.'

'We all have to respond to the changing external environment.'

1. Planning of restructure

Impact: **'Opportunities'**

4. Recovery of the old organisation

Impact: **'Improving'**

'It's beginning to work well.'

'This makes sense.'

2. Launch of restructure

Impact: **'Acceptance'**

'We can make it work.'

3. Break-up of old structure

Impact: **'Can-do!'**

more buoyant areas of the organisation, early retirement, leave of absence, study leave, secondments to other organisations, part-time work, 'encouraged' holiday leave, pay cuts, job sharing and selective voluntary redundancy (retaining and rewarding talent, however).

Second, if they do need to move faster than this as a result of unexpected externally driven forces—for example, happenings in the marketplace or economy—then they do it according to 'best practice'.

Case Study

A finance company decided it needed to centralise operations, reduce staff head-count and develop more of a customer focus. At the time I was called in to provide coaching, the company had not been performing well in terms of financial results and other benchmarks. It appeared to be overstaffed, and head office seemed to be unable to control the highly decentralised organisational structure and state-based operating business units. A recent customer survey suggested that the company was overly product-driven, and inadequate in understanding and attending to the real needs of customers.

A new managing director had recently been appointed from a consumer product manufacturing and marketing background. In his previous position he had turned a substantial food product group from a loss to a healthy bottom line by:

> successful new product development based on extensive consumer market research, supported by innovative 'above and below the line' promotional campaigns;
> centralising operations and closing down marginal plants;
> substantial head-count reductions, undertaken according to best practice;
> development of morale and productivity through his own inspirational leadership and the progressive implementation of a range of rebuilding initiatives.

Although the board of directors knew there was some risk in hiring a new CEO from a non-financial services background, they felt reasonably secure knowing that the company's senior executive team was composed of excellent people with strong finance company track records. What they felt they needed was a strong new leader with a customer and employee orientation who could breathe new life into the organisation and turn around its performance through the development and implementation of innovative business strategies.

I recognised these qualities in Dan Small (not his real name), the new managing director, when I first met him, and since then I have admired the way he approached what turned out to be an enormous task, the outcomes of which exceeded even the board's expectations. I was called in early enough to get involved in some initial business strategy development sessions conducted off-site, led and facilitated by Dan himself. In this way, each member of the senior executive team personally bought into the need for change, as well as the need for specific business development and profit improvement goals and supporting strategies.

Coaching input concentrated on the human factor and the need for meticulous planning of the restructurings, and the team agreed that anything less than best practice would be inadequate and unacceptable. The restructuring and downsizing was going to be significant, with some 350 people needing to leave over a 12-month period, from top to bottom in the organisation and throughout Australia.

The first phase of the restructuring process mirrored the earlier insurance company example: an ethos of open management was initiated by managers walking about more, frequently articulating core statements about the state of the financial services industry and the need for change, together with the active solicitation of feedback to management from all employees. Concurrently, the organisation went into planning turbo-drive to ensure that all aspects of the change program were thought through and linked to time frames, actions and responsibilities in a comprehensive master plan. A project planning software system was used to facilitate this.

An initial element of the schedule was further coaching of the line managers in successful change management practices, and in how to communicate with their staff about the job losses, whether voluntary or involuntary. Included in this coaching was how to recognise and handle the emotional responses of departing staff at the time of announcing the restructure and job losses, how to risk-manage the exercise from humanistic and legal perspectives, logistics on the day of termination, and how to communicate with and manage the 'stayers'.

The next phase looked into dismissal avoidance strategies: natural attrition, early retirement, part-time work, job sharing and selective voluntary redundancy—all being fully considered and deployed where practicable. The voluntary redundancy option was offered to all employees for their consideration, but with no guarantee it would be granted in every case. Loyalty bonuses were promised to key staff where their requests for voluntary redundancy were declined, the bonuses payable after restructuring and when the company had attained its business growth and profit improvement goals.

As the restructure was launched, there was a dual emphasis on vision and values for the stayers, and attendance on-site by a team of outplacement consultants for individual and group meetings with departing staff. These meetings focused on the staff themselves, allowing them to express how they felt about

234 | NAKED LEADERSHIP

their changing employment status. A brief introduction was given to the outplacement programs that were to be provided.

In selecting an outplacement provider offering best practice, Dan Small and his team attained exceptional results: 76% of departing staff found new jobs within 16 weeks. These staff were treated well during their career transitions and they reported this back to remaining staff and customers alike; this, as predicted, enhanced employee and customer perceptions of the company, morale, productivity and business results.

As the break-up of the old organisational structure was occurring, the firm continued to adopt best practice by prioritising the key elements of successful leadership of change. Goals and roles were clearly identified and linked from the organisation to each individual. In moving to the recovery of the organisa- tion, all managers—topped up with additional coaching—increasingly allowed their teams and direct reports to decide on and implement improvements 'on the run'. In fact, managers were by now truly leading from behind, rather than micro-managing from the front.

Additionally, at the break-up and recovery stage, the coaching consultants were called in to advise on, and provide progressively, a range of rebuilding interventions including counselling, coping and managing, new team building and career focus.

Time and again, organisations seem to underestimate the impact of restruc- tures on remaining staff, which is why such rebuilding initiatives are invariably needed, in order to:

➤ facilitate the timely attainment of performance improvement goals after restructuring;
➤ enable managers to cope with change better and manage others more successfully at times of organisational change and uncertainty;
➤ offset the risks of remaining staff feeling betrayed or becoming angry, anxious, depressed or resentful about staff departures and necessary internal changes;
➤ similarly offset the risks associated with such emotional responses, including reduced productivity and risk taking, role ambiguity, increased absenteeism and bailouts of talented executives, managers and staff (often the first to go when the organisation is in strife).

Thus the objectives of special rebuilding initiatives are based around rebuilding morale, productivity, performance and commitment. In this, coaching often represents the first step, as was the case with Dan Small's company. He was advised that, at the break-up stage, he would need to have coaches avail- able, both to advise line managers on how to attend to any anxiety, trauma or grief experienced by remaining staff and to be available themselves for direct intervention where needed.

Development of coping and managing skills was provided by the coaching consultants in two forms. First, a skills development workshop was provided to all line managers, which focused on:

➤ how to cope with changes personally;
➤ how to manage others at times of change and uncertainty;
➤ how to recognise and handle the predictable elements inherent in organisational restructuring;
➤ how to minimise the intensity and time frame of reduced productivity during transitions;
➤ how to develop leadership of change competencies.

The outcome was a much more confident and positive management group who became a better-equipped and more effective group of change leaders. Back to back with this, the coaches provided half-day 'coping with change' workshops for all employees; these addressed similar topics but from the employee's perspective.

The double impact of managers developing their leadership of change skills and employees developing their coping skills has a highly potent effect. Dan Small remarked that he felt these particular interventions enabled the organisation to accelerate through the break-up stage to recovery far faster than he had seen before in his 20+ year executive career.

As new teams were brought together, the consultants were able to assist through the provision of new-team-building profiling and group discussion sessions. The objectives and outcomes of these initiatives were the rapid development of interpersonal relationships between new team members, and the enhancement of team composition and processes.

Finally, as the organisation nudged towards the refiring stage, and the 'I win/ You win' theme of improved motivation, productivity, organisational performance and individual reward increasingly became an attainable reality, career focus was addressed by providing career coaching at mid-to-senior levels in the organisation. Outcomes sought and invariably attained were a greater sense of control by executives and staff over their own destinies, better development of ideas and strategies as to how to advance their careers within the restructured, flatter organisation, and a greater alignment between personal and organisational goals.

Dan Small's company refired and attained 'I win/You win' within its desired time frames. The company quickly achieved sought-after employer status!

All companies can do what Dan Small's company did and derive the same benefits. Out with slash-and-burn! In with restructuring best practice!

HOW TO PLAN AND MANAGE RESTRUCTURES

This checklist of executive and manager actions required with their teams at each stage of the restructuring process will ensure best practice.

Stage 1: Planning of restructure

Planning can be either a good news or bad news story. Even the most confidential planning process imposes change on executive routines, and staff notice this. Those extra meetings, those off-site seminars, all generate signals and speculation that something is going on, 'probably another restructure'. The best planning environment is one where, through a climate of open management, all staff realise and accept that organisations have to respond to the changing external environment, and see this as representing opportunities.

Open management requires *proactive leadership* of the restructuring process, an *open environment* and the *encouragement of feedback* from direct reports.

Proactive leadership includes:

➤ a preparedness to discuss the need for change, and the drivers of it, in organisational life today;
➤ management by walking about, rather than from behind closed doors;
➤ frequent use of core statements emphasising the party line and the need for continuous adaptability in the face of ever-increasing external pressures.

An *open environment* requires that teams are encouraged to learn and to convert criticism to remedy, *making* necessary improvements rather than complaining about the need for improvements. Team meetings may also benefit from the position of chair being rotated, and from participation in team meetings by others from elsewhere in the organisation experiencing change.

Encouragement of feedback requires further development of the means for upward communication—feedback from the team and individuals about issues or concerns. These matters need to be discussed and shared, and should be acted on.

When I share restructuring models of this nature with executives, I sometimes receive the initial response of 'If we suddenly start emphasising open management at the planning stage of a restructure, we are at risk of causing the worst case scenario—employees will read the signals that another restructure is being planned'.

My response is usually twofold. First, you should graduate the open management approach and initiate it in the context of improving the organisation's management practices, rather than implying—or allowing it to be inferred—that a restructure is imminent. If one is imminent, the signals will be seen anyway and open management will improve the chances of success. Second, employees expect and prefer open management, and perform better as a result of it, so executives should be practising it anyway. It's never too late or too soon to move further down the path of open management!

Stage 2: Launch of restructure

The launch of a restructure will either be received with scepticism by staff, who feel they have seen it all before and believe it will not work, or it will be accepted positively and seen to make sense. To ensure the latter, vision and principles need to be emphasised at this stage: the vision of where the organisation is heading should be presented with impact; the principles—guidelines on what is important to the organisation and how it should operate—need to be shared to gain group commitment.

The vision needs to emphasise benefits for all parties and be presented in a way that means something to the listener. For example, rather than long-winded statements about continuous improvement, a short and sharp headline statement such as 'We will be the best in our industry' is more effective. This may seem trite to senior management, but their intended audience, staff and customers, can understand and accept such headline statements.

Vision also needs to define how the organisation will look in terms of structure, as well as the impact the restructuring will have on teams and on each individual. All the key elements of vision need to be emphasised—where, when, why and how: 'We will be the best in our industry within two years. Our customers deserve and expect this, and we will attain market leadership by providing uncompromising customer service and delivering best value for money. For this to happen we need to decentralise and work in independent business units based on each of our major product lines. You will be working in smaller groups'.

Principles need to cascade down to individual teams, so the way each team should behave and operate should be discussed and agreed by team members. Behaviour is addressed at the individual level in terms of what is expected and what is unacceptable. The agreed principles and behaviours need to be referred to regularly; they represent the 'glue' between team members—'the way we behave and operate around here'.

Stage 3: Break-up of the old structure

At the break-up stage and in the worst case scenario, resistance can often be fierce and a dogged determination not to accept the changes can prevail. However, a 'can-do' atmosphere can and needs to be created by executives clearly detailing goals and roles. Goals should be specific and clearly understood and new roles should be defined, sold to, and accepted by each affected individual.

To be meaningful, organisational vision and goals should be clearly linked to individual goals. Achievement or otherwise of individual goals needs to be monitored and any adverse variances quickly and positively addressed.

Roles are invariably altered at times of organisational change, usually with an emphasis on 'doing more with less, faster'. This is a good opportunity to make jobs and work content more streamlined and thus more efficient. Efficiency improvements should be tested and modified as necessary on the run, to maximise effectiveness and productivity. No matter how well planned the restructure or the definition of new roles, modifications will always be necessary and are to be expected.

Stage 4: Recovery of the organisation

As noted, it is estimated that two-thirds of restructures fail to achieve their goals within the desired time frames. For recovery to happen more rapidly, teams need to feel empowered in their new roles in the new structure and be able to make decisions and act promptly. Self-improvement through education should continue to be encouraged. In this, the manager needs to delegate more, to enact the role of resource rather than controller, to monitor progress and to manage by exception.

Self-improvement also means that staff are encouraged to seek their own solutions, so that the work environment becomes more participative and less autocratic, and so that managers concentrate on leading from behind rather than micro-managing from the front.

Stage 5: The organisation refires

For the organisation to refire, all parties need to 'win' in the context of high levels of motivation, productivity and rewards. Motivation and productivity are optimised through a sense of achievement and commitment. For this to occur, staff need to own, believe in and be inspired by the changes that have been implemented.

Rewards are two-way. The organisation derives bottom-line benefits, and so should individuals, in order to create a truly 'I win/You win' situation. Individual rewards can be intrinsic, in the way that individual jobs have developed—inherently more interesting and satisfying—and extrinsic, via improved remuneration. 'Shared gain' should be the ethos as the organisation refires and benefits from improved productivity and bottom-line performance compared with before restructuring.

And don't underestimate the impact of coaching support, all the way through and after the restructure!

Chart 6.6 highlights how to manage restructures successfully.

MORE CRITICAL SUCCESS CONSIDERATIONS FOR RESTRUCTURING

Finally, I note a range of other critical success considerations for restructuring, downsizing, acquisition or merger.

> Required internal changes (controllable) are usually caused externally (uncontrollable); change won't stop, it will only accelerate, wave after wave, before each wave has passed; certainty has gone, ambiguity prevails; understand and adapt accordingly.
> Change is uncomfortable and problematic, despite planning; change is hard and causes resistance which consumes energy, saps morale and affects performance and productivity; there can be a 40–50% productivity drop over the transition period.
> Leading major change is like a troop commander taking their squad through the battleground; so look after yourself and each other, make haste, focus on the priorities, route and end-game; dodge the obstacles and bullets; communicate frequently; lead proactively; seek and celebrate early wins.
> Major change means losing things from the past; it creates confusion, uncertainty and suspicion and makes people put self first; leaders spend time with poorer performers; talent left largely unattended; search consultants woo and poach them to greener pastures (but are they greener?).
> Resistance to change is active (recognisable) and passive (unrecognisable); resistance is caused by worry: 'What's going to happen to me and the organisation?'; 'What will we lose from the past?'; 'What's in store for the future?'.
> Communicate, communicate, communicate; many times, even if it is known where the organisation is heading, continually if this is not known; even if you have nothing much to say, *listening* is the key to such communication.

CHART 6.6   How to plan and manage restructures

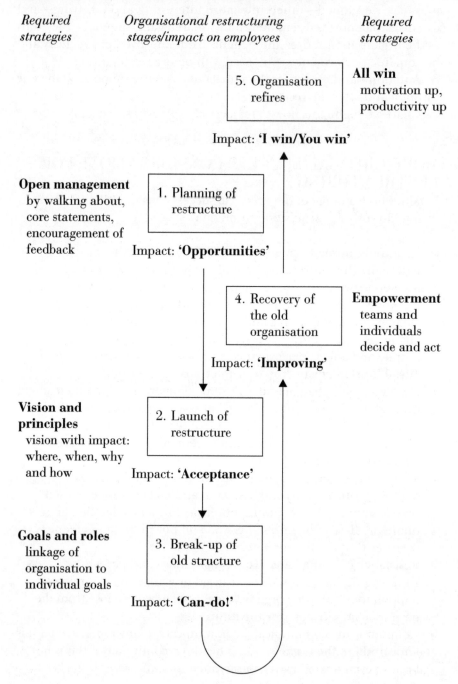

*Required
strategies*

*Organisational restructuring
stages/impact on employees*

*Required
strategies*

5. Organisation
refires

All win
motivation up,
productivity up

Impact: **'I win/You win'**

Open management
by walking about,
core statements,
encouragement of
feedback

1. Planning of
restructure

Impact: **'Opportunities'**

4. Recovery of
the old
organisation

Empowerment
teams and
individuals
decide and act

Impact: **'Improving'**

**Vision and
principles**
vision with impact:
where, when, why
and how

2. Launch of
restructure

Impact: **'Acceptance'**

Goals and roles
linkage of
organisation to
individual goals

3. Break-up of
old structure

Impact: **'Can-do!'**

➤ Don't let things get out of hand—i.e. internal focus rather than customer/competitor focus; time spent on things that don't count or have effect, or on things outside your control; leaders charging ahead of others in understanding, accepting and pursuing the end-game; assumed management responsibility for implementing major change, whereas everyone in fact is responsible/accountable.

The bottom line in all of this is putting people first, constantly communicating with them, helping them to see the advantages of the way forward, helping and encouraging them to jump the hurdles in getting there—all of which will help to generate the sought outcomes.

A CLOSING WORD ON TRUST

By developing more trust, you will reap the rewards of superior payoffs.

➤ You will be seen as a source of valuable advice—'wise counsel'.
➤ Your people will let you know of problems sooner rather than later (and/or trying to cover them up) and will give you early warning of important matters coming up.
➤ People will give you the benefit of the doubt and forgive you for mistakes.
➤ Others will share information more readily with you and let you know what's going on.
➤ They'll respect you more, confide in you more and treat you more as you wish to be treated.
➤ They'll seek your advice and recommendations.
➤ They'll pull with you, which creates better opportunities for joint success: leaders and managers can't do this just by themselves, for themselves!
➤ Your influence and performance as an executive will surpass even the level you currently aspire to.

ROB BALMER ON **TRUSTING**

One thing that staggers me in today's business world is the amount of time and money organisations spend getting external management consultants to tell them *what* they need to do in a merger, downsizing or restructure. Large organisations spend tens of millions of dollars with consulting firms every year, and these sums continue to grow with the ever-increasing need to evolve.

By comparison, minimal time and money is spent by these organisations in 'creating the *how*' in a merger or restructure. The fastest way to create the *how*, in my opinion, is to get the living vision and fundamental values of the newly created organisation (after merger, downsizing or restructure) defined and pursued by everyone. This is the best way to get everyone up to speed as quickly as possible and to realise the (elusive) benefits that were originally envisaged from the merger or restructure.

I'm not saying that management consultants aren't good at telling organisations what to do. I experienced personally how good they can be when our management consultants defined what needed to be done in the biggest merger in the history of the IT industry. In the case of this merger, both organisations had been competitors. They both had long heritages of innovation and success. And they both had extremely proud, loyal employees and strong cultures. All of this presents a huge 'creating the *how*' challenge.

Yet it was my perception that almost all the attention was given to *what* the new organisation would look like, *what* products would be sold or not sold, *what* divisions would be retained or eliminated. After six months with our consultants, many senior staff in both organisations were set up to deal with all the *whats*. But the *how* challenges around merging cultures, heritages and people into one united, new organisation, intended to be greater than the sum of its original parts, were less well attended to.

In many ways, the merger I experienced was handled very professionally, by both the external management consultants and the senior executives from within the two merging organisations. However, I think it was a really good example of how even professionally run mergers can fail to concentrate sufficiently on the *how* issues.

The result of failing to 'create the *how*' in mergers and restructures is a failure to engender what Peter calls 'the quintessence of leadership'—trust! Without trust, people in the organisation don't feel safe to express their thoughts, ideas, emotions and concerns. Without trust, no-one really believes in the vision and mission statements that the organisation's leaders profess and so they don't buy into the big picture of the organisation. Without trust, the merger, downsizing or restructure simply won't realise the benefits that it was designed to achieve.

LEADERSHIP MYTHS	LEADERSHIP TRUTHS
➤ Agreeing on and articulating values is a challenge.	➤ Communicating and upholding them, making them real, is the greatest challenge!
➤ Executives should lead the business.	➤ All employees can lead the business!
➤ Leadership of change requires charismatic leadership.	➤ It requires adaptability, entrepreneurism, resilience and open two-way communication.
➤ If you restructure you'll cut costs and improve your bottom-line performance.	➤ If you restructure, do it well and you *may* cut costs and improve your bottom-line performance!
➤ Staff morale after restructuring is the biggest problem.	➤ Poor leadership of change at times of, and after, restructuring is the biggest problem.

DON'T HIDE!

➤ Employees will give of their all only if they trust you.
➤ Always walk the talk of vision and values.
➤ Don't hide as you move into restructuring mode; step up your availability and increase open two-way communication.
➤ Best practice restructuring needs painstaking planning, and meticulous implementation and follow-up.
➤ There's enough experience around in restructuring for best practice *always* to be pursued and attained—no excuses.
➤ Work hard to develop trust and reap the rewards of superior payoffs.

YOUR FRIDAY REVIEW

1. Have we kept our organisational vision and values to short lists of the fundamentals?
2. Are we communicating and upholding our vision and values at all times—the greatest challenge?
3. Have we developed appropriate living vision and fundamental values; do we walk them, not just talk them? As a result, do we find that policies, operating principles, codes of conduct more or less take care of themselves?

4. Are we suffering from weak vision and values, creating the need for more rules and controls? Or are we benefiting from strong vision and values which create trust and provide employees with freedom to achieve?

5. Are employees achieving greatness to the full as business leaders in their own roles?

6. Do we cherish trust as the quintessence of leadership?

7. Are we adaptable, entrepreneurial, resilient and engaging in open two-way communication in our leadership of change?

8. Do we restructure well, according to best practice, and so derive true and lasting economic benefits?

9. Are we leading change so well that staff morale is never a problem?

10. Do we engage in painstaking planning and meticulous implementation and follow-up at times of restructuring, and realise that there's enough experience around in restructuring for best practice always to be pursued and attained?

11. Do we work hard enough to develop trust?

Assignments

These assignments are designed to help you implement new, more effective leadership practices and behaviours. They refer to each chapter and are numbered accordingly.

In completing these assignments, where you identify a personal development opportunity, try using the Self-Management of Personal Development process below. Note the development area you are focusing on at the top of the form, and then complete the sequence (on p. 247) as shown in the example (p. 246).

You have a couple of options regarding the completion of these assignments. The 'in-depth' option is to go over all the questions. The 'quick and dirty' option is to go over just the last question in each set of chapter assignments, which relates to the daily reviews.

As always, your time availability and time management will influence what you decide to do!

ASSIGNMENTS FOR CHAPTER 1

Don't forget to use the Self-Management of Personal Development process, as shown earlier.

Having read Chapter 1:

1. Using Chart 1.1, place a cross (x) between the left-hand side of Industrial Age and the right-hand side of Information and Knowledge Age as to where you see your organisation positioned. Hint: many organisations are in transition between the two ages, some closer to one age than the other.

EXAMPLE   Self-Management of Personal Development

Development area (i.e. competency I am trying to develop): improve my chairing of meetings

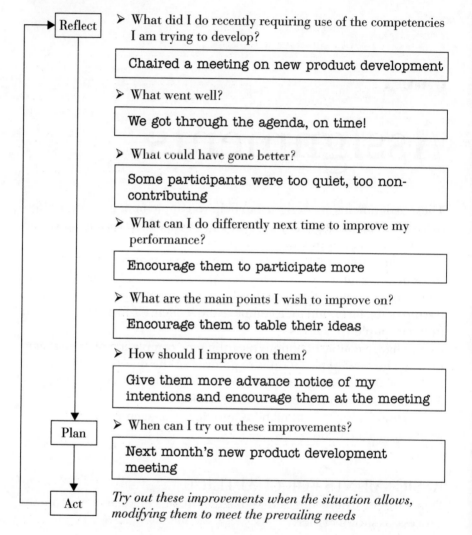

Reflect

> What did I do recently requiring use of the competencies I am trying to develop?

> Chaired a meeting on new product development

> What went well?

> We got through the agenda, on time!

> What could have gone better?

> Some participants were too quiet, too non-contributing

> What can I do differently next time to improve my performance?

> Encourage them to participate more

> What are the main points I wish to improve on?

> Encourage them to table their ideas

> How should I improve on them?

> Give them more advance notice of my intentions and encourage them at the meeting

Plan

> When can I try out these improvements?

> Next month's new product development meeting

Act

Try out these improvements when the situation allows, modifying them to meet the prevailing needs

TIPS

> Seek feedback from others about your progress—line manager, direct reports.
> Accept criticism with an open mind and use for 'Reflect'.
> Continuous improvement is the maxim, rather than one-off improvement.

Self-Management of Personal Development

Development area (i.e. competency I am trying to develop):

Reflect

➢ What did I do recently requiring use of the competencies I am trying to develop?

➢ What went well?

➢ What could have gone better?

➢ What can I do differently next time to improve my performance?

➢ What are the main points I wish to improve on?

➢ How should I improve on them?

Plan

➢ When can I try out these improvements?

Act

Try out these improvements when the situation allows, modifying them to meet the prevailing needs

TIPS
➢ Seek feedback from others about your progress—line manager, direct reports.
➢ Accept criticism with an open mind and use for 'Reflect'.
➢ Continuous improvement is the maxim, rather than one-off improvement.

2. Using Chart 1.2, place a cross (x) between the left-hand side of Industrial Age Executive and the right-hand side of Information and Knowledge Age Executive as to where you believe your personal leadership and managerial style is perceived by others to reside. Hint: it may be in the same position as in Chart 1.1, or it may not. No matter. Try to assess your style as it comes across to others and then place your cross.

3. Do the same exercise as Chart 1.2 above for each of the fellow members of your team—your line manager and your peers—by writing their initials where you believe their personal leadership and managerial style, as perceived by others, resides. Now compare your results on Chart 1.1 and Chart 1.2. What does this tell you?

4. Refer to Chart 1.3 and the accompanying text. Develop your own chart with your own numbers and types of contacts. How many possible communication lines do you have around you? What are you going to do about this?

5. Referring to the section 'The Drivers of Executive Leadership Effectiveness' (p. 14), and using Chart 1.7 as a scoring template, score each of the five essential elements 1 to 5 for the degree to which each is evident, in a positive sense, in your organisation:
   1. not evident at all
   2. evident, but poorly
   3. evident
   4. evident quite well
   5. very evident.

   Score each a second time for the degree to which each is evident in you! (Put a circle around each score to distinguish it from the first set of scores.)

6. Turning to the section 'Your Organisation' (p. 21), use the thought-prompters to undertake a mini-audit on your own organisation, as to where you perceive the greatest opportunities to move the organisation forward. This book should help you do this!

7. Go over 'Your Weekend Review' (p. 25), but change the focus from 'we' to 'I'—in other words, make yourself the focus of the review. If you have worked through questions 1 to 6 above, skip any duplicate questions in your review.

ASSIGNMENTS FOR CHAPTER 2

Don't forget to use the Self-Management of Personal Development process, as shown earlier.

Having read Chapter 2:

1. Answer the questions raised under 'Power' (p. 28).
2. To what extent do you believe in and prioritise 'It's not *what* you know, but *who* you know!'?
3. To what extent do you sell yourself externally?
4. Any chances to develop further your own 'Board of Management Advice' (p. 33)?
5. How can you become increasingly involved in customer contact?
6. What goals might you set for more personal selling and influence development internally and externally?
7. Go over 'Your Monday Review' (p. 92), but change the focus from 'we' to 'I'—in other words, make yourself the focus of the review. If you have worked through questions 1 to 6 above, skip any duplicate questions in your review.

ASSIGNMENTS FOR CHAPTERS 2 AND 3

Don't forget to use the Self-Management of Personal Development process, as shown earlier.

Having read Chapters 2 and 3:

1. What is your main operating style as you come across to, and are perceived by, others? Reality-check your thoughts with someone, preferably several people who know you well in the work setting. Don't just assume that what you feel and believe about yourself is how you come across in your main operating style!
2. Based on the definitions in Chapter 3, make a note of the senior people (along with their main operating styles) within the organisation with whom you seek to further your influence. (Chapter 2 also refers.)
3. Later in Chapter 2, it is suggested that there may be people externally with whom you need to develop your influence further. Make a note of their names and operating styles.
4. Similarly, list the names and operating styles of your customers and the key external contacts.
5. Thinking of your own main operating style, what might happen if you overuse these positive attributes—that is, what would be the caveats in your own case? How can you offset such caveats? (Chapter 2 again refers.)
6. Complete the checklists that follow, 1 to 7, for yourself, for each of your peers in your team, and for the leader of the team. In completing them, respond according to how you believe each team

member comes across to other people—that is, how you and your work colleagues are perceived by others.

Name of individual who is the focus of the survey: _____

In thinking about the individual who is the focus of the survey, award points for each statement below by circling the relevant number as follows:

1. Never   2. Sometimes   3. Often   4. Usually   5. Always

Checklist 1 (Commander/Doer)

* is preoccupied with results, has a strong output orientation and can direct others, quite forcefully when needed	1	2	3	4	5
* is very energetic; never sits still and puts a lot of effort into things; finds it hard to relax	1	2	3	4	5
* has a down-to-earth attitude, relying on commonsense approaches, and learns by doing rather than reading	1	2	3	4	5
* prefers tangible, concrete objects to airy-fairy ideas or feelings	1	2	3	4	5
Total					

In the context of the above statements, please add any other observations about the individual:

Checklist 2 (Responder/Initiator)

* has a capacity both to get involved and to stand aside	1	2	3	4	5
* can be both action-oriented and reflective	1	2	3	4	5
* talks and listens; is an excellent two-way communicator	1	2	3	4	5
* seeks tangible results and is also oriented towards people	1	2	3	4	5
Total					

In the context of the above statements, please add any other observations about the individual:

In thinking about the individual who is the focus of the survey, award points for each statement below by circling the relevant number as follows:

1. Never   2. Sometimes   3. Often   4. Usually   5. Always

Checklist 3 (Empathiser/Humanist)

* operates in a hands-off way and is calm by nature	1	2	3	4	5
* is regarded as an excellent and active listener, and as very friendly and approachable	1	2	3	4	5
* evaluates people situations with care and with special consideration for those involved	1	2	3	4	5
* displays highly receptive behaviour, understands other people, their ideas, attitudes and behaviour	1	2	3	4	5

Total

In the context of the above statements, please add any other observations about the individual:

Checklist 4 (Evaluator/Detailer)

* tends to act alone and can remain detached from groups and other individuals; can appear cold and unemotional	1	2	3	4	5
* can be non-committal, but on the other hand is factual and analytical	1	2	3	4	5
* enjoys planning and detailed work and evaluates matters down to the smallest detail	1	2	3	4	5
* takes care over tasks and decisions, sometimes seen as cautious; likes to do a job well and dislikes sloppiness	1	2	3	4	5

Total

In the context of the above statements, please add any other observations about the individual:

In thinking about the individual who is the focus of the survey, award points for each statement below by circling the relevant number as follows:

1. Never   2. Sometimes   3. Often   4. Usually   5. Always

Checklist 5 (Idea Generator)

*	changes from one operating style to another, exhibiting extremes of behaviour	1	2	3	4	5
*	has flashes of inspiration and creativity, exploring 'endless possibilities' and the 'big picture'	1	2	3	4	5
*	appears more interested in the future and the longer term than in the 'here and now'	1	2	3	4	5
*	changes his/her mind or course of action and thrives on variety; can disagree with others' ideas	1	2	3	4	5

Total

In the context of the above statements, please add any other observations about the individual:

Checklist 6 (All-rounder)

*	seldom if ever shows extremes of behaviour	1	2	3	4	5
*	exhibits a balanced yet flexible style	1	2	3	4	5
*	can be the stabilising factor in teams	1	2	3	4	5
*	can help the team reach consensus, can compromise	1	2	3	4	5

Total

In the context of the above statements, please add any other observations about the individual:

In thinking about the individual who is the focus of the survey, award points for each statement below by circling the relevant number as follows:

1. Never   2. Sometimes   3. Often   4. Usually   5. Always

Checklist 7

* Knight: at team meetings, seeks to come out on top in discussions and debates, to win with his/her point of view; can clash with other team members in so doing	1 2 3 4 5
* Clone: at team meetings, agrees with and supports others, particularly the Chair or leader, and exhibits similar views and other characteristics of this person	1 2 3 4 5
* Rook: at team meetings, holds back and 'sits on the fence' until the team makes up its mind and is ready to make a decision; then 'goes with the flow' and joins the emerging consensus of opinion	1 2 3 4 5
* Henchman: actively contributes at team meetings, at the same time encouraging each team member's own contribution, all of whom perceive him/her as a loyal personal supporter	1 2 3 4 5

No total needed here

In the context of the above statements, please add any other observations about the individual:

7. Based on your checklist responses and the information provided in Chapter 3, assess how each team member comes across to their work colleagues—how they are perceived—in terms of their specific operating style (there's usually a dominant one) and their specific in-team behaviour, including yourself. Although re-examining your own operating style may appear repetitive, since reading Chapter 3 you may have sought feedback and reflected further on your operating style as perceived by others; hence the reason for this reassessment.

8. Would you like in some way to modify how you are perceived—that is, change the way you are perceived by others in terms of your

operating style or in-team behaviour? If so, what and how? Remember, we are all able to modify our style and behaviour and be perceived differently by different categories of people—for example, a direct report, customer, supplier, CEO or partner at home; we are likely to modify our style and behaviour with each of them.

9. In Chapter 3 there are some tips about modifying your operating style further to improve relationships with colleagues exhibiting other operating styles. How can you personally use these tips in your own team setting? Record your thoughts.

10. Now examine team composition by plotting each self-perceived operating style on the model in Chart 3.3 (refer to Chart 3.4 for an example of this) by writing in your own and other people's initials. What are the results and implications in terms of team composition?

11. What have you learned about operating style in terms of enhancing your team's effectiveness?

12. Which different operating styles are likely to 'clash' under pressure? How can you help to avoid this and release the potential synergy created by combining diverse operating styles?

13. What are the implications of a narrow spread of operating styles— that is, where one or more operating styles are missing in a team? What can you do about it?

14. What have you learned about in-team behaviour in terms of enhancing your team's effectiveness?

15. Complete the following checklist on Team Processes just once (p. 255).

16. Compare scores for each statement and add up the total score. Where are your team's apparent strengths and development opportunities? What is your personal developmental action plan to enhance team processes?

17. What is your team's vision and how does it dovetail into total organisational vision?

18. What are your team's values and how do these dovetail into total organisational values?

19. How well does your team alternate between being a leadership team and a functional group? What about other teams in the organisation?

20. How well do you believe teams interact with each other within the total organisation? How would you further improve inter-team relationships and 'I win/You win' between them?

21. Go over 'Your Tuesday Review' (p. 117), but change the focus from 'we' to 'I'—in other words, make yourself the focus of the review. If you have worked through questions 1 to 20 above, skip any duplicate questions in your review.

Team Processes

In thinking about your team, award points in the box for each statement below:

1 Not at all like this   **2** Not much like this   **3** Partly like this   **4** Quite like this   **5** Very like this

1. The team has a compelling vision of the future and clearly defined and well-communicated statements of purpose. Plans are developed collaboratively and work is managed against goals or objectives. When priorities are revised, the need for change is discussed and agreed to by the team.
Your observations and comments:

2. Work is organised to support the team's functions. Roles, relationships and accountabilities are clear to everyone. Members are technically qualified to perform their jobs or have immediate plans for acquiring needed knowledge and skills.
Your observations and comments:

3. The values and principles used to support and manage the work of the team attend to both 'output' and 'human' needs. Output needs refer to the activities required to accomplish work objectives, including problem solving, decision making and conflict management. Human needs refer to recognition, participation, appreciation and general quality of team life.
Your observations and comments:

4. Interpersonal relationships are of high quality. Each team member interacts fully with every other team member. A high level of trust exists within the team, facilitating problem solving and making teamwork satisfying.
Your observations and comments:

5. The team does not compete inappropriately with other teams in the same organisation. 'I Win/You lose' situations between teams do not exist; 'I win/You win' situations do. The relationship between teams within the organisation is productive and satisfying.
Your observations and comments:

6. The team resembles a *leadership team*, whose members are highly committed to and mutually accountable for their reason for being, approach and total business performance. The team comprises no more than 12 people (8–10 ideally) with complementary capabilities and a strong commitment to each other.
Your observations and comments:

7. The team resembles a *functional group*, people who operate more as functional heads, their leader assigning them priorities, establishing performance expectations, facilitating encouragement and motivation, consolidating functional results into total business results and holding all accountable for their individual input.
Your observations and comments:

8. Team members operate flexibly somewhere between a functional group and a leadership team. They reserve leadership teamwork for major opportunities, threats or challenges. They focus on and balance their leadership team and functional responsibilities, rather than trying to operate as a single, all-purpose ongoing team. They learn not to trade off one for the other or to compromise leadership team and functional performance.
Your observations and comments:

9. The team decides when to operate as a leadership team, selecting times and events judiciously, where real opportunities exist for collective leadership team input. They understand that addressing all business performance matters as a leadership team inevitably leads to frustration, even a sense of boredom. They recognise the need for different types of meetings: sometimes as a functional group with a full agenda and tight schedule to get through the business of the day; sometimes as a leadership team with a smaller agenda and looser schedule, tackling just a few key issues.
Your observations and comments:

10. When operating as a leadership team, the team pursues a common purpose, intent, performance goals and monitoring. They commit to a mutually agreed and acceptable approach to how they work, including shared values and team processes and procedures. They believe in and practise mutual accountability. They embrace and synchronise the diverse capabilities and operating styles of members, maximising synergy.
Your observations and comments:

TOTAL	
Maximum possible	50
% Attained	%

ASSIGNMENTS FOR CHAPTER 4

Don't forget to use the Self-Management of Personal Development process, as shown earlier.

Having read Chapter 4:

1. Referring to Chart 4.5 (p. 139), complete the following table for previous actual and/or potential new delegation examples in your own setting.

Delegation Table and Exercise

Style of delegation and description of the task delegated (insert)	Priority of task *and/or*	Impact of task *and/or*	Capability of delegatee *and/or*	Motivation of delegatee	Degree of monitoring/ control required by delegator
Direct (hands-on)					
Delegate (as Helen Spencer described earlier)					
Abdicate (hands-off)					

2. What are your leadership traits (having reality-checked your conclusions, preferably with several people who know you well in the work setting)? What are the desirable leadership traits sought by the organisation for your current position? If there is a gap, what are you going to do to narrow the gap?
3. *Modifying leadership style.* Taking leadership traits to the next level of application, behavioural flexibility is the key to information and knowledge age leadership—that is, facilitating superior results with people of varying levels of capability and motivation, and in varying degrees of complexity and priority.

   Decide which leadership trait might be used most effectively according to different types of people and situations.
4. Go over 'Your Wednesday Review' (p. 157), but change the focus from 'we' to 'I'—in other words, make yourself the focus of the review. If you have worked through questions 1 to 3 above, skip any duplicate questions in your review.

ASSIGNMENTS FOR CHAPTER 5

Don't forget to use the Self-Management of Personal Development process, as shown earlier.

Having read Chapter 5:

1. Refer to the definitions of occupational interests (p. 161) and rank them by order of your greatest interests first and your lowest priorities last. NB: Do not be caught in the trap of assuming your current or last job represented your interests. Take a clean sheet of paper and rank your interests as though you did not have to work for a living! Select your three or four, maybe five, greatest interests, the ones you would particularly like to deploy in your career ahead, and make a note of them.

2. Refer to the definitions of motivational capabilities (p. 163) and rank them by order of your greatest capability first and your lowest capability last. Write down the full rank order of your capabilities.

3. Now re-rank this list of your motivational capabilities according to your level of enjoyment in using these capabilities. Select your three or four, maybe five, greatest motivational capabilities, the ones you would particularly like to deploy in your career ahead.

4. Now turn to the career areas matrix that follows (p. 260). Using a highlighter pen, draw horizontal lines across the page against your greatest interest areas and greatest motivational capabilities—that is, in each case, those you would particularly like to deploy in your career ahead.

5. Then check those career areas, A to L, that contain most of your interests and motivational capabilities on a percentage basis. Example: career area D you score six ticks (✓) out of a possible maximum of ten, which equals 60%.

6. Refer to the career areas code below, and to the career area descriptions in Chapter 5, in order to ascertain which career areas seem to offer the closest match (i.e. job fit) and make a note of them.

Career areas code

A   Practical careers
B   Technical careers
C   Analytical careers
D   Scientific careers
E   Creative careers
F   Careers in design
G   People-oriented careers

Career Areas Matrix

Interests												
Scientific		✓		✓								
Social				✓			✓	✓	✓		✓	
Persuasive					✓		✓	✓	✓	✓		✓
Literary					✓							
Artistic					✓	✓						
Clerical			✓								✓	✓
Practical	✓	✓			✓	✓	✓			✓		
Musical					✓							
Computational			✓	✓		✓					✓	✓
Outside	✓	✓										
Technical		✓				✓						
Medical		✓		✓			✓					
Motivational capabilities												
Memory		✓	✓	✓		✓					✓	✓
Verbal					✓						✓	✓
Numeracy		✓	✓	✓		✓					✓	✓
Spatial	✓	✓	✓	✓	✓	✓			✓			
Perception		✓	✓	✓	✓	✓	✓	✓	✓	✓	✓	✓
Fluency					✓		✓	✓	✓	✓		✓
Reasoning		✓	✓	✓		✓	✓	✓	✓	✓	✓	✓
Creativity			✓	✓	✓				✓	✓		
Social					✓		✓	✓	✓		✓	✓
Clerical			✓								✓	
No of ✓ 'hit'												
Max ✓ possible	3	10	8	10	11	10	8	6	8	6	10	10
My % of ✓ 'hit'												
Career areas	A	B	C	D	E	F	G	H	I	J	K	L

H   Managerial careers
I   Enterprising careers
J   Entrepreneurial careers
K   Administrative careers
L   Professional services careers

7. What are your job requirements and values? List and rank them by order of importance, having given very careful consideration to all possibilities.

8. *Whole-life balance.* 'Doing more, with less, faster . . . and with longer working hours' is a set of experiences confronted by many executives. Whatever happened to that promise that automation and computers would give us all more leisure time?

How balanced are you, in terms of your whole life ? One way to answer this is to examine your diary for the last month or for four typical working weeks. Now add up the hours spent on the following items and the % of total time available given over to each particular item.

	Hours	% of available time
Sleep		
Travel to/from work		
Time in work meetings		
Other time at work		
Business work at home		
Exercise		
Hobbies		
Personal/professional development (outside work time)		
Spiritual		
Social		
TV		
Reading		
Other time with family		
Other time at home		

Now go back and review what would represent a better whole-life balance by writing down new 'hours' and '% of available time' in a different-coloured pen. Then record your action plan to accomplish this.

If you found the adjustment and action plan hard to accomplish, there are other alternatives:

> ➤ a better understanding and acceptance of the situation;
> ➤ a view that shorter-term 'pain' will generate longer-term gain, i.e. a trade-off;
> ➤ changing your needs and expectations;
> ➤ communicating with others about any concern with a view to changing organisational and/or family expectations;
> ➤ 'retreating'—moving on or out, perhaps to a work environment or organisation more considerate of whole-life balance. After all, you have only one life!

Record a few notes about preferred alternatives.

Finally, did you involve your partner and family in this exercise? If not, why not go over your results and considerations with them now?

9. In summary, record your developmental action plan regarding your main interests; main motivational capabilities; suggested main career areas; main job requirements and values; outcome of whole-life balance exercise; implications of all the above on your job fit; action plan to enhance your job fit; and how you are going to use all this thinking to enhance the job fit of your direct reports.

10. What are your atmospheric needs and to what extent does your existing organisation satisfy them?

11. How are you going to use all this thinking to enhance the atmospherics of your work colleagues—in a 360° sense, as you are part of the atmosphere of not only your direct reports but also your peers, senior colleagues and stakeholders?

12. Regarding Talent Management (p. 178), make notes about your developmental action plan, having considered such questions as:

> ➤ What is your annual staff turnover %?
> ➤ What is the average annual employment cost of a leaver?
> ➤ What is the annual cost of your staff turnover?
> ➤ What do you believe are the causes of your staff turnover?
> ➤ What other talent management problems do you experience? What are their causes?
> ➤ What might be some solutions to all of the above?
> ➤ What is your company image as an employer?
> ➤ What type of work environment do you offer and operate?
> ➤ What improvements can be made regarding company image and its work environment?
> ➤ To what extent are you hire-and-fire, churn-and-burn?
> ➤ What dismissal avoidance possibilities are there?

> ➤ What is the bottom line of all the foregoing?
> ➤ What are you personally going to do about all of this?

13. Go over 'Your Thursday Review' (p. 207), but change the focus from 'we' to 'I'—in other words, make yourself the focus of the review. If you have worked through questions 1 to 12 above, skip any duplicate questions in your review.

ASSIGNMENTS FOR CHAPTER 6

Don't forget to use the Self-Management of Personal Development process, as shown earlier.

Having read Chapter 6:

1. Source your organisation's current vision and values statement and critically appraise it against the chapter, up to and including Chart 6.3.
2. Review from Chart 6.3 up to the start of 'From Talk to Walk' (p. 218) and again critically appraise your organisation's performance.
3. In thinking about your responses above and reading the section 'From Talk to Walk', what might your organisation do to enhance the development and implementation of living vision and fundamental values?
4. What might you do personally?
5. In reviewing the atmospheric needs of Chapter 5, 'Energising', what short list of fundamental values would you try to instil in a company of your own?
6. How does this list compare with your current company's list?
7. If there is a gap or mismatch between your answers to questions 5 and 6, what are you going to do about it?
8. On reading the section 'More Tips for Developing Trust' (p. 219), to what degree do you practise these tips? (Score yourself against each on a % basis.)
9. What might you do more of in the above context?
10. From items 1–9 above, what additional benefits from developing more trust might you and the organisation derive?
11. Go over 'Your Friday Review' (p. 243), but change the focus from 'we' to 'I'—in other words, make yourself the focus of the review. If you have worked through questions 1 to 10 above, skip any duplicate questions in your review.

Coaching and cascading

This appendix is designed to help you coach your direct reports and others in *executive leadership effectiveness*, with a view to cascading this through your organisation—in other words, they will then coach their direct reports, and so on.

The suggested sequence is:

➤ Provide each of your direct reports with their own copy of *Naked Leadership*.
➤ Ask them to read Chapters 1 and 2 and complete the relevant assignments in Appendix A.
➤ Lead a one-day or half-day group coaching session on the above, using the suggested agendas in this appendix.
➤ Conduct individual follow-up coaching: first, to help them understand how they can apply the learning in their own roles and work; second, how they can deliver the program element to their own direct reports.
➤ Your direct reports can then undertake all the above with their own direct reports.
➤ The sequence continues with Chapter 3, followed by Chapters 4, 5 and 6.

This is summarised in Charts B1 and B2.

Clearly, there is a time commitment in all this, so in Chart B3 I suggest a sample work program showing the approximate time commitment for

CHART B1 Executive leadership effectiveness sequence

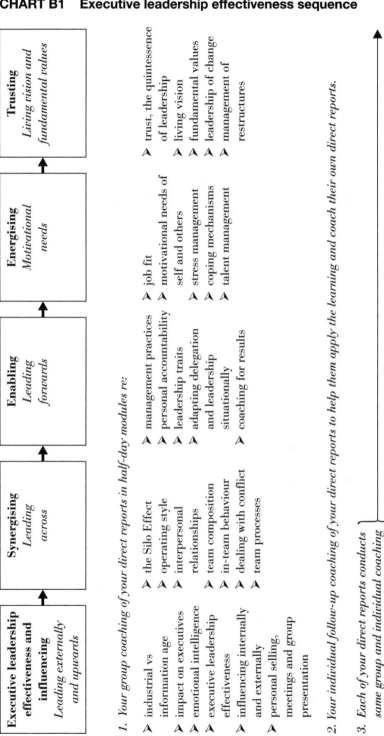

Executive leadership effectiveness and influencing
Leading externally and upwards

→ **Synergising**
Leading across

→ **Enabling**
Leading forwards

→ **Energising**
Motivational needs

→ **Trusting**
Living vision and fundamental values

1. *Your group coaching of your direct reports in half-day modules re:*

Executive leadership effectiveness and influencing:
➢ industrial vs information age
➢ impact on executives
➢ emotional intelligence
➢ executive leadership effectiveness
➢ influencing internally and externally
➢ personal selling, meetings and group presentation

Synergising:
➢ the Silo Effect
➢ operating style
➢ interpersonal relationships
➢ team composition
➢ in-team behaviour
➢ dealing with conflict
➢ team processes

Enabling:
➢ management practices
➢ personal accountability
➢ leadership traits
➢ adapting delegation and leadership situationally
➢ coaching for results

Energising:
➢ job fit
➢ motivational needs of self and others
➢ stress management
➢ coping mechanisms
➢ talent management

Trusting:
➢ trust, the quintessence of leadership
➢ living vision
➢ fundamental values
➢ leadership of change
➢ management of restructures

2. *Your individual follow-up coaching of your direct reports to help them apply the learning and coach their own direct reports.*

3. *Each of your direct reports conducts same group and individual coaching of their own direct reports.*

CHART B2   Sequencing

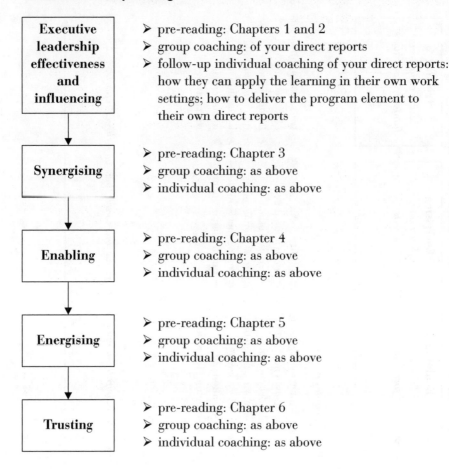

Executive leadership effectiveness and influencing

➢ pre-reading: Chapters 1 and 2
➢ group coaching: of your direct reports
➢ follow-up individual coaching of your direct reports: how they can apply the learning in their own work settings; how to deliver the program element to their own direct reports

Synergising

➢ pre-reading: Chapter 3
➢ group coaching: as above
➢ individual coaching: as above

Enabling

➢ pre-reading: Chapter 4
➢ group coaching: as above
➢ individual coaching: as above

Energising

➢ pre-reading: Chapter 5
➢ group coaching: as above
➢ individual coaching: as above

Trusting

➢ pre-reading: Chapter 6
➢ group coaching: as above
➢ individual coaching: as above

yourself, the leader, and for each direct report participating. Given the potential returns, you will see that the investment in core office time is quite modest.

CHART B3 **Sample work program for each direct report participating**

	Program element	Activity	Time commitment
Week 1	Enabling	Self-paced pre-reading of Chapter 4 and completion of relevant assignments in Appendix A, by each participant	4 hours (non-core office time)
Week 2	Enabling	Group coaching by you, of your direct reports	4 hours
Week 3	Enabling	Individual follow-up coaching of your direct reports	8–12 hours
Week 3/4	Enabling	Your direct reports prepare for their delivery of program element to their direct reports via group coaching	2 hours (non-core office time)
Week 4	Enabling	Your direct reports deliver program element to their direct reports	4 hours
Week 5	Enabling	Your direct reports provide individual follow-up coaching to their direct reports	8–12 hours
			3–4 days core office time per 6–8 weeks for each direct report; $2-2\frac{1}{2}$ days core office time for you, the leader

NB 1. The pattern repeats itself for each of the five program elements: executive leadership effectiveness and influencing (which may need a one-day group coaching session), synergising, enabling, energising and trusting (which need only a half-day group coaching session each).

2. Elapsed time frame: $7\frac{1}{2}$ to $9\frac{1}{2}$ months.

GETTING STARTED

Clearly, you will need to read *Naked Leadership* and complete the assignments yourself. And before you go about the business of group and individual coaching of your direct reports in *executive leadership effectiveness*, please pay particular attention to, and use:

> ➤ your operating style (Chapter 3);
> ➤ influencing at group meetings and in group presentations (Chapter 2);
> ➤ coaching for results (Chapter 4).

Each of these important topics, correctly understood and applied, can pave the way to success in 'coaching and cascading'.

In Charts B4 to B8 you will find suggested agendas for the group coaching sessions for each of the five program elements.

When your direct reports have read Chapters 1 and 2 carefully and completed the relevant assignments (in advance of the group coaching sessions), you are then ready to conduct the group coaching session, with the suggested agenda shown in Chart B4.

As noted in the last item of the agenda, each participant is encouraged to select three key personal development areas from the group coaching session and work out an appropriate action plan for each one, using the Self-Management of Personal Development process exhibited in Appendix A. A prudent leader will ask for completed copies (a) to make sure it gets done and (b) for your ongoing coaching of your direct reports.

Additionally, assuming you intend to take the cascading process this far, your help in preparing your direct reports for their delivery of the program to their own direct reports—conducting group coaching sessions exactly along the lines they will by now have participated in—will be invaluable.

One final point: if/when you need some discussion prompters as you go through the following sessions, do not hesitate to use the relevant daily reviews at the end of each chapter.

CHART B4 Executive leadership effectiveness and influencing: Chapters 1 and 2

Group coaching session agenda: one full day (suggested)

8.30	**The Information and Knowledge Revolution** (Chapter 1, Chart 1.1)	All
	➢ discussion about transition from industrial revolution, plotting where you see the organisation and discussion	
	➢ team action planning	
9.30	**Impact on Executives** (Chapter 1, Chart 1.2)	All
	➢ discussion about extremes of each leadership/ management style	
	➢ plotting self/others exercise and discussion	
	➢ team action planning	
11.00	**Leadership Introduction** (Chapter 1, Charts 1.3, 4, 5, 6, 7 and 8)	All
	➢ discussion about all these charts and the sharing of scores for the executive leadership effectiveness assignment question 5, and the sharing of conclusions regarding the mini-audit assignment question 6	
	➢ team action planning	
1.30	**Influencing** (Chapter 2)	All
	➢ discussion about why senior people in an organisation might like their reports being more open and frank with them, earlier, i.e. influencing upwards. How to encourage, any dangers of overuse? If so, how to avoid	
	➢ team action planning	
2.30	**Influencing** (Chapter 2, Your Monday review)	All
	➢ discussion about all the assignment questions with an emphasis on team action planning	
4.00	**Self-Management of Personal Development and Wrap-up**	Leader
	➢ the leader encourages each direct report to select three key personal development areas from the above, and to work out an appropriate personal action plan for each, using the Self-Management of Personal Development process in Appendix A, copying the leader	
NB	Plus appropriate breaks	

CHART B5 Synergising: Chapter 3
Group coaching session agenda: half day

8.30   **Operating Style**   All

➢ 'I believe my operating style and in-team behaviour is . . . and I'd like to try to modify my operating style and in-team behaviour more towards . . . (if applicable)' and feedback by colleagues as to *their* perceptions of each individual's operating style, in a supportive positive sense

➢ plotting of operating styles on model (Chart 3.3) and discussion about team composition and what to do if out of balance

➢ discussion about conflict—where it may reside in the team; how to handle it

➢ team action planning

10.30   **Team Processes**   All

➢ volunteer totals up all scores and presents, followed by discussion on strengths, development opportunities and team developmental action plan

➢ special discussion on vision:
    (a) criteria for establishing/revisiting
    (b) individual vision statement contributions
    (c) possible consolidation into one (and/or requiring later attention)

➢ special emphasis on functional group/leadership team

➢ team action planning

12.15   **The Sports Coach Analogy for Leadership and Teamwork Self-Management of Personal Development and Wrap-up**   Leader

➢ having overviewed the sports coaching analogy, the leader encourages each direct report to select three key personal development areas from the above, and to work out an appropriate personal action plan for each, using the Self-Management of Personal Development process in Appendix A, copying the leader

NB   Plus appropriate breaks

CHART B6 Enabling: Chapter 4
Group coaching session agenda: half day

8.30	**Leadership Traits and Management Practices**	All

> 'I believe I usually display the following leadership traits . . . and I'd like to try to modify them more towards . . . (if applicable)' and feedback by colleagues as to *their* perceptions, in a supportive positive sense
> plotting of leadership styles on model (Chart 4.8) and discussion as to when/how to modify leadership style
> discussion about the effectiveness of management practices in the organisation
> team action planning

10.15	**Motivational Delegation**	All

> 'I believe my motivational delegation style is . . . and I'd like to develop it further by making the following changes (if applicable)' and feedback by colleagues in a supportive positive sense
> plotting of motivational delegation on model (Chart 4.4) and discussion as to when/how to modify delegation style (Chart 4.5)
> special emphasis on how to create an even more motivational environment organisationally
> team action planning

11.45	**Coaching for Results Sports Coaching Analogy**	All

> discussion about coaching for results, whether or not the sports coaching analogy is relevant in the business setting, and whether it can be used as a leadership paradigm in the organisation
> team action planning

12.15	**Self-Management of Personal Development and Wrap-up**	Coach

> the leader encourages each direct report to select three key personal development areas from the above, and to work out an appropriate personal action plan for each, using the Self-Management of Personal Development process in Appendix A, copying the leader

NB Plus appropriate breaks

CHART B7   Energising: Chapter 5
Group coaching session agenda: half day

| 8.30 | **Job Fit** | All |

> ➤ 'The implications of the assignment on my personal
>   job fit are . . . To obtain better job fit, I'd like to do
>   more of . . . and less of . . . and differently . . . (as
>   applicable)'
> ➤ discussion about how to use job fit elsewhere in the
>   organisation
> ➤ team action planning

| 9.45 | **Atmospheric Needs** | All |

> ➤ 'The implications of the assignment on how I feel my
>   atmospheric needs are met/not met and what I'm
>   going to do about this are . . .'
> ➤ discussion about how to use atmospheric needs
>   elsewhere in the organisation
> ➤ team action planning

| 11.00 | **Talent Management** | All |

> ➤ sharing of individual responses to assignment
>   questions on talent management
> ➤ discussion, consideration, action planning
> ➤ team action planning

| 12.15 | **Self-Management of Personal Development and
>   Wrap-up** | Leader |

> ➤ the leader encourages each direct report to select three
>   key personal development areas from the above, and to
>   work out an appropriate personal action plan for each,
>   using the Self-Management of Personal Development
>   process in Appendix A, copying the leader

NB Plus appropriate breaks

The job fit and atmospheric needs discussions may be seen by some of
your direct reports as too personal, in which case replace them with a
discussion of their responses to Your Thursday review at the end of
Chapter 5.

CHART B8   Trusting: Chapter 6
Group coaching session agenda: half day

8.30   **Trusting I**   All
- ➤ sharing of responses to the first six items in Your Friday review
- ➤ discussion, consolidation
- ➤ team action planning

10.30   **Trusting II**   All
- ➤ sharing of responses to the last five items in Your Friday review
- ➤ discussion, consolidation
- ➤ team action planning

12.15   **Self-Management of Personal Development and
         Wrap-up**   Leader
- ➤ the leader encourages each direct report to select three key personal development areas from the above, and to work out an appropriate personal action plan for each, using the Self-Management of Personal Development process in Appendix A, copying the leader

NB Plus appropriate breaks

About The Stephenson Partnership

The Stephenson Partnership was formed in 1998 by Peter Stephenson to provide specialist professional services in the areas of Executive Coaching, Career Coaching and Mentoring. We continue to specialise in these areas and have grown to become a preferred supplier in this field of many Australian corporates, by excelling in three areas: our performance, our people and our processes.

Our philosophy is that we are only as good as the results we deliver (i.e. our performance), and so our emphasis is on delivering real economic benefits to our clients and successful outcomes for each executive participant. Our programs are needs-driven, personalised and confidential with an emphasis on analysis, action planning and implementation in the workplace. We believe so strongly in our approach that we offer a Performance Guarantee for all our assignments.

The Stephenson Partnership engages only coaches of the highest level. Every one of the firm's coaches has either CEO, general manager or director experience. Our coaches maintain links to industry through non-executive directorships and active involvement in key industry bodies. They are fully trained in The Stephenson Partnership's executive coaching processes, are fully aware of and connected to business realities, and are dedicated to successful outcomes.

All our work is based around The Stephenson Partnership's proprietary processes. These are based on more than eleven years' Australian empirical research, overlaid with international best practice. Our experience base includes more than 600 executive, managerial and senior professional coaching and mentoring cases, and regular feedback from our 100-member Executive Network.

OUR PROCESSES

➢ *Executive coaching* further develops executive effectiveness and focuses on leadership, behavioural, interpersonal and communication skills.

➢ *Career coaching* further develops self-motivation through a greater sense of personal career direction, control and alignment with the organisation.

➢ *Executive mentoring* is provided in confidence to the CEO or senior executive, where an objective, independent and highly experienced confidant can make all the difference to how the executive performs, makes decisions, feels, and is perceived to be operating.

➢ *Team coaching* optimises executive teamwork through enhanced interpersonal relationships, team composition, in-team behaviour, conflict resolution and team processes. Creates a high-performance star team, rather than just a team of stars.

➢ *Executive leadership effectiveness*—our range of programs on how to leverage human talent: the five essential elements with universal and time-enduring application for the information and knowledge age executive . . . all as described in *Naked Leadership*! Multi-organisation programs are also available.

➢ *Executive talent development* via multi-executive and/or multi-organisation coaching and mentoring programs, for newly promoted, high-potential and up-and-coming executives.

➢ *Coach-the-coach or mentor* coaches executives and managers in The Stephenson Partnership's proprietary coaching and mentoring processes, enabling them to put leadership well and truly into action—through coaching or mentoring—which can then cascade powerfully throughout the organisation, often resulting in leveraging the organisation's human resources potential far beyond its competitors. Multi-organisation programs are also available.

➢ *The Adeptus Process®*—a multi-level survey and self-assessment diagnostic process enabling executives to analyse themselves, their leadership and executive competencies, as well as their personal and career development opportunities.

➤ *Executive career transition* for those executives moving to another role within the organisation or externally; we offer an individually tailored program drawing on the strengths of our career coaching, executive coaching and mentoring processes.

For further information, please visit our website at: www.thestephenson-partnership.com.au

Bibliography

Adair, J. 1988, *Developing Leaders: The Ten Key Principles*, Davies-Black Publishing, Palo Alto, California.

AMA Survey: *Corporate Downsizing, Job Elimination, and Job Creation 1996*, American Management Association, New York.

Belasco, J. & Stayer, R.C. 1993, *Flight of the Buffalo: Soaring to Excellence, Learning to Let Employees Lead*, Warner Books, New York.

Bennis, W.G. 1993, *An Invented Life: Reflections on Leadership and Change*, Addison-Wesley, Reading, Mass.

Bennis, W.G. 2000, *Managing the Dream: Reflections on Leadership and Change*, Perseus Publishing, Cambridge, Mass.

Birchall, David & Lyons, Laurence, 1995, *Creating Tomorrow's Organisation*, Pitman Publishing, London.

Birkman, Roger. Birkman Career Management Profile™

Blake, R. & Mouton, J.S. 1994, *The Managerial Grid*, Gulf Publishing, Houston.

Blanchard, K.H. et al. 1985, *Leadership and the One Minute Manager: Increasing Effectiveness through Situational Leadership*, Morrow, New York.

Blanchard, K.H. et al. 1999, *Leadership by the Book: Tools to Transform your Workplace*, William Morrow, New York.

Blount, F. et al. 1999, *Managing in Australia*, Lansdowne, Sydney.

Brass, Charles. Life Without Jobs, *HR Monthly*, April 1995, Australia.

Bridges, William. 1995, *Jobshift: How to Prosper in a Workplace without Jobs*, Nicholas Brealey Publishing, London.

Cascio, Wayne F. The Cost of Downsizing, *HR Monthly*, February 1994, Australia.

The Centre for Creative Leadership. 1998, *Handbook of Leadership Development*, Jossey-Bass, San Francisco.

Champy, J. & Nohria, Nitin. 2000, *The Arc of Ambition: Defining the Leadership Journey*, Perseus Books, Cambridge, Mass.

Clancy, D. & Webber, R. 1999, *Roses and Rust: Redefining the Essence of Leadership in a New Age*, 2nd edn, Business and Professional Publishing, Sydney.

Covey, Stephen R. 1990, *The 7 Habits of Highly Effective People*, Information Australia, Melbourne.

Crosby, Philip B. 1990, *Leading: The Art of Becoming an Executive*, McGraw-Hill, New York.

Dent, Harry S. Jr. 1995, *Job Shock: Four New Principles Transforming Our Work and Business*, Bookman Press, Melbourne.

Dessler, G. 2000, *Management: Leading People and Organizations in the 21st Century*, 2nd edn, Prentice Hall, Upper Saddle River, New Jersey.

Du Pree, M. 1987, *Leadership is an Art*, Michigan State University Press, East Lansing, Mich.

Freeman, Richard D. 1996, *Corporate Amnesia*, London School of Economics, London.

Gertz, Dwight L. & Baptista, Joao. 1995, *Grow to be Great: Breaking the Downsizing Cycle*, The Freeman Press/Simon & Schuster, New York.

Goldsmith, M. et al. 1999, *Leading Beyond the Walls*, Jossey-Bass, San Francisco.

Gordon, David M. 1996, *Fat and Mean: The Corporate Squeeze of Working Americans and the Myth of Managerial Downsizing*, The Free Press/Simon & Schuster, New York.

Greenleaf, R.K. 1977, *Servant Leadership: A Journey into the Nature of Legitimate Power and Greatness*, Paulist Press, New York.

Hamel, Gary & Prahalad, C.K. 1994, *Competing for the Future*, Harvard Business School Press, Harvard, Mass.

Handy, Charles. 1994, *The Age of Unreason* and *The Empty Raincoat*, Arrow Books, Random House International, UK.

Huey, John. 1994, Take me to your Leadership Books, *Fortune*, vol. 130.

The Karpin Report—Renewing Australia's Managers to Meet the Challenges of the Asia-Pacific Century 1994, Australian Government Publishing Service.

Katzenbach, J.R. 1996, *Real Change Leaders: How You Can Create Growth and High Performance at Your Company*, Times Business, New York.

Kets de Vries, M. 1995, *Life and Death in the Executive Fast Lane: Essays on Irrational Organizations and their Leaders*, Jossey-Bass, San Francisco.

Koch, Richard & Godden, Ian. 1996, *Managing without Management*, Nicholas Brealey Publishing, London

Korn/Ferry and the Economist Intelligence Unit. 1996, *Developing*

Leadership for the 21st Century, Korn/Ferry International, New York.

Kotter, J.P. 1990, *A Force for Change: How Leadership differs from Management*, The Free Press, New York.

Kotter J.P. 1995, *The New Rules*, The Free Press/Simon & Schuster, New York.

Kotter, J.P. 1999, *John P. Kotter on What Leaders Really Do*, Harvard Business School Press, Boston.

Kouzes, J.M. & Posner, B.Z. 1995, *The Leadership Challenge: How to keep getting Extraordinary Things in Organizations*, 2nd edn, Jossey-Bass Publishers, San Francisco.

Lans, Jenni. 1996, *If it Wasn't for the Money, I Wouldn't be Doing This*, Harper Collins Publishers, Sydney.

Leaders on Leadership: Interviews with Top Executives. 1992, Harvard Business School, Boston, Mass.

Leana, Carrie R. & Feldman, Daniel C. 1992, *Coping with Job Loss: How Individuals, Organizations, and Communities Respond to Layoffs*, Lexington Books/Simon & Schuster, New York.

Levering, Robert. 1993, *The 100 Best Companies to Work for in America*, Doubleday, New York.

Machiavelli, N. 1950, *The Prince, and the Discourses*, Modern Library, New York.

Mackay, Harvey B. 1995, *Sharkproof: Get the Job you Want, Keep the Job you Love . . . in Today's Frenzied Job Market*, Harper Collins Publishers, New York.

Mant, A. 1997, *Intelligent Leadership*, Allen & Unwin, Sydney.

Meyer, G.J. 1995, *Executive Blues*, Franklin Square Press, United States.

Neff, T.J. & Citrin, J. 1999, *Lessons from the Top: The Search for America's Best Business Leaders*, Currency/Doubleday, New York.

O'Toole, J. 1999, *Leadership A to Z: A Guide for the Appropriately Ambitious*, Jossey-Bass Publishers, San Francisco.

Porras, Jerry I. *Built to Last: Successful Habits of Visionary Companies*, Stanford Business School/Harper Collins, California.

Quinn, R.E. et al. 1996, *Becoming a Master Manager: A Competency Framework*, 2nd edn, John Wiley & Sons, New York.

Rifkin, Jeremy. 1995, *The End of Work: The Decline of the Global Labour Force and the Dawn of the Post-market Era*, Jeremy P. Tarcher/GP Putman's Sons Publishers, New York.

Sarros, James C. & Butchatsky, Oleh. 1996, *Leadership—Australia's Top CEOs: Finding out what makes them the best*, Harper Collins Publishers, Sydney.

Schein, E. 1992, *Organizational Culture and Leadership*, 2nd edn, Jossey-Bass, San Francisco.

Scott-Morgan, Peter. 1994, *The Unwritten Rules of the Game: Master them, Shatter them, and Break through the Barriers of Organisational Change*, McGraw-Hill, New York.

Seglin, Jeffrey L. 1999, Straight to the Source, *Inc*, vol. 21, no. 18, December.

Slater, R. 1999, *Jack Welch and the GE way: Management Insights and Leadership Secrets of the Legendary CEO*, McGraw-Hill, New York.

Sloan, Allen. The Hit Men, *The Bulletin*, 27 February 1996.

Spears, L. 1995, *Reflections on Leadership: How Robert K. Greenleaf's Theory of Servant Leadership influenced today's Top Management Thinkers*, J. Wiley, New York.

Stephenson, P. 1997, *The Bulletproof Executive*, Harper Collins, Sydney.

Stephenson, P. 2000, *Executive Coaching: Lead, Develop, Retain Motivated, Talented People*, Pearson Education, Sydney.

Stewart, Thomas A. Looking Out For Number 1, *Fortune Magazine*, January 1996.

Thompson, John A. & Hennigsen, Catharine A. *The Portable Executive*, Simon & Schuster, New York.

Tichy, Noel M. & Sherman, Stratford. 1993, *Control your Destiny or Someone Else Will*, Transworld Publishers/Doubleday, New York.

Ulrich, D. et al. 1999, *Results-Based Leadership*, Harvard Business School Press, Boston.

Voss, Bristol-Lane. Leadership: Copy or Build, *Journal of Business Strategy*, vol. 20, no. 5, Sept/Oct 1999.

Waterman, Robert H. Jr. 1996, *What America Does Right*, Norton Publishing, New York.

Wheatley, M. 1999, *Leadership and the New Science: Discovering Order in a Chaotic World*, 2nd edn, Berrett-Koehler Publishers, San Francisco.

Zaccaro, S.J. 2001, *The Nature of Executive Leadership: A Conceptual and Empirical Analysis of Success*, American Psychological Association, Washington, DC.

Index